# HAVE ALL YOUR DREAMS COME TRUE?
# HAVE ANY OF THEM?
# ARE YOU READY TO MAKE THEM HAPPEN?

Barbara Sher can help you make the rest of your life *the very best time of your life*. She has a gift for seeing the fears and responsibilities, prejudices and doubts that have been holding you back . . . and for showing you how to conquer them! Age, time, money—none of them needs to stand in your way. Not anymore. Find out about:

- **A thirty-year plan** . . . the craziest and very best strategy for experiencing an exciting future.
- **True love** . . . it is probably impossible before the age of forty. Discover how, and why, you can now, finally, experience the real thing.
- **An energy jump-start** . . . the one thing you need to get you going.
- **Myths about getting older** . . . here's one: "Old people are lonely and depressed." The truth is the loneliest, most depressed people in the United States are actually teenagers.
- **Reclaiming wonder** . . . you can travel the world or travel through the unexplored caverns of your own soul. Turning forty is the first step in the journey.
- **A two-week unannounced strike** . . . a warm-up for the biggest change you will ever make.
- **Going for greatness** . . . there are only four rules for doing it, and they're simple. Really simple.

**IT'S ONLY TOO LATE IF YOU DON'T START NOW**

ALSO BY BARBARA SHER

*Wishcraft*
*Teamworks!*
*I Could Do Anything if I Only Knew What It Was*
*Live the Life You Love*

# it's
## only
## too
## late
# If You Don't
# *Start Now*

How to Create Your Second Life
at ANY AGE

# Barbara Sher

A Dell Trade Paperback

A DELL TRADE PAPERBACK
Published by
Dell Publishing
a division of
Random House, Inc.
1540 Broadway
New York, New York 10036

ISBN: 0-440-50718-9

Reprinted by arrangement with Delacorte Press

Printed in the United States of America

Published simultaneously in Canada

April 1999

20 19 18 17 16 15 14 13 12 11

BVG

*To life*

# ACKNOWLEDGMENTS

I want to extend my thanks to Andrea Reese, Stephanie von Hirschberg, Susan Brauser, Katinka Neuhof, Gail McMeekan, Lenore Goldberg, Jan Niemi, Katy Lazar, Paul Nadler, and all the readers and friends and editors who went through these pages, shared their own midlife experiences, and said things like "What about people who *don't* have children?" and "What if you've been having a midlife crisis since you were twenty-four?" and "Let me tell you about my uncle who took up sculpture when he was fifty-five and now has a studio in Paris!"

Thanks to Bill Connington, Gayle Morgan, Elaine Ryan, Cyndi West, Rich West, Karen Holvik, Stephanie Fuller, and Tom Anthony for praising me when I needed it, catching mistakes when I needed that, and never giving up their efforts to drag me away from the computer for a good movie or furniture-rearranging party or weekend by the shore, or trip to Topanga (with a little recording on the side since I was there anyway), even though they never—well, hardly ever—succeeded. Thanks to my wonderful mom for keeping me company on the telephone every night that I took time out to wash the dishes. Sitting by my computer all those long hours for over two years was never lonely because of them.

Most of all, I want to thank my hardworking, sharp-eyed editors: Adam Nadler, for his brilliance at creating structure and continuity (no small task when working with me), and for his delicate and pointed finesse with line-editing. His creative input and long hours were invaluable to the project. Matthew Pearl, for his astonishing eye for detail and for always understanding exactly what I was trying to say and helping me out when I didn't quite say it, and Diane Bartoli who went over this manuscript with care, enthusiasm, and intelligence. They have earned my deepest admiration.

Thanks to my agent, Kris Dahl, and her team at ICM and to Leslie Schnur and the merry gang at Dell for help far beyond the call of duty.

And to all my clients and the readers who have written me, many thanks for helping me develop my thinking and for sharing your stories. I hope I have returned a fraction of your generosity in the coming pages.

# Contents

# CONTENTS

BOOK TWO
## RECLAIMING YOUR ORIGINAL SELF: YOUR SECOND LIFE

# CONTENTS

# Introduction

How would you like to wake up tomorrow feeling young and fearless, full of creative energy, unworried about anyone else's opinions, knowing exactly what you want to do with your life, and having the unswerving intention of doing it?

I know that sounds like pie in the sky, especially to someone who's entering midlife. To you the future looks all downhill. Young again? You figure you'll be lucky to grow old as slowly as possible, right? The direction life takes after forty is so obvious that you can't understand why we're even discussing it.

You're not the only person your age who sees it that way. I see that same certainty on the face of every newcomer to the middle years.

"These are the facts. The party's over. There were dreams I had, but it's too late for them now. I have a few years of health, and then I have to be prepared for the worst. Time to face up to the grim news: I will never be young again."

Does that sound pretty close to what you're thinking?

You're in for a surprise.

You're turning a big corner all right, and walking down a new street. As a matter of fact, this is one of life's most significant turns. But the minute you step around that corner what you're going to see will astonish you.

You're not heading for any kind of decline. In fact, you're about to embark on an amazing new beginning. The era you're entering is so different from your first forty years it's completely justifiable to call it your second life.

I want you to understand that this is no variation on what's come before. Your second life is a different world, as different from your first life as college is from grade school. And it all starts as soon as you wake up from the illusions of your youth, the ones that govern your first life.

What illusions am I talking about? The ones that midlife seems to be taking away from you: the youth and beauty that gave the promise of great romance and glory, the delicious sense of endless tomorrows with endless possibilities, the certainty that you'd never grow old (because nothing could be worse) and that you'd never die. None of these beliefs is holding up too well against the passing of time, but your impulse is to hang on for as long as possible.

And that's not a good idea.

If you struggle to hang on to those illusions, you might not wake up for years to the opportunities waiting in your second life. And then you'll look back and say, "Why couldn't I have seen this fifteen years ago? Oh, the things I could have done with all that time!"

So let me say it loud and clear: *Your first life belongs to nature. Your second life belongs to you.*

What's coming is a gradual loosening of the hold that culture and biology have on you, and the arrival of your authentic self. You are losing nothing real by getting older. In fact, you're moving into a life that's sure to be more conscious, centered, creative, and energetic than anything you've known so far. And there is no way to live a life this exciting *until you're over forty*.

If you're reading this with cynicism or doubt, or you think I'm about to launch into some candy-coated Pollyanna bromides, think again. I'm a tough realist. I never make a habit of looking at the rosy side of things. In fact, I'm as surprised as anyone to be able to tell you what I've found on the other side of midlife. As you read these pages, I predict you're going to be surprised too.

But why is it so hard to see that good times are coming? Why do we suffer so when we begin to lose our youth? I pondered that question for some time, and when I first got the answer, I almost laughed, because what causes our blindness is so hidden and at the same time so obvious that it's almost like a trick.

Nature *wants* you to hate getting older. It's part of your biological makeup that you feel anguished about it. Because if everything after midlife looks distasteful, you will naturally resist getting older. And as you'll see, that makes you a lot more useful to your species.

Right now this explanation may not make much sense, but it will. And it certainly doesn't make your present situation any easier to bear. Because whatever the reason, your feelings tell you that something has gone wrong. You weren't supposed to stop being young. Not yet. There was so much you wanted to happen, so much that didn't turn out the way you expected. To you, it looks like the dice have been thrown, and this is what you got. The shine is off tomorrow. You have definitely fallen out of love with your life.

Well, I'd like to show you how to fall back in love with it again.

I know this sounds like a tall order. There are lots of books and magazine articles trying to help you cope with the scary changes that are happening to you, but I'm not talking about coping. I don't think you don't need to *cope* with life; you need to know a new way to *live* it. And you know perfectly well that you feel too young for the books that tell you how to live after retirement. Even I feel too young for them.

And when great thinkers like Carl Jung say it's time to slow down and begin giving something back to the generations behind us, and Erik Erikson implies that creativity is over and it's time for maintenance, I find myself thinking, "Who are you talking to?"

*Nothing's over, and it's time to make a movie or study the ocean floor. Or start a poetry journal. Or go to medical school. Or open a bank.* Or do anything else you've got the brains and talent to do.

But great thinkers all agree on one thing, and so do I:

**It's time to quit wishing you could stop the clock.**

You've got exciting work to do and a whole new way of living to learn, so it's vital that you outgrow your fear of the future as soon as possible. If you don't, you'll waste precious years mourning the loss of youth or, worse, trying to hang on to it.

Look at this all-too-typical scenario: You wake up one day and you're forty. Shock sets in, and you use the next ten or fifteen years fighting the "downward spiral" with everything you've got. You start joining gyms and getting face-lifts; you dream of driving through your birthday cake in a red Bronco or running off with someone half your age. If none of that makes you feel young again—which it won't—you might even decide to sell all your worldly goods, buy a sailboat or a Winnebago, and disappear into the sunset.

None of which might seem so bad for the first three days, but after all that, you wake one morning and still have to figure out how to live.

After a number of years, however, you might come to realize that all your fears of getting older were unfounded, that you've been handed a much better life than you ever expected. It happens to a lot of people.

The problem is, it might not happen to you until your late fifties or sixties.

*Do you really want to wait that long?*

"That would be like paying for a ten-day vacation and arriving on day seven!" a friend told me.

If the years between now and then were good years, I'd say, Who cares? But they're not. In my personal experience and other stories people have told me, they're usually miserable and stressed, loaded with turmoil and feelings of being abandoned, even betrayed, by fate. Few people look back on them with pure pleasure.

Now let's imagine a different scenario.

You hit midlife with no resistance at all, understanding what a special stage you've come to. You realize what a dangerous illusion your feelings of immortality have been. You start paying attention to your dreams to decide how you want to live. You begin to write the books that are in you, or go into the theater and become an actor like you've always wanted, or you become an Arctic explorer, or a business owner, or you build the community you've always known was possible, or you head out and see the world you've always longed to see.

*In other words, you start to live your life to suit who you really are.* You go after your own dreams with new respect and a clear mind because you don't have to prove anything. You're not trying to impress anyone. The top item on your list of priorities says, "Find the life I was born to live." Everything else comes after that.

The trap has opened, and you're free. Fears of getting older or less beautiful, of not being wanted or successful all disappear. You don't have to walk out on your life and escape to the South Seas like a latter-day Gauguin because your feelings of being trapped are gone.

What will show up in their place? Your original self.

A self you haven't seen since childhood—if ever. It's who you were before puberty changed you forever and threw up a mountain range of aches and urgencies, so high you lost sight of the original creature you were. And this time, when that side of you returns, you'll have the know-how and independence you never had as a child. It's a new life, and this time you're going to have a lot of choice about how to live it.

Now that's a nice scenario, isn't it?

And you can have it.

Why waste those years trying to hang on to what you were—

and what was never really you? A waste of time is a waste of talent. It's a waste of happiness. I can't leave you alone and let you come to your senses in your own good time. I have to do whatever I can to wake you up. That's why you're going to hear me saying it over and over, as strongly as I can: *If you're dreading midlife, you have made a big mistake. Run, do not walk, to the first chapter of this book and start reading now.*

Here's what you'll find.

**Book One, "Nature and Instinct: Your First Life," is all about where you are now and how you got there.**

In it you're going to have some major revelations about what's really been driving you all these years and why you now fear midlife. As a woman in one of my workshops said, "I feel like I've been let in on a terrible secret!" What's the secret? Well, here's a big piece of it: When you thought you were doing what *you* wanted, it was usually what *nature* wanted. In your early teens biology flipped the switch, and you jumped onto a treadmill; you started flying in search of what everyone else wanted: love, success, immortality. All at once they seemed so indisputably the only goals worth having. And you still want them today.

That's why you'll have some tough realizations ahead in Book One. Almost every one of your most cherished assumptions is going to be turned on its head. Do you think time is flying by too fast, stealing your years from you? You're going to find out the opposite. Do you think mortality takes your life away? You're going to see that it actually gives your life to you, like a birthday present. Everything you thought you understood—the meaning of aging, that to be beautiful is to be lucky, that romantic love is the greatest of all treasures, that success is the best and failure is the worst thing that can happen to you, even the real causes of your midlife crisis—is going to change forever.

You're going to find out why you believed in illusions masquerading as the truth in the first place and develop a new respect for the greatest playwright of them all: nature. In other words, you're going to start waking up to where you've been for the last twenty-five years.

And every time one of those illusions collapses, you're going to become freer to be yourself. Then your second life, with all the remarkable possibilities it holds, will fall into your hands like a winning lottery ticket.

**Book Two, "Reclaiming Your Original Self: Your Second Life," will show you how to break away from the leftovers of your past and claim your second life.**

You gave away a lot of personal rights in your first life because you were struggling for love and status and you thought you had to. You gave away the right to be an individual with your own personal style, the right to say no, to use your time any way you saw fit, to live your life to suit who you are. But now you've got to begin the process of taking those personal rights back.

You'll have a fight on your hands. Since infancy you've encountered powerful forces in the form of approval and disapproval specifically designed to keep you in line. By this time most of them aren't as real as they appear, but you've internalized them, so they're as tough as ever. You're still scared that if you speak your mind and make your own choices, you'll be punished or rejected or you'll feel painfully guilty. That if you love, you'll have to give your life away to your loved ones. And that if you go after your own dream, you'll wind up alone. You're about to find that none of this is true.

And when you stop being afraid to take it back, you'll be ready to start living that second life of yours. You're going to go on a mission to find your gifts and bring them into your day-to-day life. And I think you're going to surprise yourself with your own originality and productivity. As a matter of fact, I'm going to make what probably sounds like a recklessly bold statement, but I feel sure you'll agree with me by the end of this book: *The goals you pursue in your second life, because they come from your deepest gifts and are unimpeded by the obstacles of youth, can lead you to greatness.*

Not just happiness. Greatness.

Because if you refuse to fritter away your future trying to regain your past, you'll see something amazing start to happen. You'll find yourself looking forward to getting up every morning because it's *life* you love, not some person you have a crush on. You'll start to see everything around you with open eyes instead of the tunnel vision of a hunter looking for prey. You'll feel excitement about what you're going to create, because without doubts and inner conflicts to sap your energy, or fear of disapproval to make you overcautious, you're going to sail! You're going to create things no one but you could possibly create, find out that nothing is more fun than hard work you love to do. And you're especially going to enjoy the precious hours you give yourself in which to do absolutely nothing.

How's that for a nice second life?

I don't make reckless promises. If you're familiar with my earlier work, you already know that. So come along with me and let's get started on your education. I have some fascinating things to show you.

"But I was so much older then,
I'm younger than that now."
—Bob Dylan, "My Back Pages"

# BOOK ONE

Nature and Instinct: Your First Life

# PART ONE
## YOU ARE HERE

"I hate being a grown-up. Having to learn things I
didn't want to know really pisses me off."

(overheard)

# 1
# Don't Panic, It's Only a Midlife Crisis

"I am forty now, and forty years is a lifetime; it is
extremely old age. To go on living after forty is
unseemly, disgusting, immoral! Who goes on living after
forty? Give me a sincere and honest answer! I'll tell
you—rogues and fools."

Fedor Dostoyevsky

"It was only in my forties that I started feeling young."

Henry Miller

You've pretty much gotten your life shaped up. You have a decent
career, a nice place to live, a loving spouse. Maybe you're a
middle manager with a husband who's a good guy and two kids who
are very self-sufficient, or you've got your own business and you're
getting by all right. You've accomplished certain goals and have accepted that some others are unattainable. Your life may not be perfect,
but it's better than a lot of other people's. Anyway, it's always seemed
okay until now.

But something's wrong. You've got so much of what you wanted
you should be feeling fine. But the excitement isn't there like it used to
be. Life was supposed to feel more complete than this. Instead the
emptiness is undeniable. Have you made a terrible mistake? Have you
been on the wrong path? Or is it just all over, and now you're going to
be dumped into a big pile of middle-agers, soon-to-be has-beens? This

1

*looks like the end of the time of wonderful possibilities. From now on it will just be more of the same, except, oh, yeah, your health will start declining. Slowly, if you're lucky.*

*Before you put a down payment on your retirement home, there's something you should know. Life doesn't end with youth any more than it ends when you graduate from high school. All that's happening is you're leaving one world and entering a very different one. You've simply begun to outgrow the first stage of life, and you're in the middle of a major transformation into one far more interesting.*

*You're in a transition, not a decline.*

*It's very important that you know the difference. If you can see this upheaval for what it really is, you can avoid making some costly, unnecessary mistakes and wasting precious time. If you don't understand what's happening, you can't help wanting to go back, trying to find some way to retreat from the future.*

*But it's a transformation, that's a promise. And the right direction is straight ahead.*

---

What is a midlife crisis? And are you sure you're having one?

Try answering the following questions and let's see.

1. Do you find yourself spending hours at your desk in the office just staring off into space, or daydreaming about where you'd rather be?

2. Do you find yourself resenting the twentysomethings at work for their ideas and enthusiasm?

3. Are you starting to utter clichés with absolute conviction to people younger than you, like "People who live in glass houses shouldn't throw stones"? Do you ever think, "Wow, a stitch in time really does save nine!"?

4. Have you noticed a renewed interest in playing high-impact sports like basketball? Do you insist on playing with people younger than you are and get depressed if you

can't perform at their level? Do you get angry with yourself for waking up with a bad back the next morning?

5. Do you find that though you're getting older, the women or men you find attractive are staying the same age—and you realize that now there's a twenty-year difference? Do you get confused when you look at attractive young people because you can't decide whether you want to sleep with them or take the cigarettes out of their mouths?

6. Do you search the mirror every night, looking closely for signs of new wrinkles in your face and panic if you see one? Do you read plastic surgery ads and keep a secret file with the phone numbers of surgeons? When someone says he or she has had a face-lift, do you ask for more information?

7. Do you feel—about your career or your town or your marriage—"I've been here too long. I'll never get out if I don't move soon"?

8. Do you catch yourself in horror giving young people unsolicited advice, saying things like "When I was your age . . ."?

9. Do you feel your chances to do certain things have passed you by? Do you sometimes remember that you always wanted to live in Paris for a year or to try your hand at show business or modeling or sports?

10. Do you feel that having children has turned you and your spouse into caretakers and workhorses and you can't remember how to have fun anymore?

11. Do you feel with some regret that you didn't turn into the person you thought you'd be or have the life you expected to have at forty?

If you answered yes to even one of those questions, consider yourself positively diagnosed. You're having a midlife crisis.

**What is a midlife crisis anyway?**

"It's when you finally get there and find out there's no there there," said a friend, paraphrasing Gertrude Stein.

Something odd has happened, as if the wind has dropped and the boat stopped moving. It seems as if the whole thing you called your life, your purpose, has gone into a slump. At first glance it's hard to see what's causing these feelings. Your energies and values haven't changed, and chances are you're as strong and healthy as you were ten years ago. But your whole world is starting to look different. Everything you see and feel makes you certain that some game you've been involved in your whole life is winding down and will soon be over. Everything you saw on the road ahead, everything you pursued and hoped for—success, admiration, love, power, adventure—has either disappeared or doesn't look nearly as good as it used to.

This state isn't caused by failure, and it isn't fixed by success. If you didn't achieve your goals or you've had to start over in your career or your personal life, you may feel discouraged; but even those who did reach their goals—who found their perfect love, became successful, showed the world how good they were, made worthy contributions to the world—also find that something is missing.

"Everything's so anticlimactic," said a successful casting director. "I mean, my life's okay, but I always looked to the future. Now I can't see anything there."

"I guess I have to accept it," a college dean told me. "I couldn't wait to make it, and finally I did. But it's kind of ordinary. Just another thing. I guess that's part of growing up."

"I just think that the rest is about such sad stuff, getting old, losing your parents, just terrible stuff," said a forty-year-old journalist.

"All I see ahead is less of the same," said a forty-three-year-old executive. "Less strength, less youth, less sex, less time until the party's over or I get too old to dance at it. I love my wife and

4

kids, but I have very strong impulses to do something dangerous, like fall in love with my twenty-year-old secretary."

"I feel stuck in my job and my life," said a working mom who just hit forty-five. "My kids are getting to the point where they don't need me as much, and my career has kind of stalled. Am I facing twenty more years of the same routine?"

You've never felt this way before. What has happened? I'll tell you. Your future just changed. What used to lie ahead was an endless amount of time, full of the magic of potential. You felt that the satisfaction and fulfillment you were struggling for would show up sooner or later.

Well, sooner has passed and later just showed up.

Pretty scary, isn't it? Well, let me tell you something you couldn't have known during all your years of building a career and a home. Life until now was just a warm-up. Now comes the good part.

**Oh, right. Getting old has its compensations? Thanks for nothing.**

I can see your unbelieving smile. Another person telling you that when the good times wind down, you'll be given some kind of consolation prize, like a gold watch. I don't mean that at all. *The truth is, there's somebody inside you who hasn't happened yet, who's been waiting to come on the scene and create a new life. One that was never possible until now.*

Nothing you've been told has predicted this; quite the contrary. Every piece of evidence you have shows this to be an ending, the beginning of the downward spiral.

I remember feeling exactly like you, during a few very uncomfortable years when I couldn't decide whether to fight the tide and join a gym or buy a rocking chair and learn how to grow old gracefully. When I thought about the future at all (which I tried not to do), all that came to me was "Is this how my life turned out? Is this my final score? Is the game really over?"

And then, in what seemed coincidental at the time, a very

difficult decade slammed into my life. Years passed. I had jumped on a roller coaster and was careening so fast that I forgot all about my face-lift versus rocking chair dilemma and just prayed to get out alive. Midlife crisis? What was that? I was too busy. I surged ahead with a determination I never had before. Instead of complaining about how hard things were, I started a business and jumped into an impulsive marriage. For a few years both projects burned very hot, but then they sputtered and died out in a series of dizzying events that were painful and bewildering. At the end I was sitting in a pile of rubble, dazed, unable to see clearly what had happened. I had no thought of what could possibly come next. My resources, financial and emotional, were entirely depleted. It was all over. Or so I thought.

But when the smoke cleared and I managed to get to my feet, the most amazing thing had happened. I didn't feel incomplete or empty at all. For the first time in my memory, I no longer felt lonely.

*Most curious of all, I stopped feeling old.*

This was completely illogical. A decade had passed, but I felt three decades younger. What on earth was going on? I felt more like the eleven-year-old I once was than the over-the-hill midlifer I was supposed to be. Only this time, unlike that eleven-year-old, I was free to do any damn thing I pleased!

I still feel that way, another ten years later. The more time I spend in this new stage of life, the more my youth looks like a storm of confusion and desperation. I never thought of myself as a driven person—until I stopped being one. And I was shocked to discover how hungry I had been. Now, for the first time, nothing is missing. I still want a lot out of life: to see the world, to meet new people, to write another book, to study history, to keep up with my kids' lives . . . many things. But the ache of need is gone.

Where did that hunger go?

When I sat down to figure out the answer to that question, I discovered some very interesting things about myself.

*The first was that I'd had a major midlife crisis and never knew it!*

That whole roller coaster ride that made me forget the issues of midlife? That's exactly what it was for: to make me forget! One by one, I looked at what had happened when that fire burned so high. And there was the truth, plain as day. My marriage was to someone so inappropriate even he commented on it. The business was much too big for one person, especially a single parent with two young children. What on earth had I been thinking of?

But when I was defeated and the racket was over and the roller coaster ride ended, it was clear that the whole panic I'd unconsciously felt at forty was a mistake. Life wasn't over at all.

While I was busy making all that effort to stay young and vital, I had been passing through a profound transition. Life hadn't been ending. That was a skewed viewpoint, based on the self-importance of youth. I was just passing through a natural transformation! What I found was totally unexpected: I had landed in a peaceful, pleasant place with less anguish and more ease than I'd ever felt in my life.

I think that if I'd known all along what was really coming, I wouldn't have panicked, and might not have jumped on that roller coaster at all. I could have saved myself a lot of grief and a lot of time. Life has gotten so good since then that I could kick myself for avoiding it for so long.

**But why didn't I know that midlife was just a transition to a better existence?**

I should have known. My mother was a great role model. She knew how to follow her dreams and take all of us with her. When she was thirty-five, she got sick of shoveling snow in Detroit and decided to take a look at California. She and my dad bought a trailer and we all drove across Route 66 to California. They decided California looked pretty good, so we stayed. They opened a small business together, bought a little house, and on weekends my mother happily cultivated a flower garden that blossomed all year long. She continues at eighty-five to make her own decisions, live her own life, and enjoy herself. There was nothing awful about the way she lived during or after midlife. Why hadn't I learned from her?

The answer won't surprise you because I'm sure you've felt it yourself: I wasn't interested in her life. Maybe *she* liked her life, but how could I possibly want what she had? To me, she was *always* old. I would *never* be. I kept my eye on John Lennon instead, because it looked like he was going to find a way to grow up and still stay forever young. Then he was gone, and we never got the chance to see how his life would turn out.

The truth is, we don't know how to be forty and fifty anymore. Times have changed, and there's no one to show us the way. We keep trying to invent new tricks. One of the more recent ones showed up during the recent wave of prosperity, when young people expected to get so rich they'd never have to think about getting older. They would simply buy bigger houses, better cars, and retire at thirty-five to raise thoroughbred horses on their own ranches in Colorado and to ski until they were ninety. Then the tidal wave of prosperity dropped them, and the party was over. Far from retiring to the ageless world of the rich and famous, they couldn't afford to pay the maintenance on their condos. Bitter jokes were circulating: "Question: What do you call a broker with a BMW and a three-hundred-thousand-dollar apartment? Answer: Waiter!" They couldn't buy their way out after all. Now they had to deal with getting older like everybody else.

Even the survivors who were able to hang on to good careers have learned that no one is safe. The rules keep changing, you're assaulted from different corners, you're worn out from watching your back, and you could be downsized at any time. Expenses zoom out of sight. Forget early retirement. You're turning into a wage slave like your father—and you're supposed to call yourself lucky for having a job at all.

Life never turns out the way you expect.

The feelings that descend upon us at midlife have us so scared that we want to throw ourselves headlong back into the arena of youth. Certainly we have no intention of cooperating with a world that's pushing us into depressing old age.

Most of us—certainly I include myself—are too stubborn to walk away from the game of youth until we're thrown out. It's a shame to waste time fighting the inevitable, but most of us can't help losing a lot of time by being stubborn. I regret the years I wasted, but I didn't know what else to do. Now I see the whole panorama much more clearly, and I've reached a conclusion.

I did a lot of stupid things before I was forty, but I don't regret them nearly as much as I used to because I now believe that most of the dumb things you do before you turn forty are unavoidable.

*But the dumb things you do after you turn forty are very avoidable.*

And there's nothing that will help you avoid them but some radical icon toppling and a crash course in reality. It's time to stop believing all the hype about youth, love, and success everyone fed you because that hype has shoved you right into "age shock" and even near hysteria.

**What is this bogeyman of midlife that's scaring you out of your wits?**

For one thing, we're suffering from an image of aging that comes from a different time. An image that was never anything but propaganda. Think of those dear old grannies on Christmas cards, happily knitting their way into oblivion. Did you ever know anyone like that?

I was recently watching a video of *The Little Rascals*, depicting a perfect old granny and a pompous, steel-backed matron, and I said to my mother, "Whatever happened to those old ladies, Mom? I never see them. Did they all relocate to Vegas?"

"They never existed," she said. "That's the movies."

I certainly never came across them when I was growing up in Detroit during World War II. My grandfather, depressed by the death of my grandmother, came alive again in his seventies when he was hired back to work at the "war plant." My aunts and uncles, in their forties and fifties, went to work in the factories, too. At 3:00 A.M., when they got off work, they'd meet at a local diner for raucous breakfasts that were more like parties, resisting sleep because they had so much energy.

Ignoring age labels was nothing new to them. They were funny, tough, and sassy before the war too. After all, *their* parents were gutsy immigrants who had torn up roots in Europe to come to America and begin a totally new life with no money and no one to guide them. They came from villages that hadn't changed in a hundred years to the newest country in the world, carved out a livelihood, bought homes, listened to radios, talked on telephones, drove the first cars, and had no intention of missing anything.

Their children, my aunts and uncles, grew up in the Roaring Twenties, when the culture went wild. Everywhere flappers stunned their staid parents by flaunting sex, cigarettes, and booze, creating a generation gap more extreme than kids with spiked green hair and nose rings would create seventies years later. One of my uncles owned a speakeasy where you really had to knock three times and say, "Joe sent me," and an aunt of mine opened a sandwich shop at one of the first airports ever built, often leaving the operation to an assistant at the offer of a pilot to take her up for a joyride. They managed a little real estate, had families, made deals. Then they lost everything in the crash of 1929, dusted themselves off, and got started again.

And no matter how old they got, none of them ever looked anything like those grannies on the Christmas cards.

Why did they seem to lack our despair about aging? Because life was never really settled for them. It was always changing, always new. Whenever life is exciting, notions of age just fall away. People act like themselves, not the representatives of some stereotyped age-group.

As a matter of fact, age stereotypes weren't yet the commonplace they were to become. They got their real start in this country when World War II ended.

Most of us forget this, but something radical happened to our thinking in the United States when the soldiers came back from the war and our views of how we were supposed to act suddenly took a sharp about-face. We've been feeling the shock waves ever since. Women and older people had to give up their wartime jobs because the returning veterans needed them. Suddenly movies, which had come into their own as powerful propaganda machines during the war, swung into action again, churning out prescriptions for new identities; they began to portray a "good" woman as someone who took care of her home and her man, never complained or demanded anything, and certainly never humiliated her husband by holding a job. If she wasn't content with this, she was unnatural and twisted, a danger to her family's emotional well-being, and she might even have to go to one of those psychoanalysts who suddenly showed up on the scene.

Women weren't the only ones forced into a rigid role. For the country to get back on its economic feet again, men had to stop being warriors and become stable and productive. So they were pressured into becoming stereotypes too. They learned that a real man is serious and responsible, finds a job, wears a suit, and never lets his family down. And he never leaves his job no matter how it withers his soul. He acts "normal" like his neighbors and buys all the right things—suburban homes, refrigerators, stoves, cars, and barbecues. Then he trades them in for newer things when the neighbors do.

The surviving elders, both men and women, many of whom had been running production in war plants, were supposed to retire and become cute and harmless, or they might be portrayed in movies as evil and overambitious, maybe even secretly traitorous during the war (when the *good* people were away fighting). The ones who saw through it all, and found this propaganda outrageous, were nullified by being cast in the "old" stereotype: cranky, eccentric, and irrelevant.

Every child who was watching was fed these stereotypes with their morning Cheerios. Their conclusions were inevitable: Originality and individuality were okay only in children, because children weren't important. Growing up meant facing the hard truth that life isn't supposed to be fun. Adults settled down, resigned themselves to the goals set by nature (breed, then quietly become obsolete) and culture (do the right thing—however the culture defines that at any given time). Growing up was the end of playing.

This dreary viewpoint, which became so useful in the late forties and the fifties, carried all the markers of its newly useful Freudian origins: very nineteenth-century, solemn, and scientific European male thinking. Very serious. And oppressive.

Too oppressive. As soon as the children of these postwar adults got old enough, they blew the whole structure sky-high. If their parents represented adulthood, they wanted no part of it. It was the sixties, and the only right response to the responsibilities was to throw away your girdle, smoke dope, make fun of the neighbors, love people with long hair and funny clothes, do your own thing—and never, ever trust anyone over thirty. Their younger brothers and sisters, in fact almost everyone born between 1946 and 1964, watched them tear down the humorless edifices of fifties culture with rapt admiration.

Being young was absolutely beautiful.

**That's why growing older is especially hard for your generation.**

The sixties generation created a revolution in how young people saw themselves. Where they once had been taught that young people were immature and should listen to their wiser parents, now youth came to represent all that was pure and good and expansive. Age was corrupt and selfish and narrow. The rejection of the older generation was total.

But after a while many of them found they didn't want to live out their lives stoned or raise kids on a Day-Glo bus, and they began to change.

"We spotted the enemy, clear as day. But the years passed, and the enemy became us," a friend told me.

Obviously it was time to grow up, but they wanted to do it the right way. A new way. And they simply didn't know how.

Still, they did their best. Tiptoeing into adulthood, they decided maybe a career and a family wouldn't destroy them if they were extra careful, and they swore that although they had broken their promise to stay under thirty, they'd find a way to hang on to their youthful goodness and be especially vigilant about never turning forty.

And now they're breaking that promise too.

*What if none of that directly affected you?*

Even if your head was in a completely different place, your thirty- and forty-year-old identity shocked you because of an almost universal experience, a trigger that was set to go off by a force more unchanging than any particular cultural era you grew up in (as you'll see in the next chapter). Somewhere around the age of thirty-six or thirty-seven an odd realization hits you: That's usually how old your parents were when you first became conscious of their ages.

"I don't remember knowing my mother's age until she was about thirty-seven," a woman told me recently. "But now that's my age! I'm as old as my own mother!"

No wonder it's called a crisis.

**So here you are. What now?**

You've got some fresh thinking to do at this point in your life.

You've got to push aside those mythical notions of what it means to grow up, however they got there, because this crisis is a fake. You're not running down at all. You've barely broken in the engine.

Because the age myths neglected to point out that when youthful goals (competition, the search for love, the protection of children) start to move aside, a radically new kind of energy is freed up. All the effort that was tied up in trying to fill those adolescent yearnings and bend reality to your will is released and now becomes available. For what could be the first time in your adult life, you can use that energy to fuel different goals.

Once reality knocks your illusions out of the ring, you're going to find that desperation for love and glory went with them. Now those dreams will begin to look like children's toys—and expensive ones, at that. When your vision clears, you'll begin to see an astonishing new way to live.

That's what happened to me when I stood up after my disasters and stopped feeling old. To my complete surprise, I had picked up where I left off years earlier, when I was a preteen. But this was even better because now I had the benefits of my age. It was like being a kid with a car, a driver's license, and a credit card. Now when I hear people say they'd never go back to being young again, I no longer think it's sour grapes talking. They just might be feeling like I do.

It's been said that "youth is nature and age is art." If art is taken to mean "artifice," like the makeup and soft lights that are used to disguise signs of age, I disagree. But I don't interpret it that way at all. To me it means you stop being driven by instinct and wake up to a different level of consciousness—complex, subtle, and intense, loaded with revelation and insight. Art means you see familiar things as if they were new, like an artist sees them. It means you stop trying always to bend reality to suit your taste, and you face your subject like an artist does, with respect and admiration. Your materials become life *as it is*—not as you wished it would be.

Because when you give up your youthful urgency to control

every outcome, you can finally throw yourself wholeheartedly, without conflict, into whatever matters to you. For the first time, *all you're responsible for is what you can do*. The rest belongs to fate. The change is so radical and thrilling that you'll never again regret leaving behind the drives of youth.

**Transformations like these are nerve-racking, no doubt about it, but they aren't endings.**

To paraphrase Mark Twain, the reports of your demise have been greatly exaggerated. So don't sell your business and run off to Tahiti with the baby-sitter, and don't lock yourself up in a dark room with the TV remote grafted to your hand. Nothing bad has happened. There's simply a life-changing shift in your outlook coming up. If you stop being afraid, you can pass through this transformation faster than you think and get a head start on your second life without wasting a lot of time.

So, let's begin by finding out where you are now.

## EXERCISE 1

### *What I really think—the cosmic questions*

You're probably not going to want to do this exercise because it's a rough one. But I want you to ask yourself some questions you don't like thinking about. You know, the big questions: Why am I here? Where am I going? What does it all mean? These are frightening issues, and I wouldn't ask you to drag them up, except you know perfectly well that they're floating around in the back of your head anyway. So, instead of being alone with them, pull them out, and we'll work on them together. We need these questions now, here at the beginning of this book, because I'm going to ask them again at the end, and I'll make you one promise: Whatever your answers, or your inability to come up with *any* answers yet, your feelings about them are going to change.

Once you've read through these pages, I promise you won't

mind the questions anymore. They'll become excellent tools you'll want to work with.

So, for the sake of taking the fangs out of this exercise, jump right in. Pick up a pencil, and write the answers down without pausing to think. You may be surprised at what comes out.

**The big questions.**
Where am I going?
Did I do the right thing with my time so far?
What's ahead?
What are my greatest fears?
What do I really want in my future?
What do I definitely not want any more of?
What regrets would I hate to have when I look back on my life in later years?
Why am I on this planet?

**Take a look at how some other people answered.**
Len, stockbroker, forty-four:
*Where am I going?* I have no idea. Daily emergencies eat up all my time.

*Did I do the right thing with my time so far?* I always wonder about that. I keep thinking I must have done something wrong, or I would have wound up somewhere better.

*What's ahead?* Well, I'll never be a millionaire. I just hope for status quo, but that's not very appealing.

*What are my greatest fears?* That I'll never find out what I'm supposed to be doing.

*What do I really want in my future?* I don't know, but being a broker isn't it.

*What do I definitely not want any more of?* Confusion. Not knowing which direction to take.

*What regrets would I hate to have when I look back on my life?* That I wasted my time. That I should have married whatsername.

16

*Why am I on this planet?* That's the question that cuts the deepest. I don't know, and I'm afraid I never will.

Gwen, forty-one, accountant, divorced, no children:
*Where am I going?* Somewhere more pleasant than where I've been. Somewhere where I am fulfilled rather than doing the fulfilling.

*Did I do the right thing so far?* I'm not sure. I probably underachieved to avoid the pain of rejection and failure.

*What's ahead?* Sometimes I think it will be new horizons, learning, loving, living. But sometimes I think it's all going to be the same as now, frustrating with some good times and watching my face get older.

*What are my greatest fears?* That this is it for me, that I'll be lonely and forgotten, that I won't grow.

*What do I really want in my future?* Everything. Myself to be independent and alive and happy with a mate.

*What do I definitely not want anymore?* People who don't know how to love.

*What regrets would I hate to have when I look back on my life?* That I never found anyone to love, that I never found the right kind of work for me.

*What am I on this planet for?* To make the most of it. Whatever that means.

Sophie, forty-four, ex–club singer:
*Where am I going?* Haven't a clue.

*Did I do the right thing with my time so far?* Yes, so far.

*What's ahead?* Not sure I want to know.

*What are my greatest fears?* How am I going to support myself?

*What do I really want in my future?* Happiness.

*What do I definitely not want anymore?* The last six years of fear and my period.

*What am I on this planet for?* To discover and understand so I can make choices.

Randy, fifty-two, librarian, divorced:

*Where am I going?* Forward, but I don't know what's up there.

*Did I do the right thing with my time so far?* No, because I thought things would always stay the same, and now I think I've blown my chances.

*What's ahead?* Who knows? I don't much like to think about it.

*What are my greatest fears?* Death. What else?

*What do I really want in my future?* Money and security.

*What do I definitely not want any more of?* Things.

*What regrets would I hate to have when I look back on my life?* That I didn't have enough happiness.

*Why am I on this planet?* Parents put me here.

If some of those answers—or your own—made you say, "Ouch!" I don't blame you. But remember, your answers just indicate the starting point. They'll begin to change almost immediately, as soon as you begin to understand where this viewpoint really comes from. But even now I wouldn't trust those answers too much. Try this exercise, and you'll see what I mean.

## EXERCISE 2

### *Your changing viewpoints through the years*

Here's a free-association exercise that will show you how your viewpoint has changed over time. You can write your answers on a sheet of paper or speak them into a recorder.

*What did the following words mean to you at age five? Fifteen? Twenty-five? Today?*

Potential

Someday

When I grow up
Happily ever after
Married people with good careers
Midlife
Maturity
Thirty years old
Forty years old
Sixty years old
Artist
Businessman
Cowboy
The best years of your life
Never married

If you're like most of us, all those terms meant one thing at one age and a different thing at another. That's just as true right now. The way the future looks has everything to do with the stage you're going through.

## EXERCISE 3

### *A glimpse of the future*

Now I'd like you to think for a moment about how it would be if this problem completely disappeared. Imagine you stopped seeing midlife as any kind of decline and began to see it as a transition to something better. What would you do differently? And what would you stop doing? Really take some time to imagine this happening. Now write down your answers to those questions. You've just gotten a preview of your second life. Nice, isn't it?

With that promise in hand, turn the page and take a closer look at the biological programming that makes us all, no matter how smart or sophisticated, plunge into a midlife crisis. I think you're in for a few surprises.

# 2
# You Are Not the Favorite

"I lost the conviction that the lights would always turn
green for me, the pleasant certainty that those rather
passive virtues which had won me approval as a child
automatically guaranteed me not only Phi Beta Kappa
keys but happiness, honor and the love of a
good man. . . ."
Joan Didion, "On Self-Respect," *Slouching Towards
Bethlehem*

"Don't you think my narcissism is the most interesting
thing there is?"
Norman Rush, *Mating*

*T*he stage is set from the moment we're born. We start our lives as complete narcissists. When we're hungry, we don't listen to reason; we scream with astonished outrage for food. If our parents are sleeping or busy or tired, that's their problem, not ours. It's not that we're bad or unloving creatures; in fact, we're loaded with love and affection. But only as long as we get our way.

Fortunately this self-centeredness causes a positive response in our parents. Because no matter how sane they may be on other issues, they're a little crazy when it comes to their babies. Our parents are fiercely protective, they want us happy, and most important of all, they find us so adorable that they put up with our selfishness with amusement, even pride. Like our narcissism, their adoration is a powerful force for the survival of our species.

And to us, their love seems absolutely appropriate. We figure we deserve it. They smile at us, and we smile back, thinking how nice it is that we're the most important thing in the universe.

But that illusion starts to fade after a very short time.

Every day, every year of our lives, our cheerful self-centeredness is under terrific assault. As we grow out of infancy, we are continually surprised, then outraged, and finally frightened to find that adults don't always want to cater to us. Or that sometimes they even get angry with us. Or that they actually love someone else in addition to us! Terrified and wounded, we struggle fiercely against these injustices and pull every trick in the book to get things back to where they were at the beginning, when we were adorable and beloved, the center of our universe with the power to make adults jump to our every whim.

It is this response, our endless effort to get back our most-favored-baby status, that runs our first life.

If that seems like an exaggerated claim, that's because as adults we have trouble understanding what a jolt this loss of importance deals to the system of a small child. But just imagine you were on your way to work one day and without warning all the oxygen in the atmosphere disappeared for one minute. You'd be gasping with shock, not sure what had happened. And if it happened twice, you'd spring into action. No effort would be too great to make you feel safe again. That's the kind of impact we suffer growing up, every time our narcissism collides with reality and we glimpse the fact that we might be unprotected, without special privileges, not fate's favorite at all.

We're not maladjusted. We're right in step with the program. We just don't know it yet.

There's a biological purpose behind this painful process. The drama of this loss of unconditional love and our relentless struggle to get it back again is brilliantly—if unkindly—designed to save our species. It starts a domino effect that ensures we will leave our childhood homes to find mates, reproduce as often as possible, and protect our children until they're old enough to do the same.

That's why we compete obsessively with our siblings for attention. That's why we walk out on our unfair families at adolescence, in *search of someone who will love us as we should be loved. That's why we try to be beautiful and successful and worthy of being adored again. That's also why we respond to the love our own infants feel for us— and only us—by falling madly in love with them.*

*And that's why we're thrown into panic at midlife. Because we suddenly realize we're going to lose the battle.*

*After about four decades we look up and the handwriting is on the wall. We will not be the lucky ones who have no sorrow, no failures, no losses. What happens to everybody else can happen to us as well. And as if that weren't bad enough, we're delivered the final blow: We are mortals. It's unbelievable but true. We too will die one day, just like ordinary humans.*

*There it is. No matter what deals we have made, what capitulations and accommodations, the news is finally unmasked: Nature is going for unconditional surrender. Our frantic struggle to fight off the inevitable is failing. Inside, we can feel ourselves beginning to tire of this battle, but we know we have to struggle harder than ever before just to stay in place, because what's coming is too depressing to contemplate: We'll end up like the old lions in nature documentaries, once powerful but now on a terrible downhill slide.*

*The party's over.*

*But struggling to maintain some version of center stage is becoming exhausting: We don't really want to exercise four hours a day to have flat stomachs; we don't want our shoes to be uncomfortable. And we're not as confident as we used to be that winning hearts will give us everything we really want. But how can we stop trying? What's the alternative, the descent into a permanent state of second best?*

*How's that for a dreary picture? Some of you are shaking your heads vigorously and denying that you ever think that way at all. But more of you are wondering how I read your minds. The answer is that I've heard this sad expectation voiced by everyone I've ever spoken to who was suffering from the crisis at midlife.*

*But none of this is going to happen at all!*

*Then why do we all believe it? Because we're supposed to. It's part of the drama of your first life, the one that began when the curtain went up at birth and you found yourself at center stage. Midlife has brought you to the final act of your first life, this intense, decades-long, dynamic drama that's had you battling to regain that position.*

*What you're not supposed to know yet is that beneath all this striving and torment is an authentic, original self who never was a narcissist at all. And that this superb creature doesn't even appear until the narcissist loses its struggle to be the favorite, the drama is over, the curtain falls, and you walk out of the theater into a beautiful reality.*

*Because you're about to discover a remarkable fact: All these relentless assaults on your narcissism have handed you your ticket to a wonderful second life.*

---

**Narcissism drove the whole show.**

In Greek mythology, Narcissus was a demigod, so beautiful that everyone fell in love with him. Including himself. He became so enraptured with his own image in a pool that he couldn't stop looking, and he wasted away and died. Some versions of the myth say he tried to kiss himself, fell in, and drowned. In either case, the myth is a clear warning against being too self-centered.

But we can't help ourselves. Why?

Because the first forty years of life belong to biology, not to us.

You see, if nature has a favorite at all, it's not the individual, it's the species. We think that narcissistic feelings like jealousy, rivalry, competitiveness, obsession, even the depression that follows any loss are all unfortunate aberrations and point to a wobbly psychology or a faulty upbringing. But everything indicates that these emotions are both biological and inevitable, put there by nature for specific survival purposes, present at birth.

Your mother's rapture for you as a newborn baby is a universal trait, found everywhere among animals. You started life with

24

that rapture directed at you. That's what made you cheerful, secure, and interested in living. Very good for your species. Both you and your mother believed that she would feel that rapture for you forever, and for a while you were the most important thing in her life. When you looked up at her, you saw a love she showed no one else. And if another baby came along, she was genetically programmed to look at *that* baby with the same eyes, so that baby would be safe and happy like you were. And so you would go crazy.

Again, very good for your species.

Even if no other babies came, that change was still terrible and far more incomprehensible; you watched her attention gradually turn to the rest of her life and away from you without ever understanding what you had done wrong.

Either way, this loss of center stage was the first and most powerful of a series of emotional triggers, all designed to make you follow the plan nature had for you. Your future moves were set up by this first ripping away of the rapturous love you needed so desperately and its terrible aftermath, an unshakable sense of loss that you would spend many years striving to undo.

Your misery at that betrayal, your rivalry and jealousy, your struggle to regain the lost love, all these feelings that are so hard on children, are utterly essential to the survival of your species. They are the force that pulls us into the biological race.

How can I be so sure these impulses are biological? Well, anytime you see a human characteristic—like narcissism in infants, for example—appearing everywhere, even in isolated groups of humans who've had little contact with other groups, you can assume that it has some kind of survival value, that it's been handed down through the generations since the species was young. Millions of years of washing out the problematic traits of our ancestors have resulted in our present ways of responding to the world around us.

That means nature "likes" what remains. It's been found useful and is now part of the plan to protect the species.

Now, we know there's no lady named Mother Nature who's wearing a garland of leaves and making decisions about springtime. But when a species of plant or animal has survived and flourished, that means it handed down traits that would help its offspring also survive and flourish. When that happens, you can say nature or biology favored it. Because if ever a trait stopped an individual from reproducing successfully or stopped him from caring for his offspring, his genes would have died with him and vanished from the gene pool.

Narcissism is therefore obviously a survival trait. It's useful when we're infants because it makes us insistently attach ourselves to our parents. It's useful when we're adolescents too, when it pushes us to fill our erotic need to mate. And narcissism is useful again when we fiercely protect our children, finding them far more valuable than anyone else's. As a result, our narcissism makes us formidable allies in the war for the survival of our species.

**We may not realize it, but our species' fight becomes our fight.**

We don't know it, but we want passionately to do everything our species needs from us. We're irresistibly compelled to try to be strong, beautiful, and smart, to compete for the best mates, and to grab the biggest piece of meat for our offspring. We have plenty of drive and big emotional needs to fill. And we want satisfaction.

Of course we think we're pleasing only ourselves. However, once the individual has accomplished the tasks that ensure the survival of its own kind, the usefulness of its irresistible compulsions declines very rapidly. But at midlife our drive may be only slightly slower, and the goals still look like the only game in town. We still want to be in the competition, but we're no longer needed like we once were.

We don't know this either. But we do know we're having

more trouble getting the best mates and the biggest piece of meat. And we don't feel very good about it.

That's pretty cold for the individual, but it works out fine for the species.

**It's kind of heartless to be dumped like this.**

Or maybe the heartless thing is that we were drafted in the first place. After all, we've given a lot of energy and years to the survival of the species, and we haven't had a chance to concentrate on what we as individuals wanted from life. But that's the price of admission to being alive. Without it we wouldn't be here to have this discussion in the first place.

The truth is, we're *supposed* to be unhappy about this. If we try to hang in for as long as we can, attempting to stay young, we just might produce one more baby.

But when the hormones finally do kick out, the biological favor is transferred to the breeding members of the group, who are adorned with attractive bodies, thick hair, all the features of mating that at forty begin to fade. Even the health of these younger, more fertile members is sheltered by a strong immune system, while ours is allowed to decline.

Wasn't there any survival value in having experienced older members of a tribe to guide the others? Yes, probably. But their numbers had to be balanced against the available resources. Who was useful in a small group of humans was probably much clearer long ago, when food was in short supply, mates were not plentiful, many mothers and most infants didn't survive childbirth, and life expectancy was painfully short. We're living so much longer now that this pattern isn't as easy to see anymore. These days we *all* feel important, whether we're useful to the species or not. We don't live under the same hardships anymore because we've done an amazing job of fighting back. Humans have created impressive technology to bend the rules. With all our advances in medical science, we stay young and live much longer than our ancestors. Nature keeps dropping us, but technology often catches us before we hit the ground. People with illnesses or accidents that would have killed them off in earlier times are now living to tell the tale.

Yet the fact remains that at forty we're starting to be thrown out of the popularity game while we're still in the mood to get all our narcissistic needs filled. Unlike cavemen, we have the luxury of worrying about all those years ahead waiting for us, obviously (to us) empty of personal pleasure. This clash between our urgent longing to be desired and our diminishing powers to attract is so like the first feelings of the infant narcissist that the similarity is impossible to miss.

Yet during our lives there are some interim periods of happiness and contentment when this raging battle disappears almost entirely.

**Our narcissistic drive kicks into full gear at three times in our lives. In between, we get some intermissions.**

Our extremes of self-absorption aren't constant. They rise and fall at certain times in our lives. Sometimes we absolutely must get our own way, and other times we relax and enjoy the environment.

The obsession to fill our personal needs becomes activated at three crucial periods in our lives: as infants (hanging on to our mothers for dear life), as adolescents (driven by the same intensity and hunger to find that same kind of love in our mates), and as the parents of small babies (powerfully attached to our own infants). At these three times we belong to our biological urges, not to reason. We're driven by powerful impulses to do what it takes to stay near our mothers, to possess our lovers, to protect our children.

But in between those intense periods we relax and experience something very different.

Our first intermission comes just before adolescence, from roughly eight years of age until we're about eleven. Just at the age a human can first begin to take care of itself, we start to let go of our desperate need for our parents. We begin to accept how powerless we are to remain our mother's favorite being, console ourselves with the promise to fix that injustice when we grow up, and put the whole struggle on the back burner. For a few years we are free to pursue our own interests instead of those of our species. At this time we're very exceptional creatures, at our most clear and creative, interested in friends, curious learners. Girls aren't afraid to be smarter than boys because they're not yet trying to win love. Boys are not yet trying to prove they're men. For a while we're actually quite sane.

Then, at around thirteen, our hormones kick in, and all those wonderful characteristics fall under the onslaught of adolescence.

But when the dust settles, somewhere in our twenties or early thirties, if we've managed to find a satisfying love relationship, we marry and relax into another pleasant intermission. We even grow a little surprised at how intense we were about setting up this relationship in the first place as our mates change from fantastic objects of desire into regular people like us. Yet all things being equal, we don't mind. We have babies or we plan for the future, and do our best to make secure homes, and enjoy the comfort of our lives.

For a while.

And then, just when you'd expect to hear less and less from those hormones, we get restless again. Our babies and our projects aren't enough to entertain us anymore. And we start to miss the intensity of *longing* for love and prefer it to the satisfaction of actually *having* it. The love that looked wonderfully durable starts to look dull. We worry that maybe we're not really in love, maybe we're missing something. Something essential.

*We're having our midlife crisis.*

Why *now*? Because nature has no intention of letting us be comfortable yet. The war for the survival of our species isn't over yet, and nature wants us to become as itchy as warriors after too much peacetime.

Love is a major issue at midlife, and I've dedicated a whole chapter to it later on. For now, let's admit that one mark of nature's mischief is that the very best addictive drugs are produced by our bodies when we're in romantic/erotic love. We find ourselves with vivid memories of the paradise of sex when it was fueled by the ache of longing. We recall the feeling of completeness with another person that we haven't felt since infancy (or our last bout with romantic madness). We feel bereft and bored. The solid, sunny warmth of a good friendship-love begins to feel drab by comparison.

So even a good relationship won't keep us sane forever. The devil makes work for idle hormones, and at midlife often one or both partners start finding other people very attractive. Insecurity that our spouses will feel the same way throws us into occasional wobbles, bringing back the uncertainty, urgency, and pain that are suspiciously like adolescent love. This terrible discomfort is a huge threat to a stable marriage.

But what's the purpose of all this madness? Why would nature want us to feel like adolescents again?

Because adolescent love produces babies. It's that simple. And if a little temporary madness will get us reproducing, so be it.

Once again, this may not be very pleasant for the individual, but it's obviously useful for the survival of our species.

**And what of our relationships with our children during these times?**

If we have children, our relationships with them run alongside the calms and turbulences of our relationships with our mates. When they're infants, we're on twenty-four-hour alert, afraid that they might hurt themselves. Year by year we worry less as they become more self-reliant. When our kids are about eight years old, having their period of relative sanity, we have the opportunity for a lovely intermission. At that point we often have our best, most egalitarian relationship with them. They require less of our attention to keep them safe, but they're friendly and they still like us because they haven't hit puberty yet.

**Adolescents make us crazy again.**

A lot of attention has been given to how crazy adolescents get. But when our kids hit this phase, we get crazy too. We feel afraid of them, overwhelmed, angry. Having them in our lives is like having a herd of high-strung racehorses running through the house. We're terrified that they'll get hurt, and it's our job to take care of them, but they're too big to control, and they're busting up the furniture! We don't want all this trouble. We still love them a lot, but we've put them first for a long time, and now we want our own lives back.

Instead we're right back on alert, putting our own lives on hold again, just as we did when they were infants. Except this time they decide to reject us!

You can see why. We have become difficult and unreasonable too, partly because it all seems so unfair to us and partly because we're terrified. We act like we'll have a breakdown if they get a buzz cut or pierce their noses. At the same time, their own biological urges make them push us away and seek love elsewhere. They may still need us, but they're impatient with our ideas, and they don't like to hug us anymore.

You could almost go so far as to say they shove us out of the nest!

The rejection makes us feel hurt and lonely. To add fat to the fire, their high-hormonal presence stirs our own. Rejection and hormones are a powerful mix, and if we don't watch ourselves, we might even go out in the world and start acting like adolescents ourselves. Right now at midlife.

Notice that your chances of producing offspring just spiked off the charts. Just before your fertility is about to disappear, you're starting to think about mating with someone new. Will you look at that?

Nature doesn't miss a bet.

**Don't think you're safe if you didn't have kids.**

The same thing happens even if you didn't have kids. You might have been comfortable with your life and your career, living in a clearheaded intermission into your late thirties. But then suddenly you look over your shoulder, and there they are, those hard-bodied young people breathing down your neck at work or trying to steal the ball on the basketball court. Even if they're not a real threat to your position, this is another dent in your narcissistic self-image, and a big one. They're more beautiful than you are, and they have more drive because they're pushed by the urgency of youth, and these young people want everything you've got, and more.

Until they showed up, you were starting to grow into your life. You had accumulated years of work experience, done a lot of the things you wanted to do, and become simply less driven. Visions that once were dazzling from a distance didn't look so glamorous up close. You'd burned your hands a few times and developed some respect for fire. Unlike those safety-be-damned young people hard on your heels, you'd learned how to estimate the cost before plunging after another goal.

Then one day, when you were about forty, a bunch of twenty-year-olds showed up at work, raring to go.

*The threat shocks us awake, and we lose our hard-won serenity.*

Their sudden appearance in our arena scares us to death. Not only are we afraid they'll take our turf away from us, but we envy their enthusiasm.

"It makes me sad that I'll never be that excited about a job again, no matter how much I like it," said Marty, a high-level executive in a major corporation.

"I watch those young women primping in the mirror and marvel at their self-absorption. I'm lucky if I get to work with matching earrings after getting the kids off to school in the morning," Leslie, an editor, told me.

And there's something else, even harder to face, in their eyes. Us.

They're looking at us in exactly the way we used to look at forty-year-olds: with condescension. We know they're just ignorant, but some part of us is still their age and agrees with them. We see ourselves as has-beens, slowing down, starting to plod, never to race again.

These thoughts jolt us awake. Wait a minute, we're not finished yet! What's going on here? Suddenly, we who had done our best to create some peace of mind and comfort for ourselves want to flee our safety zone and go hunting again. We start becoming uncertain of our worth. We begin to fuss about our appearance like worried teenagers. We fear that no one will love us. We have moments of panic. Is our day over?

Maybe not. But our contented intermission is.

**Looks like you are not the favored one after all.**

After some fevered attempts to clutch at our fading youthfulness, we realize that the outcome of the game has already been determined, and all we can do is try to hold off the inevitable for a while. Here we are, getting older, suddenly wanting what young people want again, but seeing so clearly that the future won't give it to us. All we see ahead is less beauty, less power, less status, less health, less love. And unbelievably, up there in the distance, waiting for us, is our own death. We thought we were special, but look at how things turned out. We're getting the same cards that fate deals to everybody else. The world isn't about us at all.

This is not what we were promised.

Is it any wonder after a lifetime of steadily losing most-favored-child status, doing our best to calm down about it, and suddenly being blindsided by the biggest blows of all that we're in a crisis at midlife?

It seems quite reasonable to become bitter.

**Philosophy 101: Life sucks, then you die.**

Now you're a disillusioned veteran. You know what life is

really all about. You figure you've got all the news, can finally see the big picture, and you've dropped your childish illusions about happiness and good fortune.

I recently overheard this attitude perfectly stated: "Midlife is when you decide not to kill yourself because you realize you're going to die anyway."

But don't relax just yet. You're feeling much older and wiser than you actually are. Your bitterness is just another stage, another attempt to get back in charge. Cynicism is only the first stage of disillusionment and won't protect you for as long as you think.

Now, have I come close to describing what you're feeling?
**Ask yourself these questions:**
1. Do you find it shocking that the same bad things happen to you as to anyone else?
2. Does it feel as though you were led to expect someone would come along and give you a great life and you got stood up?
3. Do you ever feel that you worked hard to do everything right and still didn't get the success you had coming?
4. Do you ever despair about the way your life turned out, even though other people don't think you did badly at all?
5. How do you feel when someone younger gets the kind of attention you used to get? Do you feel that *you* were supposed to get that attention, but now you'll never get it when there's someone younger around?
6. Do you find it impossible to forget that you're over forty?

If you answered yes to any question, you can be sure you've been programmed to hang on to center stage.
**I want to persuade you to give it up.**

It's not easy to ignore a feeling of injustice. The entitlement that's been betrayed puts a wound in the most powerful and primitive part of you, the infant you used to be. Being tormented by this injustice is at the heart of your efforts to try to stay youthful and adored. But the struggle will suck up all your energy and steal too many of your precious years. So although reason is a weak tool to use against such a strong emotion, let's at least begin to take away some of the myth around the prize of becoming the favorite once again.

Because unless you're a professional performer whose special art requires center stage and the attention of an audience, being a star isn't all it's cracked up to be.

Here's why.

*First, when you're working for star billing, you can't have a self.*

You'll always be the central person in your own life; that's unavoidable and appropriate. And to live the right life for you, you need a strong sense of self. But *self* and *star* have two different meanings. As a matter of fact, they're exactly opposite and can't exist together. Why? Because your self listens to what's inside you, so you know what you really want and need, and watches what's outside you, so you know where to step next. But your star listens only for applause and watches only for its reflection in the eyes of others. You can't attend to both at the same time.

*Second, you've already outgrown it.*

Like being carried everywhere in your mom's or dad's arms, being the favorite was great, but it doesn't work for you anymore. It's suffocating and takes away your autonomy. Adults, no matter how much they try to stay children, have no tolerance for large doses of protection. If someone actually adored and cared for you the way a parent does for a child, you wouldn't like it. You'd become restless, fretful, irritable. Because you've gotten too old for that.

"I always fantasize about being adored, but whenever someone starts looking at me with worshipful eyes, I get uncomfortable, and all I can think is, 'This isn't who I want. I want to be worshiped and adored by someone, uh, by someone . . . who doesn't adore me so much.'"

I don't much trust worship and adoration in adult relationships. It comes from people who either want to baby you or place you above them. Although neither of you may be aware of this at the beginning of the relationship, this kind of adulation is usually a form of jealousy and a thin mask for anger. It's possible to be highly valued by your partner in a healthy way, but this requires a partner with a good opinion of him- or herself. And it is impossible to be worshiped by such people because true, solid love has no adoration in it.

But it isn't good for you to be adored anymore. You should give it up because like mother's milk, adoration is too rich for an adult's digestive system. You'll do better without it.

*Third, you'll have to give up star billing because it's being taken away anyway.*

"You can't fire me. I quit!" goes the punch line of an old joke.

You can't win a race you've been denied entry to. Anyway, the passion to win isn't there the way it was, and it shouldn't be. You're supposed to be getting ready for a better way to live. A lot of other people want top billing, and they're very enthusiastic about getting it. It takes a certain lack of information to be that enthusiastic, and you're too educated. But don't waste too much sorrow about losing your belief in Santa Claus until you understand what you're really leaving behind and what you're gaining in its place. When you admit that you won't win this game, you get the biggest prize: a self that doesn't need center stage at all.

*Fourth, you have work to do, and it can't be done by a star.*

In your second life you'll be picking up the dreams you neglected and developing the gifts that weren't valued in your first life. Like a master cabinetmaker or silversmith, you'll find your greatest happiness by focusing on your chosen work. Becoming a master is a position reserved for people who are willing to direct their undivided attention toward their craft and who are too passionately engaged to waste precious time seeking admiration.

*Fifth, you should give up star billing because being a narcissist is boring.*

It's boring because you can't learn anything except what will serve you personally. All the data you're able to process have to be about you. "How do I look? How am I doing? What will I get?"

A world that's full of only you, your opinions, your status, your efforts to look good is a poor world indeed. Instead of seeing the amazing variety around you, you're locked in a house of mirrors and can see nothing unless it's useful to you. After a certain number of years of focusing on such a narrow field, even you are beginning to get sick of it. Your intellect has developed, and it wants something more interesting to do. It wants to let go of its grasping. It wants to stop being hampered by self-consciousness.

The good news is that you're ready to get back to learning. Learning is what our souls were born for, but you can't learn anything when you're determined to make everything "relevant" to you. That's a refusal to see an idea, an object, a person for itself.

Once you start looking around, seeing things for what they are instead of how they can serve in your personal climb to glory, the world turns into a great university. Everything becomes fascinating, and everything becomes new.

*Sixth, you're getting worn out seeking applause.*

"I feel so incomplete without admiration, but I'm tired of working for it every day," a client told me recently.

When you feel incomplete, you are obviously driven to do something to become complete. Like most addictions, you don't really want to give it up; you just want your emptiness filled. But like drugs, applause doesn't satisfy for long, and the need has to be filled over and over. After a while you can't help wishing you didn't need to struggle so hard. It wears you out to get the price together day after day—to win another race, to charm, to please, to manipulate for more attention.

\* \* \*

There they are. Six good reasons to give up your craving for star billing. Six good reasons to stop seeing midlife as a crisis and just pick up and walk away, to stop caring about the unfairness of losing everything you counted on. Sounds like the right thing to do, doesn't it?

Unfortunately, *knowing* it and *doing* it aren't the same thing. That's why there's one more question to be answered.

*When should we give up star billing?*

You probably wouldn't ask that question because you think you know the answer: right away, of course. In fact, that's not my answer at all. *I say you should give up your star billing as soon as you're ready, but not a second sooner.* If you try to give it up before you're ready, you're sure to fail. Ending your narcissistic outlook is no mean trick, and a simple rallying cry to inspire you isn't enough. There's a stubborn little pit bull of an infant still inside you with a single-minded, even fanatical determination to drag things back to the way they once were. As long as you believe you still have a chance to be the favorite, you have no intention of stepping aside. And you probably do believe you still have a chance. *Not because any evidence confirms it, but because you can't bear to believe anything else.*

But you're about to get some help. In the pages that follow, you're going to turn a bright light on many of the most cherished certainties of your first life and uncover some truths you may never have seen before. What seemed sterling in the morning of your life will be shown to be tinsel after all. What you're grieving as a great loss will reveal itself as an illusion.

"Ah, but it's sad to lose your illusions," a friend told me.

It won't be. Not when you realize you're clearing space for the real thing. What does the real thing look like? Well, oddly enough, it looks a lot like that first intermission you experienced, the one that occurred when you were about eight years old.

**Back to the first time-out from the biological struggle.**

All things being equal, barring exceptional circumstances,

all our intermissions are good times for us, because during them we're secure enough to relax and be ourselves. But the intermission that comes in the few years just before puberty is the purest and most complete. When it's happening, of course we take our state for granted, but in fact, it's quite extraordinary. For the most part, we're not trying to get attention from our parents anymore, like we did as babies, and we're not yet trying to shape ourselves into some ideal in order to win romance.

*We simply know who we are and have some freedom to act on it.*

There we are, for the most part uninvolved in a competition, more interested in being with our friends and exploring the world than in noticing whom our parents love most. Our innate curiosity stays active, and now we have some independence too, so we begin to learn about the world around us. We start to show the signs of individuality in our interests and abilities. We're not greedy or self-centered, but we know what we want. At this time you could say that we are most truly "ourselves."

If we had been able to stay that way, there's no knowing what we might have done. But of course, as we've seen, that first intermission didn't last very long. The onset of puberty pushed it aside with the force of a deluge. The later intermissions came and went, but it wasn't until now that the floodwaters have really begun to recede.

Now here's the interesting part. That centered, conscious self you had before you entered your fertile years is the same self that is about to return now that you're leaving them. This is a remarkable gift, of no obvious use to nature. Why do we get it? Is biology kinder than we imagine?

**Selfish and unselfish genes.**

The writer Samuel Butler once noted that a hen is just an egg's way of making another egg. Robert Wright, author of *The Moral Animal*, agrees: ". . . those genes that are conducive to the survival and reproduction of copies of themselves are the genes that win . . . however the genes get the job done, it is selfish from *their* point of view. Hence the title of Richard Dawkin's book, *The Selfish Gene*."

I'd like to propose the possibility that there is an "unselfish gene," not strictly designed for survival at all, and that it operates in these times that we are in our sane intermissions—that is, when we're out of the grip of biological demands. And that it's from this "unselfish gene" that we are given the potential for a surge of creativity, curiosity, energy, and intellectual growth that characterizes a successful second life. It's very common to hear people talk of it, as Margaret Mead did when she spoke of her "post-menopausal zest."

But what could it possibly contribute to the survival of our species?

After all, the amazing clarity and sense of self, the uncon-flicted ability to love learning, to experience unpossessive affec-tion for friends, and to try out our budding gifts might have had some use when we were young and fertile, but after midlife they appear to be *gratis*. Of what possible use can they be now, at an age our ancestors almost never reached? And this time the inter-mission apparently doesn't end. We can even experience brain growth into very old age.

"The dendrites' [nerve cells'] projections are like muscle tis-sue. They grow the more they're used. Even in old age, if you learn a new language it's dendritic fireworks,"* says Arnold Scheibel from UCLA.

So maybe there's an unselfish gene after all. Or maybe there's no explanation for the arrival of the "permanent intermission" that shows up in your second life at all. All the same, it's yours if you want it. All you have to do is let go of some of the illusions that originate in the narcissism of your first life, and this excep-tional second life will be waiting for you.

---

* Quoted in Betty Friedan's *Fountain of Age*.

## EXERCISE 4

### *Are you ready for a pop quiz?*

Have I been talking about you? Answer these questions and you'll find out.

### Questions

1. If you have siblings do you want to say, "Mom always loved you best"?
2. If you were an only child, did you think schoolmates should pay attention to you without your having to work for it?
3. Do your adolescent feelings of rejection rank among the most painful times of your life, even though you've been through greater actual tragedies?
4. When you got married or settled into a relationship, were you enormously relieved? If you felt safe in the relationship long enough, did you find yourself becoming bored?
5. Do you agree that your children are cleverer, better-looking, and more interesting than all other children?
6. When reading these pages, do you keep wanting to say, "What about people who had children later in life?" or, "What about people who didn't have siblings?" or, "What about my particular situation?" with some indignation?
7. If you have teenagers, do you find yourself flirting with their friends or their dates?
8. Do you find yourself digging out your old Rolling Stones records and playing them at top volume?
9. When you're driving, do you take personal offense at traffic that goes too slow or too fast for you?

*Can you smile and forgive yourself for all the yeses you answered?* I hope so, because that means you're beginning to develop a proper respect for the ingenious ways nature works on us all.

## EXERCISE 5

### *Another glimpse into your future*

All right, I'd like to ask you to do something tricky.

Fantasize your life without any narcissistic desperation at all. It's almost impossible to do for more than the briefest moment, but you can get an idea if you imagine that you don't have the slightest interest in being anybody's favorite or any kind of star. See if you can catch a glimpse of how that would feel. Then ask yourself these questions.

1. What do you think you'd have done differently in your life if you'd always felt that way?
2. What would you do differently now?
3. What would you stop doing?

Give it some thought for a few minutes.

Can you see how different your life would be? Well, that's what you can expect in your future.

But first, you need a little deprogramming.

# PART TWO

## ILLUSIONS

Disillusion—verb: to break the spell, to debunk,
to open one's eyes, to embrace reality.
noun: disenchantment, freedom from illusion,
the return to reality, enlightenment.

"Thoroughly unprepared, we take the step into the
afternoon of life; worse still, we take this step with
the false presupposition that our truths and ideals
will serve us as hitherto. But we cannot live the
afternoon of life according to the programme of
life's morning—for what was great in the morning
will be little at evening, and what in the morning
was true will at evening have become a lie."
Carl Jung, *Modern Man in Search of a Soul*

# 3
# Time Limits

"... I thought that time must lead me from sunshine
to darkness. I never wanted any season but spring."
Judith Viorst, *Necessary Losses*

"It was now 1986 and I realized that if I kept my health
I would enjoy perhaps twenty-five years of peak
performance. This doesn't mean that the public will
retain an interest in me or my work for twenty-five years.
It means that I know that's how much time I have left
to work at this white-hot temperature. The knowledge
that I would never be young again startled me. It didn't
depress me—just woke me up."
Rita Mae Brown, *Starting from Scratch*

*At forty, you think you understand time and mortality perfectly, for the first time.Where once you carelessly let the years slip through your fingers like pennies from a millionaire, it's suddenly crystal clear that your supply is not endless and now you're desperately trying to pick them back up from the ground.*

*Clearly the passage of time is chewing up your choices. Maybe earlier in life you could go out and find another job, another spouse, another city, but as you get older, that will no longer be true. It seems so obvious that the best is behind you and the worst lies ahead like a trap that you can't imagine why I'm calling your view of time an illusion.*

*Suddenly you want nothing more than to be young again, to go back to your past, or at least throw your arms around the present and hang on for dear life. Your sense that time is running out, that your choices are becoming limited, and that death on the horizon makes everything pointless looks indisputably true. You feel like you just wised up from an illusion; you thought time was endless, but you finally got smart, and now you're facing the awful truth, right?*

*Wrong. This new "truth" is an illusion too.*

*At forty you understand less about time and mortality than a child does.*

*You see, time isn't going anywhere; its passing simply got visible. But because time's behavior feels very new to you, you need to sit down and do some thinking before making any emergency decisions. When you're in unfamiliar territory, it's better to have no map at all than the wrong one, because if you become frightened by this new face of time, you might start running in circles just when you're finally free to start moving ahead. That would be a costly mistake. Not only because you can't stop time, but because everything you need for a superb second life lies in the direction time is carrying you.*

*So let's take a cool look at what's really going on with time at this stage of your life. I think you're going to be pleasantly surprised to find out that far from becoming limited, your life choices are expanding for the first time in your life and that your awareness of mortality won't take the delight out of the coming years; it will add more. Contrary to what you believe, being conscious of your mortality isn't a church bell announcing a funeral. It's a bell that starts a boxing match.*

*And it's saying, "Wake up, dreamer, and come out fighting!"*

---

**Time. It's amazing. But what is it?**

It's been a source of curiosity throughout human history. Everyone has made an attempt to get a handle on it, probably for the same reason you want to: It's very slippery, but your life depends on it.

More than fifteen hundred years ago St. Augustine said, "What, then, is time? If no one asks me, I know what it is. If I wish to explain it to him who asks, I do not know."

The Greek philosopher Archytus took it even further. He said time couldn't logically exist at all: ". . . how could it exist in reality, if its past is no longer, its future is not yet, and its now is partless and indivisible?"

Tell that to yourself on your next birthday, and see if it consoles you. It didn't do a thing for me.

"If the years keep passing this fast, I'll be dead soon!" a scared young woman told me the other day. "Or I'll become one of those awful old people who say, 'Where did the time go? I still feel sixteen!' "

Her conclusion seems inevitable: Everything will be ending sooner than you believed possible. Time waits for no one. That's a fact of life.

Is it?

*Or is it just another midlife illusion?*

You may not think of time as an illusion. After all, you wear a watch, your birthday comes at the same time each year, your bills come due each month, and you were a lot younger twenty years ago than you are now. But as you note with horror how fast the days, weeks, and years slip away, you're caught in a very dangerous illusion. You're certain time is speeding up and running out. You're convinced your life is heading for a disaster—and at frightening speed.

This is as dangerous as someone wrongly shouting "Fire!" in a crowded theater, causing a panicked rush to the exits.

**And it's equally untrue.**

In fact, time has completely changed its face over and over throughout your life. But you've forgotten those changes. Instead, since you passed thirty-five, you've noticed time gain a frightening amount of speed, as if you turned your back for a moment and a year had passed. To you, the pattern seems obvious: The older you get, the faster time flies. After all, look how slowly it went in childhood.

Remember when summer vacations were so long you could

hardly find your classroom when you got back to school? When grown-ups said you couldn't go swimming until the weather warmed up, or you couldn't have a puppy until you were old enough to take care of it? You felt you'd been told to wait for eternity.

"When you're a kid, your whole life is ahead of you, so it seems slow. But as you get older, there's less time left, so it seems to be going faster," a forty-four-year-old friend explained unhappily. "And in the future it will go even faster for the same reason because there's so much less of it left."

Do you agree with her theory?

*Well, I think she's got it all wrong.*

I see a very different reason for the slow pace of time in childhood. This is when our steepest learning curve occurs. When we're barely able to survive, we must learn to navigate gravity, speak a language, understand the meaning of an incomprehensible environment, get along with people, and avoid getting killed. Not only that, but everything that happens—a doorbell rings, a cat walks by, we sneeze—is so astonishingly new it gets our complete attention. In order to deal with so many unfamiliar experiences at once, we need enormous focus and presence of mind. If we'd been as panicked about time then as we are at midlife, we might have gotten hurt. But time always slows down for us when we most need it, as you know if you've ever been in a near accident and had to think with lightning speed.

And that's why it slows down for us in childhood.

At adolescence, if my friend is right, time should have sped up steadily. But just think back, and you'll see that's not what happened at all. Instead it took on twenty faces at once. Important moments sprang upon us without warning and flew past before we could get our bearings and manage a poised response, while suffering through the agonies of self-consciousness at school dances was like roasting slowly in hell. Summers away from our friends were empty and endless. But time didn't speed up when we were on the phone with our friends. It moved like Jell-O, and we liked it anyway, even when we knew we were bored and boring. Always hovering over us was the sense that something huge was about to happen—and the equally powerful fear that it would miss us entirely, that nothing would happen to us at all, not ever. The looming potential all around us created such an intense drama that some days we were obsessed with it and others we wanted no part of it. Sometimes we wanted to retreat into the past, take out our bicycles and play with the younger children, while other times we gazed at movie stars and at classmates a year or two ahead of us and ached to be older.

*Time back then was like a whole gang of weird creatures pressing up against us.*

Then we grew up, and for the most part, time drifted from our everyday consciousness. We got into the groove, learned how to support ourselves, and took on adult responsibilities. We were building a life, and like birds constantly on the move bringing worms to feed their babies, we were caught in an ongoing present, immersed in our obligations, rarely picking up our heads to note the years passing.

"When I was a young parent, I noticed only the minutes and hours passing. At the end of the day I collapsed, and the next morning it all started over again. Time went around and around like a circle," a woman told me.

Of course we were looking ahead, making plans and dreaming of the day we could buy a bigger house or make more money or find a better lifestyle. But we never felt that the future was rushing toward us. Quite the contrary.

Our concept of the future extended only as far as next week. Time turned into "Will I get this project finished on time? Will I make enough money to pay the rent?"

"I used to look at our small apartment every day and wonder how long we'd have to wait until we could afford to get out of there."

Time didn't seem to be speeding by at all.

Naturally, if we had kids, we were amazed at the speed of their growth, but it felt as if they were moving by a different clock from our own. They seemed to change into different people every month, while we stayed the same. But for the most part, time behaved itself without our help. The weekends would come, bills would arrive in the mail, holidays would be here again. We always had more on our to-do lists than we could manage to take care of, but we learned that we could always do it tomorrow. We became average consumers of time.

*And then time changed again at midlife.*

Suddenly tomorrow has started flying out of our hands before we can catch it. Now you've awakened with a jolt, as horrified as if you'd been sleepwalking on a dangerous ledge. Why didn't you notice that time was flying like the wind? When did everybody's children get so tall? And why do your parents look so painfully old? Suddenly you wake up to something you never noticed before: Time doesn't just rush by faster and faster; *it ends.* You can actually run out of it, like sugar or coffee!

**Take a deep breath, and stop right where you are.**

You just hit a crisis, and you're so scared you could bolt into the traffic like a panicked deer. So, before you take another step, I want to tell you something you haven't realized yet.

*Time is not going to continue to speed up at all. As a matter of fact, it's about to slow down again.*

Why?

For one thing, as soon as you get past this transition and step into your second life, time will drop its speed for the same reason it did when you were little: *Everything's about to get new again.* Your viewpoint is about to change so radically that you might as well be entering a different world. Your learning curve will start soaring again. Every day will be so full of new events it will seem like a week.

For another, when your present panic disappears, time will slow down even more, for a very different reason.

Why?

Because fear gobbles time. Whenever we're frightened, we instinctively start protecting ourselves. We get ready to move fast. Our feelings disappear. Our creativity gives way to high-speed problem solving. And the only senses left awake are the ones that help us focus on the danger in front of us, so we can see which way the tiger or bear or lion will move, and calculate our response.

But when the only danger is that time seems to be rushing by, there's nothing to focus on. We have the same responses, but because we fear an illusion, the danger never passes, and the result is an impoverishment of every moment. What can we experience when we're anxious? Only the minimum of color and scent, sound and texture and taste. Instead of being happy or sad or wistful or peaceful, we feel emotional white noise. And instead of inventing or writing or painting or designing, we're watching TV infomercials to check out the latest mail-order exercise equipment.

*But when your fear disappears, all that changes.* You will actually have *more* time. When that happens, you won't need to say, "Where did the time go?" When you learn how to experience time in that calm and deep way, you're far more likely to say at the end of a day, "Is it still only Saturday? I feel as if I've been on a long journey," or, "What an amazing year this has been. I've been so many places and done so many things it seems like five years." Not only will your present time expand, but your future will open up again because you'll be looking forward to it instead of turning your face away as you do now.

**Wait a minute. Am I really saying time is not running out?** Am I living in a dream? Don't I own a calendar?

*But no one has ever lived in calendar time.* Calendars don't own time any more than a wristwatch does. They are nothing but a convention, an agreement we all make with one another so we can arrive at the same destination at the same moment. Personally experienced, calendar time has no meaning at all. Ask someone in jail how long a month is. He'll tell you it's forever. Now ask the same question of a business owner who has to make a payroll. She'll tell you it's tomorrow!

On paper they're the same month. In life they couldn't be more different.

Time speeds up and slows down; it shrinks and expands; it flies past like a hailstorm or moves gently like a stream. It can be rich and sensual or frozen and empty. Time is very fancy stuff, affected by your age and your emotions and your adrenaline and even the way your particular culture views it.

If you lived four thousand years ago, you'd have a very different feeling about the passage of time, and life, and death. Though we now assume time travels only in a forward direction, all the evidence back then was that time was cyclical: The year went through its seasons; the rains and the dry periods came; plants, animals, and humans grew and withered; then the cycle started again. The notion of human reincarnation seemed logical. The movement of the moon and stars also confirmed that nature went around in cycles, repeating itself over and over. While every culture had its own creation myth, with a beginning taking place at some point in the distant past, that beginning wasn't anchored in any particular time. These were the "nature religions."

Then the Hebrews wrote a surprising book. Unlike the repetitive, hypnotic poetry of the nature religions, the Hebrew book was written in linear prose. Even more unusual, the Hebrew creation and the stories that followed did not circle back with repeat lines like a long song; they were firmly anchored in linear time that went in only one direction. Abraham and Isaac, Ruth and Sarah happened once and only once. The generations were listed, in case you needed any reminders that reincarnation wasn't part of the plan.

Many scholars think this was done with a conscious intention of distinguishing the Hebrews from nature worshipers. By insisting that God's time was linear and not cyclical, the Hebrews meant to set themselves aside from nature itself—above animals and natural forces, governed by a force more conscious and more powerful than nature. The Christians later carried this sense of time even further, emphasizing the notion of a final and fiery apocalypse.

That's how we've come to see time ever since: as traveling straight, in one direction, to The End. It's hard for us to see it any other way, but it creates one of the biggest reasons we don't like to hit the age of forty.

**Midlife is when your mortality finally hits you.**

No matter how much you may toy with the idea of it before you're forty, you rarely really believe the inevitability of your own death until after your fourth decade. Then it wakes you up like a bucket of ice water in your face.

"I was so mad the day I figured out I was going to die someday that I wouldn't get out of bed all weekend. I'd never be young again. Someday I won't be here anymore. Well then, I would just stay in bed, and to hell with everyone," a forty-year-old accountant told me.

"I didn't know what to do first. I wanted to buy a house. Then I decided I should quit my job and go into the theater. Then it seemed very important to move to Colorado," a college professor said. "I felt like a trapped rat. I didn't know which way to move, but I couldn't bear to stand still."

"It just seemed so unfair. As if everybody else could worry about dying, but I shouldn't have to," said my neighbor, a piano teacher.

Here you are, lost in a crisis and the clock is ticking. Should you run faster than ever after the old goals, the familiar fantasies? Or should you freeze and try to be invisible like a scared rabbit when a hawk floats overhead? What is the best use of your time?

People say, "Use your time wisely," and we nod in agreement, but after they leave, we think, "What the hell does 'wisely' mean?" What *should* you do with the remaining time? In the middle of pondering that question, you suddenly hear what you just thought: "the remaining time." *You never used that phrase about your life before.*

That's when a chill runs down your back.

The future just changed its face. Where it once shone with possibility, you now see that your biggest escape hatch, immortality, just disappeared. You are having what is often called a predictable life crisis. But just because someone gave it a name doesn't mean they told you what to do about it. Should you run down the street screaming? Or become bitter about the whole thing?

**Woe and world-weariness at midlife.**

It's an interesting characteristic of dark moods that they make you feel you have all the answers. I see it in often in midlifers struggling to find a footing in the confusion of this crisis. In a knowing, disillusioned, even cynical tone, they'll tell you that your worst fears are totally real. The shine is off everything. What's the point in doing anything? You're just going to die anyway. And anyone who doesn't agree is a silly Pollyanna indulging in wishful thinking.

"I don't want to hear any cheerful garbage about getting older. My knees hurt, and I'm losing my hair," a client told me.

"Don't give me any fairy tales. I want some help facing the fact that it's not going to be all right," said another.

And I want to say to them, "Sorry. *It's going to be all right.* Maybe the handwriting is on the wall, but you can't read it yet."

Because something very suspicious is going on when you suddenly discover your mortality at midlife.

**Why don't we get the picture earlier?**

Why do we suddenly discover it now? It's likely that a biological purpose is served by our becoming so suddenly aware of our mortality. The result of our shocking encounter with our own mortality is that we often crave sexual passion and throw reason to the winds. Literature and opera deal with death and Eros frequently, and not just because it makes for good drama. When soldiers return from wars, they create a baby boom, just like the one occurring now in the United States. The connection between death and eroticism has been noted in animals as well.

But right now, death has got to become less frightening or you'll sink into hopelessness, even avoid thinking about it completely. You shouldn't do that right now because you have some very important thinking to do. You've got to answer the biggest question of your adult life.

**How do you live now that you know you will not live forever?**

The major task of this time of your life is to figure out the answer to that question. It's a whopper. It's like trying to figure out how to spend your last ten dollars when you're in a foreign country without friends, a credit card, or an American Express office.

But the answer lies right in plain view because it's the cause of your problem with time in the first place. You see, whenever people say time is going by too fast, they usually mean something else entirely.

*The passage of time drives you crazy when you know perfectly well you're not using it right.*

And what constitutes using it right? Joan Didion, the essayist, says it loud and clear in her essay "On Self-Respect," when she writes of "the gifts irrevocably wasted through sloth or cowardice or carelessness."

If you're afraid time is flying out of your hands, it's because you know you're not using what's inside you. Ask people who are completely absorbed in something that matters to them, how they feel about time, and they'll probably say, "Don't bother me, I'm working."

They don't think there's ever enough time either. They resent having to die as much as you do. But for a completely different reason: *They have so much important work to do.* And chances are they don't fret about how much time has already passed because to them it's not gone at all. They have made use of everything that has happened to them, and their past is like a big bank account.

**Oh, no! I should have thought of this before!**

No, you shouldn't have. When it comes to answering the big question: How do you live now that you know you will not live forever? You couldn't possibly have dealt with it before.

Why?

Because nature and narcissism made you think you would live forever. Only now can you work on how to live from now on. As a matter of fact, now you can't avoid it.

And it begins with something you're already doing: assessing what you've done with your life so far.

**Have I done the right thing with my life?**

*Yes. Everyone has.*

Look what you've done with it so far: Your life is shaped unlike anyone else's. It reflects your originality in everything you have created and your unique responses to everything you encountered. If you don't appreciate what you've done with your life so far, it deserves closer examination than you've likely given it.

Take a look at the path you chose.

Get a few sheets of blank paper and a pencil. I want you to write down down the answer to a question.

## EXERCISE 6

### *Your responses to life*

How did your responses to the circumstances of your life bring you to where you are now? Think especially of the choices you made that were different from those of the people around you.

Melanie: "I responded to my difficult homelife by going away and giving myself a new start in a different city. My friends stayed in the middle of their messes and took drugs or married people they didn't love just so they could leave home. Now I have a career I like okay, but I don't have a husband, and I wish I did. I'm different in this way, too. I just won't marry someone unless it's right, no matter what anyone says."

George: "I tried to do what my family wanted, went to law school, and did well. But when the time came to get a job, something made me pull back. I got some good offers, but I turned them all down, and I went to business school instead. After I graduated, the same thing happened: good offers of jobs I just couldn't accept. All my friends are established by now; everything's settled for them. But nothing is settled for me. I still can't bury myself in a big company."

Angela: "Unlike the people I grew up with, I married someone who wasn't a 'professional,' and I left him because he wasn't loving, to me or to our kids. Now my women friends are either divorced with lots of alimony (but unhappy all the same) or living depressing lives with husbands who don't care about them. I don't know why I did what I did, but I don't think I could do any differently today."

**Are these success stories?**

So far, yes. Because every one of these people got *where* they are because of *who* they are. That's the right reason to be anyplace.

What about you? Can you see that you too got where you are because of who you are? Can you see that the alternatives were never right for you? Even if you decide to make radical changes in your second life, there's a logic in your past choices as they accumulate through your life that gives you important clues to what you need. Until now most of that has been unconscious. Just as a fish doesn't understand water, we didn't understand time, but we always knew dozens of ways to use it all the same. *And each of us has carved out a path to the right point for our next move.*

But what about the friends mentioned above, the ones who made the "bad" decisions, like sticking with bad marriages or careers that suited their families instead of themselves? Is it all over for them? Or have they too carved a path to the right point for their next move?

*Of course they have.* Perhaps they were too frightened or hadn't developed the sense of worth they needed to make more independent moves when Melanie, George, and Angela did. *But they made the moves they were able to make at the time and learned the lessons they had to learn before they could take another step.* They just had to go to a different school and put in their own kind of time.

Do they have the strength to choose differently now? Possibly. Like you, they're probably getting stronger every year. They certainly know more about the cost of their decisions than anyone else does. If they become conscious of the passage of time and the corner they're turning, they have a better chance than they've ever had before. They may not even be behind schedule.

**It's not possible to waste time in your first life.**

"The so-called traumatic experience is not an accident, but the opportunity for which the child has been patiently waiting—had it not occurred, it would have found another . . . in order to find a necessity and direction for its existence, in order that its life may become a serious matter."
W. H. Auden

Everything was educating you. Look carefully, and you'll see it. As soon as you wake up to the fact that time gave you experience and skills and a lot of information about who you are, you stop being a has-been or a time waster and find yourself in the same place as an artist who is completing his apprenticeship. When you begin to understand that time will now give you the days and years to build something first-rate from this knowledge, you're no longer someone who's losing your youth; you're an architect who's been given material to work with.

Time is not a thief. It does not steal. Birthdays aren't bad news; they're something to push off from like a dancer pushes off from the floor in a beautiful flight into midair. Without gravity to work with, there can be no dance.

**But birthdays take away the person you were, don't they?**
No, they don't.

All you've lost is the appearance you most recently identified with. When the face in the mirror starts to look like it belongs to someone else, you think your identity has changed! *But what's inside isn't gone at all, and never will be.* You should know that in your bones, but whenever we wonder at how we feel inside compared to how we appear, we almost invariably think the appearance is the truth.

"I forget how old I am all the time," a friend told me.

Why does she forget? Because nothing essential about her has changed at all. The same is true for you. Originality, creativity, curiosity, none of them is diminishing. In fact, they may be increasing. Everything that was valuable about you when you were young is waiting inside you, intact and shining like a new set of tools, ready to use whenever you like. Your years of experience have provided you with language and feelings, know-how, strength, and memories, like the keys of a piano, ready to be played whenever you have a tune. You are all the people you ever were, and you can tap into them whenever you're ready and use them to gather even more riches.

Only the passing of time could give you that.

**But what happened to your future?**

"I lived on hope. Today didn't matter; the future would fix everything."

"The best part was always ahead; that's why life felt so exciting. Now I don't like to think ahead anymore."

You've spent the first part of your life in love with the future, always looking forward to the next stage, always expecting life to get better. Like Orphan Annie, you said, "I love ya, tomorrow, you're always a day away."

If that kind of hope keeps you going, active, doing what you should be doing, I'm all for it. Or if you're locked away in a deep depression or have a serious illness, hope will drive away despair, like a divine light.

But hope can cut both ways.

Sometimes it can harbor a chronic refusal to enjoy the present—or to improve it. After all, if your *real* life is always ahead, never arrives, just beyond the next bend in the road, then why bother? If you've been using hope to replace action, the passage of time has caught you unprepared. Because the future is here.

Does that mean it's too late for you?

**Has opportunity slipped away with the years?**

If the future isn't shining like it used to, opportunity must be gone as well, right? Again, quite the opposite. Your potential isn't gone; it's right here, right now, in your face. Instead of hovering somewhere up ahead, it has come to sit right at your breakfast table, and its name has changed from "your possible future" to "your actual present." It's now or never time.

*What you do today, this hour, will be your ticket to happiness.*

This is no ending. It's a major beginning. The years have moved you past animal instinct—the blind impulses that overrode everything else—and into consciousness, the ability to see and understand what you're looking at.

Think about that for a moment. This change is one of the most transformational in your life. It's as if you were blind and got your eyesight back. But the change isn't limited to your ability to look at the world around you. *Consciousness also wakes you up to who you are, where you are, and where you want to go.* Your car finally has a driver, and that driver is you as you really are, not as you thought you were supposed to be. Your path is real, it's here now, and it's got your name all over it.

**Time has always given you more than it took away.**

Time brought you here, washed your sorrows away, made you bloom. It gave you your present richness built out of accumulated decisions and lessons, events, skills, insights, relationships. Collisions with life helped shape you and show what you're made of. Time made regular deposits in your experience bank account. Now you're a treasure house, like the library at Alexandria. And every year that passes, you become more valuable.

Time is your medium. Whatever magnificent things you will ever do will be molded out of time itself. Like a sailor uses waves and wind, time is what will carry you. And a time limit is nothing but a dock you push off from at the start of a voyage.

**Oh, yeah? What about death?**

Try pushing off from that one, right? Find a way that death is good news? Impossible?

You'd be surprised. Wallace Stevens called death "the mother of beauty." It's also the mother of time. *One of the most peculiar characteristics of time is that you can't use it with all your heart until you've glimpsed death up on the road ahead.* There it is, your enemy, the bully on the block, the spoiler who doesn't love you enough to let you be the first person to live forever. But look a little closer, and you'll see that death is also the best buddy you ever had, the bell ringer who wakes you from your dream of endless time, the friend who will actually *give* you years!

Unless you refuse to face it, of course.

**You've got to see your death coming or one day you'll collide with it head-on.**

If you pretend death doesn't exist at all and live your life in happy denial, one day it will give you a nasty surprise. It isn't as though you can ever be ready, but the shocker comes if you forgot to use your time the way you should have. To avoid that, you don't need to know when death will come, just that it will come someday.

Some people think it's a very good thing we don't know when we will die. My friend's rabbi is one of them. "The reason we're not allowed to know the day of our death is that if we know it's far away we say, 'Well, there's still lots of time,' and we don't do what we should. And if we know it's soon, we say, 'Well, it's too late,' and we don't do what we should either."

**The D word. What is death to us?**

We know so little about death that we invent ways to imagine it. Like primitive people who knew little about science, we make up answers based on our own experiences and our worst fears, some of them embedded in memory since early childhood.

Erta: "Death is like a terrible aloneness, like a dream I had where I was floating in the dark sky looking down at friends chatting and talking without me. It was so lonely."

Joe: "Death means failure, no more chances to be somebody or do important work."

Hilary: "It means that the people who were supposed to rescue me never came."

Death seems so . . . final. Is it? Who knows? We have stranger ideas about death than we do even about sex or money. We have no idea what it is or when it comes. Only that it will.

But death is by no means the only way you can stop living your life. Stay numb and live someone else's life instead of your own, and your life ends years earlier. That's what Kurosawa's film *Ikiru* is about: a clerk in a mindless job who finds out he's dying and decides he wants to do something that matters to him. As he discovers what that is and goes after it with a courage he's never had before, it becomes clear that only now is he alive. For all the years before, hiding behind papers, trained to obstruct action, to take no chances, to avoid responsibility, he might as well have been dead. The lesson he teaches is that there's more than one kind of death, and you don't have to run out of time to experience it.

Still, our mortality shocks the hell out of us. Nobody really wants it. Everybody wants to live, even when they don't like their lives. And everyone struggles to find their own way to control death. For the entire history of humankind we have tried to convince ourselves we have some kind of power over death.

**In the Middle Ages, people tried to numb their terror of death by pretending they accepted it.**

Tormented by barbarian massacres and horrific plagues, people in the Middle Ages reminded themselves over and over: memento mori (remember you must die). Everybody tried to disarm death by figuring out what it was. If sin was the cause of death, they punished themselves and recanted their sins, hoping that would satisfy their debt. If that didn't turn the tide of their terrible misfortunes, they tried to embrace death as inevitable. But don't think for a moment that just because they walked around saying "memento mori," that they were cool about it. They were hysterical.

As soon as this dark time got a bit sunnier, there was a rebellion against their bleak view. Henry Wadsworth Longfellow called out to a receptive audience when he wrote, "Life is real. Life is earnest/ And the grave is not its goal,/ Dust thou art, to dust returneth,/ Was not spoken of the soul."

Spoken of the soul or not, death still exists, and no one has ever changed that. But no one has ever stopped trying either. We are no different. You might be amused at some of these attempts. See if they look familiar.

**How we all try to control death.**

Every one of us invents our own form of primitive magic. Some of us ignore death, thinking that might make it go away. Or we worry about it constantly so it can't sneak up on us, like the character in Heller's *Catch-22* who counts every minute on the clock to make time slow down to put off death. Some of us admit we're "fighting the clock" by getting some sagging part of our bodies lifted or dyeing our hair or buying sexy cars. Or we fight nature toe to toe by taking youth hormones. Or we dare death with reckless driving or bungee jumping, or try to outsmart it by practicing detachment and pretending that neither life nor death is real.

I know someone who believes that if he's always involved in some huge project, he can't die until it's finished. And some people try to move fast and drink deep from life's cup, using sex, drugs, alchohol, gambling, partying, or falling madly in love over and over, to prove that death can't stop them from living. Others calm themselves with the bizarre logic of remembering one can always commit suicide. Almost all of us make ourselves brave by joking about death, making fun of our fear in an attempt to drive it away.

"If I had only one hour to live, I'd probably get stuck waiting for an elevator."

But we all know perfectly well there's nowhere to hide. And these attempts keep us focused on the wrong thing. *You see, you're not supposed to control death, and trying to is a bad use of your time.* What are you supposed to do instead? Walk up, shake hands and say, "Thank you."

**The usefulness of remembering our mortality.**

Acknowledging mortality gets you in touch with the moment like nothing else in the world. Have you ever been in the presence of a dying person? It's a powerful experience to watch them drop all the surface games and get to the heart of each moment. Suddenly "here and now" shows up like never before. A journalist friend of mine, accustomed to working sixty- and seventy-hour weeks, was confronted with the long illness and coming death of her father. She took an indefinite leave of absence and went to stay at his house. "I just wanted to be near him. Not do much, just play with the cat, make him a nice cup of tea."

That's a taste of the timelessness most of us have lost, isn't it?

But awareness of time limits also makes us swing into action as nothing else can.

*The knowledge that you will die is the beginning of accomplishment.*

## EXERCISE 7

### *Call to action*

I'll show you what I mean in this exercise.

1. First, come up with as many explanations as you can think of for why you haven't used your brains and talent and your ability to savor life to the fullest. Briefly list them on a sheet of paper, as many as you wish.

   "Not enough time."

   "Probably not really talented."

   "Just can't get around to it."

   "No money."

   "Fear of success."

   "Don't feel entitled to give this to myself."

   And whatever else comes to mind.

2. Now pretend you've just been told you have exactly two years to live. Which items on that list are you ready to cross off?

"How about everything?" a friend said, looking shocked.

If you're like most of us, you just stopped protesting and started making plans. Death sorts out your priorities very fast. Suddenly you're not as busy as you thought. You could manage to go away to a writers' workshop for a week if you planned it right. Not only that, but you just became entitled to do something for yourself. Only two years to live? Call the travel agent, and buy your plane ticket this afternoon.

*Finally, the fear of becoming everything you're capable of just* took *second place to the fear of not becoming everything you're capable of.*

**What do you want to do before you go?**

"Quit taking care of everyone and take time for myself. Just do what I want, when I want."

"Rent a studio and start to paint."

"Go to Mexico, adopt a town, and save the children."

Death sorts it all out very neatly, doesn't it?

Maybe you'd better get started.

**No frame, no painting. No deadline, no work of art.**

Time limits are woven into all our greatest enterprises. That's the ball, and you must run with it. You have big things to do, and nothing else will remind you to do them. When your resources were endless, you couldn't help wasting them. You fretted about petty matters and couldn't remember what the great ones were. That's not your fault; that just seems to be the way we're made: We waste when there's plenty, conserve when there's less. But once you understand that you will not live forever, you can—and must—begin to act on your warehoused dreams. We'll talk more about this in a later chapter, but for now you should let mortality remind you that it's your duty to use your gifts and make your unique contribution to this remarkable planet you've taken so much for granted until now.

Of course, you can't walk around thinking about death all the time, but you mustn't forget it either. Perhaps the most useful thing is to remember that although your time is limited, there's still a nice big chunk to play with. Will it be enough? Yes and no. There's no longer any time to waste, of course, but time is about to start stretching for you in an amazing way.

**Deep experience expands time.**

A woman I know told me about her last year with her husband, after he'd had open heart surgery. "We really weren't close through all our marriage. He was a busy doctor, and I had four kids. And he was a standoffish man, even with his colleagues. But he changed radically after open heart surgery: He connected up with the world as he never had before. And he fell in love with me. We went for walks every day through the beautiful woods near our house, and we talked about everything. In that last year, we lived more than we did in all the years before."

**And what of the loss of beloved people, beloved times?**

Surely I must admit there's no way to hold on to the wonderful times we had. Time stole those like a thief in the night.

Think again. We never lose times; only places. And we mix them up, one with the other.

Our biological ancestors—from one-celled animals to primates—had as one of their first survival traits a sense of place and familiarity. We are no different. We need to feel we have a safe place to settle down in order to nest and survive. As a result, changing locations is very hard on us. It may not be so clear, however, that we have woven this need into our sense of time.

The past is full of attachment for us. From our first home—the arms of our mothers—to a wonderful summer that has ended, we've always regretfully accepted that we can't hang on to happiness. We may think we remember our most wonderful feelings in terms of places—the treehouse we had as children, high school with all our friends, a great trip to Paris—because we can see those places in our memory's eye and miss them very much. But in fact, it's actually *time* we've become attached to. We make our homes in time as surely as birds make nests in trees, and these homes get into our hearts. But visit the old places again, and even if they're still standing, nothing is the same. Everything is empty and unfamiliar because the cherished time has evaporated from that place.

*But the time has not gone from our hearts.* Every memory we gathered is waiting inside us, ready to take down and view whenever we like. That's why I disagree with people who say you should forget about the past and live only in the present. That would be like forgetting the books in your library, when every read makes them come to life again.

Of course, no moment ever comes twice. Even without death you've had to learn to say good-bye many times in your life, to the charm of a puppy that would soon grow up or a splendid holiday that was drawing to a close. The passage of time has introduced us to losses, but think for a moment and you'll often find that you had to let go of one thing so you could reach for another. If you were still hanging on to your tricycle, you'd never be driving a car.

So try the following exercise, as if it were a sort of balance sheet. Let's see if the losses were worth it. Sit down, pencil in hand, and jot down any losses and gains you can remember at the ages mentioned; but especially try to pinpoint those things you could never have gained without first experiencing a loss.

## EXERCISE 8

### Losses and gains

1. What did you lose before the age of five? What did you gain?
2. What did you lose between the ages of five and fifteen? What did you gain?
3. What about the ages between fifteen and of twenty-five? What did you lose and what did you gain?
4. How about the years following twenty-five?
5. And what about the last few years? What did you lose and what did you gain?

How does the balance sheet look now? A bit different, I hope.

The lesson is clear. Simply remember to say hello with all your heart to everyone and everything you love every time you see them. Remember each moment as it happens and store it in your memory. Loss is always painful, but you invite tragedy when you forget to appreciate how good things are when you're in the middle of them and remember only after they're gone. It won't be easy. Left to our own devices, we can't help taking things for granted. We've always got our minds on the next thing. *The only thing strong enough to wake us up is the knowledge that our time is not endless.*

Face that, and time falls into your lap like a present from the sky.

It will be as though we'd spent our lives moving hurriedly through the world's greatest art gallery, looking at our watches and worrying about what time the stores close, and suddenly, as if by magic, everything changed. We stop in our tracks, look around us, and see like never before. Every painting becomes a journey for us, touches a hundred points in our minds, our memories, our feelings, stirs our vision and our own creativity. We awaken out of our distracted half-awareness into full-color life. Because understanding loss makes everything beautiful.

Is time starting to look different to you?

Let's find out.

## EXERCISE 9

### *What time gave me, or, "if I'd only known then what I know now."*

What do you know now that could have changed your life if you'd known it earlier? Take a sheet of paper and pencil, and write down as many things as you can. Here are some answers I got to that question.

"I wish someone had told me you were supposed to do things you liked. No one ever did."

"I wish I'd known that there isn't a judge sitting in the sky keeping score of your goodness and your performance. That the people you meet aren't focusing on your faults; they're thinking about their own thing."

"I wish I'd known that the problems were inside me. That I could only do my best and I'd get picked for a part or I wouldn't. I'd have felt better about myself."

"I'd always worry about unfairness, always think it shouldn't be that way. But that's just the way it is, and it's not going to change. I wish I hadn't bothered myself with it."

"I didn't understand that I should do whatever worked best for me. I could have relaxed and accepted myself for who I was."

"I had a long list of things I wanted in a person: intelligence, humor, wit, style. I left off number one: kindness. Nowadays I would put kindness ahead of everything."

"I wish I'd known that everything starts with one small step. No one ever said, 'You're just thinking about the big goal; think about the smaller goals on the way.'"

"I never acknowledged my own progress, never was satisfied until I got to the end. I wish I'd known that if you're not satisfied with little successes, you'll never be satisfied with the big successes."

What about you?

After answering those questions, are you shaking your head with regret, thinking, "Just look at what I could have done if I'd only known then what I know now"?

Of course, you could say that differently.

*Look what you can do now that you never could before.*

Time gave you that.

I hope it's clearer now that what looked like a disaster is no disaster at all. You're on the verge of beginning a wonderful new relationship with time.

Just as soon as we deal with its unpopular twin sister, age.

## EXERCISE 10

*Here's your end-of-chapter quiz:*

1. In what ways have you been trying to fight time?

2. In what ways have you been trying to control death?

3. You thought you wasted your time in your twenties and and thirties by doing _____ (fill in the blank). But now you realize this wasn't a waste of time at all, because _____.

(Use the blank space to describe how you learned from these experiences.)

# 4
# Age

"... men, like women, fear that getting older means
that things will get worse ... a background buzz of
apprehension all through mid-life commonly registers in
the conviction that just over the next rise, it is all going
to be downhill."

Gail Sheehy, *Pathfinders*

"The body is at its best between the ages of thirty
and thirty-five: the mind is at its best about the age of
forty-nine."

Aristotle, *Rhetoric*

"Mailer never had a particular age—he carried different
ages within him like different models of his experience;
parts of him were eighty-one years old, fifty-seven, forty-
eight, thirty-six, nineteen, et cetera, et cetera—he now
went back abruptly from fifty-seven to thirty-six."

Norman Mailer, *The Armies of the Night*

*N*ow here's a strange phenomenon: As you approach midlife,
somewhere between the ages of, say, thirty-five and fifty, you
start feeling old; but ask someone fifty-five or sixty or sixty-five, and
most of them will tell you they don't feel old at all. You flinch at the
sight in your mirror of wrinkles or gray hair as if they were invitations
to an old folks' home, while people fifteen and twenty years your senior
tell you of their plans to go back to school or take up photography or
visit Pakistan.

If your viewpoint was accurate, anyone with more wrinkles and
gray hair than you should feel even worse than you do. Instead they
often feel far better. Now that doesn't make any sense at all. Or does
it?

Is it possible your notion of age itself is an illusion?

I think the wisest thing you can do right now is temporarily set

*aside your notions of youth and middle age—or old age, for that mat-*
*ter—and face the possibility that you might have it all wrong. After*
*reading this chapter, you may decide to set age labels aside perma-*
*nently. I hope so, because that's the only way to keep this false feeling*
*that it's "too late" from turning into reality. You see, the more time*
*you waste fighting with the phantom of age, the longer you postpone*
*the most exciting developments in your life.*

*And there's no need for it. As you're about to see, there's nothing*
*to fight. "Age" isn't a useful concept at this time in human history.*
*And it probably never was.*

———

**Has anybody caught on to how weird it is to define yourself
by your age?**

Imagine you've just run a marathon. Would you say, "I'm the
only English major ever to finish the marathon?" or, "I'm the
only Arab ever to run in a marathon?" But how people love to
say, "George is the oldest person ever to run the marathon."

Well, you might say, that's understandable. After all, age and
physical stamina are relevant comparisons. But we get the same
reactions when someone over sixty writes her first novel too. As
though to do anything interesting over a certain age is simply
amazing.

The media have latched on to this attitude, thinking they're
appealing to an aging population. Magazine articles applaud people for being the oldest to have their own radio show or run their
own business, as if you became less capable with more experience.
TV shows feature elderly people getting married, and the inter-
viewers beam at them indulgently as if they were really cute.

Does that make you want to get older? Check out your feelings, and you'll probably discover a trace of horror. There's something about describing older people by their age that's demean-
ing, as if they're toys or freaks, not regular humans.

**How old are you? How old is anybody?**

What can we say about people that's absolutely tied to aging? Less than you'd ever imagine. You may know how many years you've logged, but what does that mean? That you have less time left than someone younger? Statistics say you could live many decades in excellent health. On the other hand, you could get struck by lightning tomorrow. And that was just as true when you were fourteen.

Well then, is it safe to say that as you grow older, you grow wiser about the ways of life? Apparently not. People of fifty who think they have all the answers usually recant by sixty or seventy and admit they don't have any answers at all. I once heard a lecturer ask a large group of people the following question: "How old would you feel if you didn't know how old you were?" Everyone in the room—whether they were thirty or eighty—came up with the same answer: They felt they were somewhere between fifteen and twenty-five years old.

If life is an education, you could say the grade levels in this particular school won't hold still. How do you know if you're a Freshman in the school of Old, or a Junior in the school of Midlife—or if different parts of you belong in many different age-groups? Or none of the above?

There's one thing to know right off the bat: When it comes to what age means, we are ignorant and misinformed. Our heads are stuffed with hopelessly garbled data. As a result, we're all trying to navigate through unfamiliar waters with a broken compass.

*But these shouldn't be unfamiliar waters!* All our lives we've watched older siblings, upperclassmen, aunts, uncles, cousins, parents, and grandparents hit midlife, pass through it, and move to the next stage. Nothing could be more familiar. But very early we drew a clear line between us and them, and we still have no desire to bridge it. We never believed that older people had anything to teach us because we always felt they belonged to some group of their own, one we'd never want to enter. As a result, instead of being interested in what they actually feel, we simply assume they must hate getting old the way people hate getting sick. If they don't hate it the way we think they should, we think they're a little crazy—and we're kind of happy for the poor things.

Well, I think you'd better start waking up and take a look at the reports rolling in that are shattering our traditional myths about aging.

*Myth:* Old people are lonely and depressed.

*Fact:* The loneliest, most depressed people in the United States are teenagers. The least lonely and depressed are over seventy-five.

*Myth:* Older people are poor.

*Fact:* The most affluent people in America are over fifty.

*Myth:* Life starts winding down after forty.

*Fact:* People in their fifties and sixties report the feeling that all kinds of new things are beginning for them. More people over forty-five travel to unknown places, start new studies, begin new enterprises and relationships than those under forty-five. Women of fifty-seven are off the charts in happiness. Betty Friedan postulates a biological spurt in mental growth among people over sixty that's beginning to be confirmed by neurologists. Many gerontologists are very irritated with her notion and would rather discuss Alzheimer's and old-age homes, but more and more the forward-looking ones are noticing the same thing.

Did you know all this? Most people don't. And what conclusion can you draw? It looks like your assumption that you have some idea how old you are, how old you will be, or how old anybody else is, doesn't rest on a very solid base. The truth is that the scripts for how to act at forty, or eighty, or ninety have vanished, and *nobody knows their lines anymore.* But one thing is sure: Baby boomers turning fifty are not the same age as granny was when she turned fifty around the turn of the century—and not simply because they're staying healthy longer.

**How old we feel and act depends on the style of the moment.**
Throughout history, whenever a society has suffered through a period of painful upheaval—like a civil war or a revolution or a natural disaster—it almost always longs for stability. This is when cultures create conventions and defend them fiercely. As a result, many aspects of culture become rigid, and one of them is the notion of age. In some societies—such as the European monarchies after the French Revolution—the elders take over and tightly control every aspect of the culture. When that happens, the old are considered wise and competent and the young are seen as impetuous, headstrong, and unreliable, in need of control.

After a while there's usually a reaction to the oppressiveness of that stability. In our country it took the form of wild unconventionality in reaction to Prohibition in the 1920s and in the youth revolution of the 1960s. When such reactions happen, young people stop believing in the wisdom of the old, and seeing themselves as having divine clarity, they set about destroying restrictions.

Society's rigidity about age also crumbles when an unusual opportunity appears, like a gold rush or a land rush, when young and old fly into action with no thought of their age. The same thing happens when disaster hits, such as a flood or fire, when every hand is needed and there are no ages, only able bodies to hand off buckets of water to each other or try to rescue flood victims.

At these times older people often jump into the fray and become very strong and capable, but when the crisis is over, they slump back into their rocking chairs and start acting old again. You'd almost suspect they had been deliberately impersonating old folks.

What's going on? We all behave according to society's latest fashion in defining age, nothing more or less.

**The definition of age is about to change for you personally as well.**

Yesterday, when I was walking on Broadway, a man passed me, probably some years older than I am, moving fast, bent a bit from age, brandishing an umbrella. I looked at his wrinkled, strong face as he zipped past and strode ahead of me, and I realized that my thinking about "old" people had changed. I used to see old people as if they had been born old and stayed that way all their lives. If they had ever been young, it was in some era so long ago that it wasn't real or relevant. But when I looked at his face and then his back moving away from me, I found myself thinking, "What did you look like in junior high?"

Something very big has changed inside me. I didn't have one thought about what it's going to be like when I become that "old." And if someone had said, "One day you'll be his age," I would have thought, "So what?" I had recognized him as an individual, not an example of age.

It wasn't always like that for me. Somewhere after the age of thirty-five, I started dreading getting older. Almost everyone does. And you know when the panic peaks: on your fortieth birthday.

**Why do so many people leave town on their fortieth birthday?**

"Forget this rite of passage, I'm getting out of town," a friend recently said to me. "I don't hate being forty or anything. I just don't want to celebrate it."

"I'm going skiing on my fortieth birthday," another friend said. "I want to ignore what happened to my youth. I want to pretend I'm still young."

Have you noticed it too? Lots of people don't want a fortieth birthday party because they don't want to hear the toasts and jokes. For the first time those jokes don't seem very funny. But they don't want to avoid the party by staying home. They don't even want to wash dishes or watch TV in their own home or go to the movies in their own city. They want to be somewhere else.

78

What a difference a day makes!

Why now? Why at forty? Think back: Getting older didn't always worry you. There was a time you couldn't wait to get older. You'd get to drink, drive, and have sex! You'd ignore authority, earn your own money, see the world, make your own decisions.

And then, at some point, usually as you neared your thirties, you got blindsided with an incredible switch in meanings. Where the word age used to be part of a school ID card (Name: George Smith. Age: 14) or, even better, a driver's license that allowed you to buy alcohol (Name: George Smith. Age: 21!), it has now become part of phrases like *old age*, and the root of terrible words like *aging*. When a word turns a corner like that, you freeze and don't want to go another step with it. And who can blame you?

**Prejudices my culture taught me or, the brainwashing of America.**

The outside world helps us right along, because we live in a nation that focuses on age like Eskimos focus on snow. "Most people assume that being middle-aged in America is akin to contracting a mild case of leprosy," says Gail Sheehy.

If you were an intelligent creature from outer space and you heard people with gray in their hair saying things like "I'm not getting older, I'm just getting better," or "You're only as old as you feel," or "Consider the alternative, ha-ha," what assumption would you make? After all, you never hear anyone saying, "I may be young, but I'm happy to say I feel old," or, "You're only as young as you feel." You'd have to conclude that there's something wrong with being older.

And that's exactly what we do conclude. It's obvious that these people are trying to cover up the bad news, trying to make the best of a very bad deal. Those cheerful slogans only increase our dread, subtly convincing us of the misfortunes of age.

And look at the magazines. Not the ones that refuse to show a face over forty but the ones that do! I call them "the investment/incontinence" magazines: how to live off your pension or your investments (or you'll surely be eating cat food in your old age) or what to do when your bladder weakens. The ads are worse: You too can grin brightly, have a twenty-five-year-old body despite your gray hair, and pose by a golf cart with an equally vapid spouse at your side. You too can stay young at the same time as you grow old gracefully (whatever that's supposed to mean).

The attitude is outlandish and alarming to us. I hear thirty-year-olds worrying themselves to death about how to prepare financially for retirement! If they save and invest every penny, can they have the $1.7 million they need to live on the interest when they're "old"? Or should they just trash their careers so they can have their last great adventure before they turn into the frightening creatures featured in these articles and ads?

Much of this media hype is well-meaning, but the decision to make gray hair, retirement, or incontinence the focus at mid-life is like making shin splints, Spanish, or seasickness the focus for twenty-year-olds. And discussions of menopause, both male and female, and how certain illnesses speed up and others slow down are simply done to death. Sure, some information is necessary and useful, *but the relentless focus on bodily changes in every documentary, magazine article, and book about aging only reinforces the dismal myth that the most significant thing about getting older is your disintegration!*

Where are the pictures of older people sitting on the ground cross-legged, frowning with concentration as they dust off pottery shards, or arguing at labor negotiations, or squinting at an airplane engine with a wrench in their hands? You know, *doing stuff*—not talking about fallen arches or grinning fiercely as if to prove they're not miserable just because they're old?

If you want to find pictures like that, you have to look in special-interest magazines about art or archaeology or architecture or history or psychology or popular science. Or in trade magazines, the ones for cartoonists, pilots, cattle ranchers, geologists, journalists, illustrators. Most tellingly, you'll find pictures of people over forty in action—political leaders, scientists, explorers, philanthropists, financial turks, filmmakers, tiger trainers, and oilfield firefighters—in business magazines and newspapers and newsmagazines. *They have to be there because these are the people who make most of the news.* There's no avoiding images of people over forty, fifty, sixty, and seventy. They run the world. They're busy.

But when you look at their pictures, you forget to notice that these fascinating people are over forty. When we think about "older people," we never think of *these* people. We can think about "people," and we can think about "older people," but we can't think about both at the same time. The same woman you find so interesting in a science magazine becomes vaguely pathetic in a magazine for seniors. Why? Because no matter how you try to avoid it, *when you select your focus based on age, you automatically pull in cultural bias.*

**Subtly but relentlessly, our prejudices about age come to the surface.**

". . . according to the prevailing mythology, to be younger is to be better; therefore, we should expect to find young people in the majority of those who reflect high well-being . . . In fact, the one finding that registered more consistently and emphatically than any other in the course of my research was this: Older is better," says Gail Sheehy.

"There is a terrible excitement to growing old, a fierce game, a devil-may-care acceleration of living well in the time left us."

"If anybody had told me at fifty that I would enjoy the mid-seventies, I think I would have laughed it away. Now I can say without hesitation that the mid-seventies are some of the best times of my life."

Where are the older people who feel this way? They're not in hiding. They're all around you. And you can see with your own eyes that they feel fine.

But you don't see what's right in front of you, and neither does anyone else. Why? What's going on? Well, not cool fact, that's for sure. Facts are supposed to hold still for you. *What you've got is a prejudice, a viewpoint turned into a bias.* A prejudice is characterized by your inability to see what's in front of you, because it doesn't fit what you've been taught to think. Ageism is just like racism or any other prejudice. You're certain there's something wrong with some group or other, but you haven't got one airtight argument to prove it. For example, in the 1940s and 1950s, it was commonly agreed that women weren't as interesting company as men. Then, thanks to the battles of many courageous people, we woke up, looked around and discovered a world full of fascinating women. Why didn't we see them before? Such is the nature of prejudice.

The myth that age is bad has put down deep roots and isn't easy to pull out. Older people are stodgy, and the young are hip, right? To hold on to that mistruth, you must ignore both older people—like Mick Jagger, for instance—and younger ones, like some of those stuffy people you knew in high school. Prejudice is irrational and powerful, and limiting. It cuts your free, creative spirit off at the knees and deprives you of the company of exciting, original people.

One of them is you.

Because while you're struggling to avoid falling into this stereotype, you're stealing time away from the real you who is sitting on the shelf waiting to happen.

At a recent career conference I overheard a man saying: ". . . so the frog speaks to the princess and says, 'Kiss me and I'll turn into a handsome prince!' but she says, 'At my age, a talking frog is much more interesting.' " A nearby woman turned to him and said, "That's ageism. Older people like sex, and you know it." She was probably right to point out that he was belittling older people, but in a way so was she. Sex is nice at any age, but one of the prizes you get with the years is that *it stops being the only show in town*. For my part, I'd never turn anything so astonishing as a talking frog into just another prince.

**The appearance of age.**

Prejudice or no, starting to look physically older throws us all into a tailspin.

Baba Ram Dass, speaking in front of a large group some years ago, held his hands in front of him and looked at them. Then he looked up at the audience.

"These are not my hands," he said quietly.

I think he's right about all of us. *At some point your body and you part ways.* When you're young, you and your body are one and the same. You look in the mirror and see someone familiar. And then one day your body starts looking like somebody else's. This is very strange, because inside, you stay exactly the same as you always were. You continue to think and see and laugh and worry and learn just like you always did. You're the same person. But the person in the mirror isn't.

How can we read this?

It could be a fantastic opportunity, finally your chance to stop identifying yourself in terms of your looks. You could say, "Look at that! If inside I'm staying the same—funny, curious, analytical, grumpy, or good-natured or whatever I've always been—and my appearance is changing, maybe my body and I are two different creatures!"

How great that could be for you! It could be your own personal Bastille Day! *You could say for the first time that you're not an animal, you're just using one for transportation.* Naturally you'd take wonderfully good care of that animal because its stamina will determine how far you get to travel. But from now on the physical side of you would be only a good friend, while your true self had a mind of its own, free to think, feel, experiment, play. Not merely react impulsively.

The appearance of age could be great for you in other ways, too.

**The power of the Invisible Man—or Woman.**

In most cultures middle-aged people become invisible. They can walk down the street without being the object of attention. That could be a very good thing, although most of us don't think so at first.

"I hate this!" said a forty-two-year-old friend. "I thought I hated men whistling and bothering me, but now they don't look at me at all! I feel like I disappeared!"

But being invisible puts a great power in your hands, the power to be yourself. It's not that you can walk into jewelry stores and swipe a tiara, like an invisible person in a movie. That's small potatoes. Being invisible lets you swipe something a lot bigger, the freedom to do as you please. *Because when people stop seeing you, they lose control over you.* It's a little gift but extremely useful, because it gives you an early taste of freedom before you're quite ready to stop feeling defined by other people's opinions of you.

"If nobody whistles at me anyway, I'm going to wear comfortable shoes. The hell with it," said a forty-four-year-old woman who had returned to college.

However, few of us take advantage of our invisibility until we're much older. When we're hovering on the borderline of midlife, we do everything in our power to stay visible. The project is enormous and full of tricky contradictions: exercise, stay hungry all the time, dye your hair, write checks to the cosmetic surgeon, dress youthfully—and at the same time, act your age and not like some old lady or man impersonating a teenager. You have to walk a fine line, trying to act more grown up than you feel, trying to be a person with the dignity adults are supposed to have so no one will make fun of you, while at the same time trying to be someone chirpy and charmingly impulsive with a good spring in your walk so people won't call you "old." Since you're neither of these, you literally have to impersonate someone younger and older at the same time!

Where are you supposed to learn how to do that? And why would you want to?

**To "act your age" is to be controlled by others.**

If someone decided you were Napoleon, you wouldn't feel you had to act like Napoleon. So why do we care when we hear people say, "Act your age"? For one thing, it's completely impossible; the way older people are supposed to act is redefined every year. For another, you never feel your own age, so you can never remember how old you're supposed to act. As a result, you constantly have to search other people's eyes for clues. A fifteen-year-old might think that a thirty-five-year-old is over the hill and that a fifty-year-old needs assistance walking. If enough young people decide you look like a cute old man or a distinguished old lady, maybe you missed your cue and you're supposed to impersonate one. Maybe that's who you became when you weren't looking.

And maybe you just shouldn't give a damn one way or the other.

Instead, maybe you should ask yourself just exactly who your viewers are. Can they do you any harm? Or any good? Will they refuse to take your money at the checkout stand if you don't act your age? Will they marry you and take you to Monaco if you do? The sooner you can replace this knee-jerk accommodation with some confidence and integrity, the better. To drop all efforts to fit a stereotype and be true to yourself in the essential acts of your life could be the first day of the best stage of your life. Your first wrinkle could be the first ray of consciousness, coming at you like a sunrise.

But we're checking out our appearance in their eyes for another reason, and this is one of the biggest reasons that we simply hate to grow older.

**Fear of becoming square.**

We shudder at middle age because our stereotypes tell us that we're going wake up and be like the adults in *Father Knows Best* or the women in *The Stepford Wives:* rigid and conformist. You can almost see the instructions for adulthood blazoned across your future: Become conventional.

Senator Claude Pepper said, "When I was young, women over forty seemed terminally grown up . . ."

"People over forty are different from us. They fuss about foolish things. They hate change. They forget they were ever young. I can't bear to turn into one of them!" a woman of twenty-six wrote me.

This is the real fear of becoming middle-aged: not death or decrepitude but the dread that you'll inevitably turn into someone else, someone who doesn't live an exciting life or have exciting dreams, a middle-aged bore who likes boring "safe" cars, travels to Europe in groups, loses touch with the good music, becomes opinionated and conservative.

But there's something you may not have noticed: Conventional middle-aged people were always conventional. If they scare you now, they probably scared you just as much when they were young and buying their first carpeting. The young and beautiful Stepford Wives were just as horrifying as the Stepford Seniors we've created in our minds. It's the Stepford part that's scary, not the years themselves.

The real culprit is thoughtless conformism. *And it attaches itself to only one age group.*

**The only age that is invariably conventional is adolescence.**

Yes, that's what I said. If you think of teenagers as being rebellious and wild, take another look. Their rebellion is only against adults. Teenagers don't rebel against other teenagers. In fact, no other group watches its peers with more intensity, scrutinizing the latest convention so they can conform precisely to it. At no other age do people suffer such agonies if they aren't allowed to copy their peers. At puberty the only thing in the world we want to know are the rules for being cool in our peer group. That intense self-consciousness, measuring worth in the eyes of others, has a powerful purpose: It's the first step in the mating process. But it makes adolescents the most conforming, conventional age-group in our species.

Your instincts to be wary of too much conformity are right on target: Whatever the benefits of stability and convention, they must be carefully watched or they will muffle our unique voices. But if it's teenagers who are the conventional ones, where does your fear of middle-aged deadness come from?

It comes from your memory of being a teenager.

The challenges you threw in front of your parents were a test, and your parents didn't pass. They always failed so hopelessly to understand you that you had to assume they were incapable of thought. From your viewpoint, you weren't a copycat; you wanted to do something very new. What was new wasn't dyeing your hair purple; everyone was doing that. What was new was leaving your family's ways and taking up the ways of young people who were deliberately shocking to your parents. But the grown-ups overreacted and flew into a panic. To them it seemed like you were turning into someone they didn't know, and even worse, you could be putting yourself in terrible danger. That started the inevitable war of the generations, fought in every household in the land.

To a teenager, the only danger worth considering is the rejection of other teenagers. But your parents obsessed about car crashes, drug addiction, and pregnancy. That made them difficult and fearful and angry, and it seemed that all they wanted was to stifle everything that was fresh, exciting, and new to you. They seemed to stand directly between you and your drive to live.

*And now you think you're going to turn into the same dreadful people.*

I know I'm generalizing about teenagers, just as I did about infants, but I don't expect to be challenged on that generalization because at these two ages behavior is predictable. The reason? These age-groups are the most important to the survival of our species: The young must live to become fertile and reproduce; they are the most carefully programmed by biology.

And by extension, you are least conventional when you have reached the age least important to the survival of the species.

**You can't emerge as a true original until you're free of the grip of youth.**

Not to say that young people don't have great surges of originality and creativity—they certainly do—but what's coming through is only half of what's inside them because they have to concentrate on two things at once: their original vision and the dictates of nature. They need to make the grade, so they must keep one eye on what they personally want to do and the other on the competition. Whatever originality breaks through is promptly slapped into service to get a good grade, a good job, or some other prize.

But once you are, as Jung would say, "abandoned by nature," you become a wild card, a loose cannon. Dorothy Sayers, the mystery writer, said, "[A] young woman can be controlled by time and trouble . . . but an older woman is uncontrollable by any force known to man."

So much for the inevitability of becoming stodgy.

**Okay, you were duped. It's back to the drawing board.**

You've just blasted your ageism out of the water. Now how old are you? Who the hell knows? You're probably every age you ever were, and there's no end in sight. Everything you do has its source in one of your warehoused ages. Whenever you're creating, you're a very young child. When you notice patterns repeating themselves and come to understand their meanings, you've lived at least thirty-five or forty years. When you forgive yourself and others more easily, understanding how hard it is to be perfect, you're probably over fifty.

Nobody ever "grows up." All your ages are still inside you. The different ages we pass through don't drop off like a snake's skin. We just add layers. You're everybody you've ever been. The more years you've lived through, the more sights, sounds, smells, events, decisions, viewpoints, and feelings you carry around inside you. It's as if you visited a lot of countries or read a lot of books. Your inner theater holds a very large cast of characters, each one stepping out on the stage to say her piece whenever it seems like the right time.

**You still don't know what's coming.**

Because you were so certain you knew, you were afraid to get older. Because you were afraid, you hesitated to launch into the next step. But now you're in a greatly improved position, simply because you understand that the meaning of age is anything but clear. Don't be discouraged. Relax and admit your ignorance. Confusion is a perfect learning state. As Carl Jung says, "When certainty goes, it is the beginning of consciousness."

Now you can begin to see your future is wide open and you've got a whole new life to design. It's time to pick up your pencil and start again. You've just changed an ending to a beginning.

**So how do you handle the issue of age?**

My advice is, forget it. When it comes to others or to yourself, pay attention to experience, intelligence, imagination, talent, energy, decency, kindness—the things that really matter in any human being—and ignore age entirely. It's irrelevant, and anyway, it's incomprehensible. Worst of all, it leads to costly errors you don't want to make, the kinds of errors I hope these four rules will help to prevent:

*Rule Number One: Don't decide you're too old to do something before you really are.*

A woman with white hair came up to me in a bookstore in Wyoming and said, "I wish I'd heard you years ago. I've wanted to do some things and just couldn't get it together and now it's too late."

I said, "Are you ill?"

"No, no, but I'm sixty-three, I really waited too long."

"You know," I said, "you might live to be eighty or ninety. Are you going to feel like a dope when you realize you thought you were old at sixty-three! You are really going to hate that feeling. You'd better get into action now."

The problem is that she, like you and me, was prematurely traumatized by her own birthdays. By the time we get smart enough to understand how young we were at forty, fifty, or sixty, we'll be seventy, eighty, or ninety!

That's why it's important to pay particular attention to anything you should not put off. If you're in good health, this is the time to go trekking. Don't put it off until you're seventy. For one thing, your body might not be able to carry you. For another, by the time you're seventy, you'll be doing other amazing things you never did before and will be too busy to go trekking anyway.

Are you noticing small physical problems already? Fine. *Make a list of what works and use it.* Don't waste any time deploring your expanding waistline or a thumb that's misbehaving. You're probably in exactly the right shape for what you should be doing at this time of your life, just as you were when you were a baby or a teenager.

Don't let yourself forget that you're never too old to do anything your body will allow.

*Rule Number Two: Time is clay. Make something.*

Remember those things you always wanted to do but felt you couldn't—like travel or dancing or writing? Now is the time to begin them. If, like most people in their forties, you're in charge of endless projects and have very little time, remember that doing what you love doesn't have to be a full-time commitment to have an enormous impact on your life. Five minutes a day of writing or singing, dancing or thumbing through travel brochures will revive you like water does a thirsty plant. And that five minutes a day will increase your chances exponentially of actually getting involved. Familiarity breeds possibilities, I promise you.

*Rule Number Three: If you've got a big dream, go for it. But never believe it's your last.*

Is there one big thing you want to do before you're "too old"? Go ahead and do it if you can. But don't fool yourself by thinking you'll be willing to grow old once you've accomplished it. One dream will never be enough for you. As a matter of fact, the best reason to go after your dream of a lifetime is to get it out of the way so you can move to the next ones. One day you'll see this one was just a warm-up.

You're entering your age of great undertakings, and your dreams are only now beginning to line up. Wait until you see what's in store for you later in this book.

*Rule Number Four: Watch out for premature regrets.*

"For all sad words of tongue or pen, The saddest are these: 'It might have been!'"

If you find yourself wondering where the years went and questioning whether you put your life to good use or not, understand that it's a good question, but *you've asked it at the wrong time.* What have you done with your life? My answer is, Who can say? There's a good chance it hasn't started yet.

## EXERCISE 11

### *Okay, ready for a pop quiz?*

1. Do you tell young cashiers at the grocery store checkout line that they should be asking for your liquor or cigarette ID and then wait to see how much they laugh?
2. Do you ever look at someone in a magazine who looks old and realize with horror that he's the same age as you?
3. Do you blurt out your age to your hairdresser or waitress and wait for a reaction? Do you feel bad when you're told you look young for your age? Do you feel just as bad when people accept how old you are without comment?
4. Do you try to guess people's ages when you're in public?

5. Pretend you're sixty-five years old. Walk around the way you think a sixty-five-year-old walks. Did you find yourself enacting a decrepit or lonely old person?

6. Now go back and remember when you thought twenty-one was old. Describe what you thought about that age then and what you think now.

7. Do the same with thirty. Remember when it seemed old to you. How has your perception changed?

8. How old do you feel when you're around people much older than you?

9. How old do you feel when you're alone, absorbed in something you enjoy?

10. Imagine you had absolutely no consciousness of age, and neither did anyone else? What would you do differently? What would you stop doing?

Answer those questions for yourself, and then take a pencil and a piece of paper and write down what you learned by your answers.

**Now what's your position on age?**

Andrea, thirty-six: "As soon as I finished reading this chapter, I went out on the street and people looked different. I looked at what they were doing, you know, shopping or driving buses or drilling in the street, not how old they were. Before, I don't think I would have noticed them at all if they were over a certain age."

Lou, thirty-nine: "I feel like a vise has fallen off my neck. I've been afraid of getting old since I was twenty-five!"

Will, forty-two: "I thought this age thing was an open-and-shut case, and now I'm confused. I don't know what to think."

Well, you're not supposed to think anything. It was all a false alarm.

If I've met my goal, you too are ready to admit your certainty about age has been shaken and you honestly don't know what it means anymore. That's the best thing that could happen to you.

Of course the disappearance of your certainty might have left you, like Will, with a big empty space where an assumption used to be. My advice is to treasure it. Uncertainty is a great asset, and you won't feel empty forever, so you must make the most of it. Remember when I said that "emptiness is a place to grow things"? You've just cleared out another illusion and made room for a radically new kind of personal growth.

It's planting time.

# 5
# Beauty

"Mirror, mirror on the wall, who's the fairest
of them all?"

Evil queen, "Snow White"

" 'And what is your fortune, my pretty young maid?'
'My face is my fortune, sir,' she said."

English Folksong

*B*eauty. *It sounds frivolous and lightweight compared to the great issues in life, but at midlife it muscles its way right into the center of our consciousness. Is it because we're immature or shallow that we start obsessing about how we look? No, this particular obsession is one of the most deep-seated concerns of our lives, and it peaks at midlife. Suddenly we find ourselves engaged in a mighty wrestling match with every hint of wrinkles or weight gain, obsessed with our image in mirrors, preoccupied with clothes that flatter and exercise that beautifies, engaged in endless efforts to hold back the ravages of time, until finally, at some age, full of sorrow, we give up and forget the whole thing.*

*And then we get happy again.*

*Very peculiar. If beauty is so important and losing it so terrible, why would we get happy again? For that matter, why does the onset of this dramatic battle for beauty suddenly peak now, at midlife? Why would something like our own beauty become such a huge concern at this particular time in our lives? It doesn't make any sense at all.*

*Or does it?*

———

Beauty has always been an issue in your life whether you are male or female, but at midlife it takes a special spin. No matter how differently each of us felt about our looks until now—happy or unhappy or totally unconcerned—at midlife we all feel exactly the same: unhappy. There's no doubt about it, you're changing—for the worse. Reason won't fix your opinion; your friends can insist you look exactly like you did ten years ago, but it doesn't help a bit. You're losing your looks, and you know it.

**For once your irrational feeling is completely accurate.**

There's a certain kind of beauty that is actually diminishing in us as we get older, and it's this kind of beauty we hate to lose. Maybe other people can't see the change, but that's because they aren't paying attention. We're looking more carefully, and it's really happening. We look better than we ever have? Yeah, right. We don't look beautiful in that special way, the way young people look beautiful.

Even people who have always considered themselves ordinary-looking are disturbed by the diminishing of their youthful beauty. Why is it such a big deal? Look closer, and you'll see that all of us harbor a belief—however unsubstantiated by our adult experience—that if we are truly beautiful, we will be loved and led into an earthly paradise. And if we are not, we will be forever outside its walls. Why do we believe such a thing?

Because we've been here before.

**Once upon a time we all were gorgeous. And then it went away.**

As I've said before, your first experience in life was to be adored. Few parents can resist their own offspring and are totally convinced of their astonishing beauty. That means that right at the beginning, when we were much too young to know how to win love, we got it for doing nothing at all, just because of how we looked. We just lay back and allowed people to look at us, and they thought we were beautiful. They said so. One of our earliest lessons, and therefore one of the biggest, was: You will be adored and protected because you are beautiful.

Most of us lost that little taste of paradise rather quickly. Either our parents got used to us, or they were overwhelmed by life's demands (including the ones we made on them), or they fell in love with the next baby. One way or another, most of us learned soon enough that we were going to have to develop something besides our good looks if we wanted to survive.

It didn't seem fair, but it was clear you'd have to earn your own way from then on. Like all of us, you came up with a plan: Be very good, or very unselfish, or helpful, or clever, and then you would be the favorite again. It didn't work, of course. You would never be the favorite again.

**But it wasn't a total loss. You won a greater prize.**

You tried hard to regain your position as favorite, and in the process you developed an entire personality. You tried out dozens of different behavior styles, learned how it felt to compete and to win, or lose. You developed your perceptions and intuition by trying to understand the strange workings of your parents' minds. You learned which losses you could tolerate and which ones filled you with despair. By trying for a prize you couldn't win, you won a greater prize. You learned how to charm, threaten, coerce, strategize, compensate, debate, plot against your enemies, and wail about injustice to the gods.

Ultimately you turned your back on the arena of your rejection and defeat, took your newfound cleverness, and marched out into the world—your neighborhood, your school. You lived two lives. Once you realized you could no longer get what you wanted at home by just dimpling up, you became a fuller person—independent and curious, perceptive and communicative and cooperative, and competent. This may have started earlier than you realize, often by five years old. But the timing was good, because at that moment, you were introduced to a new world, school.

Soon you were making your own friends, learning the ways of this world, developing a personality, and building a rich and complex imagination. You learned about other families with different feelings and values; you played with new tools and learned to read. When you were by yourself, you chose your own amusements and dreamed your private dreams. Day by day you built a history your parents knew nothing about.

You didn't even spend much time thinking about being the favorite unless you happened to see another sibling get some attention. For the most part, you preferred less painful activities, such as riding your bike, playing with other kids, learning new things. You became a very smart little person.

**But you never forgot.**

Somewhere in the back of your mind, half forgotten, the lesson was there, waiting: *If ever you could manage to become the fairest again, you would become the favorite again.* One small side of you, wounded by loss and rejection, sat in the shadows and waited for the future.

Now you were all set up for nature's program, scheduled to kick in at adolescence, the opening of the biggest beauty pageant in the history of anyone's life. After a few years of relative freedom during childhood—a time of considerable individuality and creativity—the rejected side of you woke up and wanted to try once more to be the favorite. Things that had fascinated you as a child—like whiling away a day collecting tadpoles or crawling behind bushes or playing catch—became unimportant, and two things loomed in their place: your own appearance and the appearance of other adolescents. Your mom didn't have to force you to take a bath anymore; in fact, she couldn't get you out of the bathroom. While she banged on the door, you showered, combed your hair into the latest style, tried on cool expressions, and searched for your fate in your own reflection.

Fortunately that level of intensity didn't last forever. Adolescence passed into young adulthood; you calmed down a bit, found a look you could live with, and took your place in society one way or another. You didn't really leave the beauty game, but it became more a matter of maintenance than of winning the gold medal for a number of years. After all, you'd fixed (or beaten) yourself up in front of the mirror every day for years, so once you stepped out of the house you could forget your appearance and think about other things. How you looked became a background noise, a daily half-noticed ritual, no longer central. Until you started crowding forty.

What a difference a birthday makes.

**Another beauty pageant? Why now?**

Cosmetics, diet plans, gym equipment—who do you think buys these things more than anyone else? Midlifers, by a wide margin. It makes sense that adolescents would be obsessed with beauty, but why you? Why now?

After all, you're not just a pretty face anymore. You've been in the business of building a unique personality for years. Choice and experience have given you a powerful and complex personality and a very big brain full of experiences, decisions, accomplishments, and personal tastes. When you've been tested by a hundred thousand small events and gotten familiar with how you typically respond, you start to know who you are. Not only that, but you've built a small world of your own with your home, your relationships, your work. You have your own opinions, you know how to hold your own against other people, and you're not so quick to let anyone define you.

Even your environment's changed by the time you've reached midlife. For one thing, your universe has gotten larger. You've got your personal history, of course, but you're also interested in world history, politics and nature, work, goals, creativity, projects, travel. The number of people in your universe has quadrupled as well. Not only have you met many people in the last years, but unlike an adolescent or a twenty-five-year-old, you're not interested only in people your own age. Unlike adolescents, you're not primarily a hunter, so you don't need their tunnel vision and can see more. Now you find that you're interested in kids, peers, elders, and lots of other people who are of no apparent use at all. All in all, you're in a very good place. If ever you didn't really need to be gorgeous, it's now.

But things keep happening that trigger a new obsession with your looks.

A sudden glimpse in the mirror makes you realize you're starting to look like your parents!

"It's like a bad dream. Like some force has me and I can't break free. I'm going to turn into my mom!"

"I look different. I don't like it. Just holding on to whatever looks I have is getting to be a huge struggle."

"I used to read *Vogue* magazine and think, 'What's the big deal?' Now I read it and hate all the young, gorgeous girls."

Then one day you notice that strangers are treating you differently.

"You know, sometimes I think young waitresses or salesgirls are angry with me! Like I'm somebody's wicked stepmother," said a forty-two-year-old woman. "How did I get old enough to be anybody's wicked stepmother?"

"I watched this cute young woman gaze at a handsome young guy I was standing next to in the elevator, and she didn't even see me. This is a new thing for me," said a forty-four-year-old man.

"When I'm driving, I sometimes see a car in my rearview mirror, and it's a young guy trying to catch up with me, and then he comes alongside my window, looks in at me, and his eyes glaze over, and he turns his eyes back on the road. He loses interest! I never believed this could feel so terrible!" said a thirty-nine-year-old woman.

**And an old process starts again.**

The original hurt from childhood is stung awake by these new rejections, and we start yearning to be desired again. We become hyperaware of our looks, and we find ourselves checking to see how far the loss of our beauty has gone, how much can be salvaged. We ask boxboys at checkout stands how old they think we look. We try to make it clear to barmaids that we are still very hip and cool. We look in every store window to see if we look better than we did in the last store window. Even moderately attractive young people look like the most fortunate people on earth, and we wish they'd have the brains to appreciate it.

All that richness of personality and lifestyle we've developed starts to look empty and worthless. We'd trade it all just to have our beauty back.

Why?

Because we want to feel like the favorite again.

**Back to the past, to hell with the future.**

The changes we hate the most are the ones that threaten our survival. But the loss of looks isn't going to threaten our actual survival, not at this stage of the game. You're not worried about being abandoned by your mom, and your mating strategies should have been figured out by now. But this doesn't feel like just a change; it feels like something is ending forever. Something incredibly important.

Suddenly you find yourself regretting the fact that you never appreciated your beauty when you had it: "If only I'd known, I'd have acted differently, more sure of myself, gotten something for it." Pretty revealing, isn't it? What would you have gotten? Obviously something you wish you had right now.

Love.

Beauty is a control issue. With it we imagine we have the power to get all the love we need. Without it we're convinced we're helpless. We forget that we're quite tolerant of ordinary looks in everyone else: friends and relatives, teachers, coworkers, bus drivers, character actors on the screen. When your mother looks at your favorite photo of her and says, "Look at those horrible wrinkles," you're surprised because she looks so good to you. You might be more critical when it comes to potential mates, assessing them with care on first meetings, but after you know them, their looks have much less effect. They can't lose you with plainness, and they can't win you with beauty.

*But when it comes to yourself, your demands for perfect beauty sail off the charts.* You become as hopelessly unforgiving of your imperfections as a fourteen-year-old. And equally as narcissistic. You never think twice about other people's need to get love. It's *your* need to be desirable that's got you in its grip.

**The mating game is still in full play, but you've been benched.**

Look at those beautiful young people having all that excitement. You didn't notice it so much before, but now it seems everywhere you look you see them holding hands, gazing into each other's eyes, wanting each other. *And they can't even see you.* It hits you that all your life you were a player, even if you took it for granted, but now, somehow, without your permission, you got taken out of the game, and you're horrified. It sets off another trigger in you. Even if you thought you hated the mating game, suddenly you want another shot at it.

If you're in a good relationship, it starts feeling a bit dull. What felt like comfort and friendship before is now missing some essential element. Maybe this is your last chance for the great passion. It may even be too late! Now the heartsickness, the loneliness, the urgency that once spurred you into action are back in full force. You're weighed down with the depression of a hopelessness that can only be cured by the excitement of the chase. On the horizon you think you can make out the shape of paradise. What are your chances of winning happiness this time?

*To answer this, we all go straight to the mirror.*

And what do we see there? Fatal imperfections. Nothing can ever make you feel beautiful again—except maybe if someone new came along, someone who looked at you with all your new imperfections and became weak with desire all the same.

Of course, the rational side of you wants no part of these reawakened hungers. You don't want to jeopardize a good relationship. You're no fool. You've already been an adolescent and have had time to watch others. It's a bit embarrassing and shallow to care about your surface at this stage of the game. So you figure it's just Madison Avenue and the media working on you, or all the superficial values of a youth-oriented culture. You should be able to stop caring about anything so stupid, right?

Unfortunately, you have a bigger opponent than Madison Avenue or culture: biology.

**Beauty is youth, youth beauty. And nature loves them best.**

"Beauty is truth, truth beauty—that's all/ ye know on earth/ all ye need to know," says Keats. At midlife you can change it to "Beauty is youth, youth beauty," because biology has its own truth.

Pretend all you will, find it unfair if you like, but inside, you agree, and so does everyone else. And I mean everyone. Every animal and every nation, all human groupings everywhere in the world, even in primitive cultures hidden deep in the jungles. *And that universality is a dead giveaway that biology is at work.*

Affection becomes beauty-based at adolescence. And because nature takes a very great interest in anything that encourages breeding, the biology of beauty is obviously hardwired into us. The members of every culture in the world begin at adolescence to decorate themselves so they can win the beauty contest that has now begun in earnest. That's why it's so hard to talk yourself out of it no matter how much you try. This one belongs to nature.

**The true purpose of beauty.**

The kind of beauty you hate losing is purely a breeding magnet. Plumage is designed to stir desire. You can go so far as to say that if the perception of beauty weren't useful for the survival of the species, there would be no such thing as beauty.

*And once we're past the breeding age, it's supposed to change.* After all, if older people were as sexually desirable as young ones, fertility might be wasted on people who couldn't reproduce. Every time older people wish they were still as desirable as ever, they should thank the fates that such wishes weren't granted or they might not be here to think about it.

But if you're in a comfortable, loving relationship, what difference does it make? If you're among the many people who never paid much attention to the extremes of beauty, what's the big deal? After all, although the best-looking kids in school were the envy of all the others, they were hardly the only ones who fell in love and got married. And why should you care if younger people or handsome strangers don't notice you?

But you do care. A lot.

**This is absolutely not fair!**

What does this make you, chopped liver? At first glance it looks that way. We're not the fairest of them all anymore, so you're getting the message to give up and move aside. Just bite the bullet and face the truth, that's what you're supposed to think, right?

Don't be so sure.

Nature is craftier than you think. Nature wants you to squawk right now, good and loud. Why?

It's all part of the plan.

**Nature's hidden agenda for midlifers.**

If you think nature wants you to grow up and maturely move aside for the youngsters, think again. Your biological clock has wakened the rejected child in you one last time. There's a device inside you that was timed to go off right about now and make you become as insecure and vain and needy as an adolescent. Because you still might be fertile. Perhaps you can be persuaded to make just one more baby.

**Don't fall for it!**

Don't look now, but you're being conned big time, by the best con artist of them all. By taking away your youthful looks, nature has reactivated your aching heart and cruel self-appraisement. Just like an adolescent, you've started thinking, "If only I were fantastically good-looking. Then I'd be the luckiest person alive." But you wouldn't be.

For one thing, you need that body and brain for more important matters than mere display. For another, there are so many disadvantages to being young and beautiful that ordinary-looking people would be amazed. Let me introduce a bit of debunking because it's time for you to stop envying Adonis or Venus.

**The disadvantages of beauty.**

1. *It's not as much fun (or as useful) to be beautiful as you'd like to think.*

Do you remember being happy when you were young and beautiful? Was anybody? Well, the prom queen *looked* happy, and so did the captain of the football team, but they were under a lot of pressure to keep up appearances. Where's the prom queen now? Stuck with that quarterback? Too successful too young?

In some ways, nature makes the hardest demands on its favorites, like the cultures that sacrificed their beautiful young people to the gods. Like young athletes and musicians, beauties worked every day to stay beautiful, always were in a contest of one sort or another, and depended on others to tell them what they were worth.

But midlife hits beauties especially hard, because they've had no way to develop fallback positions. Their early success actually deprives them of learning how to get along. They're given the trophy without having to play the game everyone else is required to play. Unlike more ordinary-looking youngsters, a beauty often has an easy adolescence, since he or she seldom experiences a break in the adoration of infancy.

There are exceptions, of course. Not all beautiful people were adored as children, and some of them developed a different strategy.

"I made a deal with myself that said, 'All right, I won't rely on my beauty, but I'll still use it to attract attention and then I'll also be good or helpful or clever.' But what if the phone stops ringing?"

Unlike more ordinary-looking people, beauties don't have to develop other ways to attract attention. You rarely find a beauty who's also the class clown or the one who can help you fix your computer. And beauties are keenly aware of the insecurity and loneliness of unpopular classmates who have to struggle so hard for everything they get. Like anyone would, they feel grateful to be spared. Like children who win in beauty pageants, it never would occur to them that they're missing the good times average-looking kids had.

2. *Some of your happiest times had nothing to do with beauty.*

In fact, they happened most when notions of beauty or popularity had temporarily disappeared. If you think about the best times you had with friends, you'll notice something interesting: You had the most relaxed fun when the most beautiful and desirable people weren't anywhere to be found. Because beauties stir competition and make us self-conscious.

"Beautiful women upset my stomach and make me very irritable. Always have," said a thirty-three-year-old man. But why? He's quite good-looking himself. "Not good-looking enough for the real beauties back in my school days, and it's never gone away," he answered.

I remember a conversation I had with a very beautiful woman I knew slightly in college. She told me she watched with longing the fun my friends and I had every day when we gathered between classes on the lawn.

"I walked over a few times, but the mood changed right away. The men got uncomfortable, and women stopped looking happy. That's why I never sat with you."

I remembered those times, and she was absolutely right. She was so wonderful-looking we all, even the women, were a bit in love with her. She was a nice person too. But she drove the men crazy, and she made us women feel rejected, just as she said. Even worse, the few times she sat down with us we became inhibited for her sake because she wasn't really playful and didn't know how to take part in the goofing around we habitually did. She hadn't had a chance to play in groups as we had because, like all the gorgeous girls, she was usually off with some equally impressive boyfriend.

3. *The unusual beauty often paid the price of loneliness.*

Because most people are afraid of them, you sometimes hear beauties complain that they spend a lot of Saturday nights alone; but they have another kind of loneliness you rarely hear about. I've seen a number of models in therapy, and they all report a kind of loneliness that ordinary-looking people rarely experience, a lonely center as they look at people watching them with eyes full of love *while they feel nothing.* And when beauties are approached, they must respond to their admirers. If they don't respond, it's seen as rejection. If they do, they must expect to be fallen in love with, whether they want it or not. It's a trap not easily escaped from because beauties have their own mixed feelings. They know they must put their good fortune to use by becoming stars or marrying someone rich, regardless of whom they love. In fact, more than one remarkable beauty has walked out on someone they loved because they knew they could do better.

"All my energies went into making the most of my opportunities by dressing up and going to the right places," said a forty-four-year-old woman. "You develop a technique to deal with people who are attracted to you to see if they're worth your time or if they're just pulling you away from better opportunities. Sometimes you give up and choose the guy who admires you most just because you hate to walk out empty-handed."

Like great wealth, great beauty can insulate a person from the experiences everyone else has. Even highly intelligent beauties often don't develop their intellects. And for the most part, no one challenges exceptional beauties with political or philosophical debates, even when they go to college.

"College is a microcosm of life. Beauty, like sports, gets you through on less. I could tell you stories!" a friend wrote me.

Some don't develop personalities past the level of cute children. Others are forced into passivity by the simple fact that no one expects anything of them; they can sit like statues and still be valuable. Or they learn young that being talkative, gesturing, and joking can actually make an admirer uncomfortable by interrupting fantasies of motionless perfection.

And if they get hurt or abandoned—and they do, just like anyone else—they get no more sympathy than rich people do when they lose their money.

**The flip side: the uses and misuses of being plain.**

" 'No poet worth his salt is going to be handsome; if he or she is beautiful, there's no need to create the beautiful. Beautiful people are special; they don't experience life like the rest of us.' [John Berryman] was obviously dead serious, and then he added, 'Don't worry about it, Levine, you're ugly enough to be a great poet.' "*

What became of the nerds and wallflowers from high school? Where are the ugly ducklings now? Well, a surprising number of them grew up to be very interesting. Lots of professors, writers, scientists, and computer millionaires say they were decidedly unpopular in school. Somehow they built better lives, developed

* Philip Levine, *The New York Times Book Review*, December 26, 1993.

their talents. Why? Because all unpopular kids are brainier than all popular kids? More likely, they just had a lot more time and the motivation to find substitute ways to preoccupy their minds.

They would have changed places with the beauties in a heartbeat if they could have, but that wasn't possible. Their brains were unemployed and in need of activity, so they developed rich fantasy lives. They became heroes at the computer, gallant naturalists walking in the woods, fascinating writers at work, or great readers of books. Freud called that kind of replacement sublimation. Not "repression," mind you; *repression* means burying your feelings because you reject them. But *sublimation* means transforming narcissistic drives into creative and productive activities. Because of it, many of the beauties you envied turned into "has-beens," stuck with the lives that young people want, while many ugly ducklings blossomed into having the lives that grown-ups want.

But when average-looking people believe that beauty gives love and happiness, they never quite forget the shame at not making the grade and the unhappiness they experienced in their younger days.

"I never was popular or good-looking when I was young, but now women are looking at me all the time. And it pisses me off. I'm happily married now, and not interested, but it feels so unfair. Like they should have been there when I needed them," a reader wrote me.

No matter how successful or rich their lives have become, some average-looking people still feel they missed something of incredible value. Often, if they parlayed their talent into money or position, they fantasize regrouping for another attack at the elusive (and illusory) world of the beautiful and the loved. They're the likeliest candidates for trying to marry a beauty and pay for it with money. If they hadn't felt so unattractive, they might have considered marrying someone they loved, someone who loved them, maybe someone they had a lot in common with.

Too bad. It's a waste of a lovely present to be living in the past. But there's an even higher cost, because believing you weren't beautiful enough is a smokescreen for a very devastating truth.

**The truth that's covered by the myth of beauty.**

Most of us blame ourselves—our looks, our awkwardness—for what was wrong with our social lives as kids. We're certain we were unloved because we were unlovable, and to us that meant "unbeautiful." But it's a cover-up—and a costly one because it covers up a truth that, had we known it, would have changed our lives.

What truth?

*That there never was anything wrong with us at all.*

We cling to the notion that we weren't beautiful enough to be popular because we don't want to face the truth if we can possibly avoid it. But why avoid such a wonderful truth? It should be like finding hidden treasure: There was never anything wrong with you. Step right out, and accept your overdue inheritance.

It sounds good on paper, but nothing could be more painful.

Because if it's true that there was never anything wrong with us, we'd have to go looking for another explanation for why we were unloved and lonely. And that might bring us face-to-face with something we really don't want to know.

For instance, maybe the love we wanted from our peers wasn't worth very much at all.

When it comes to popularity, some groups of school kids are tougher than others, and some are merciless. Whatever standards they set, you pay a price for being accepted and after a while, you know it. At close quarters, in-groups usually lose their luster. But if you're rejected, you never become disillusioned with the in-group.

But if it wasn't you, it was them. Maybe the people you admired from afar were never worth your admiration. Certainly at the time they didn't have it in them to really care about anybody.

The love you wanted didn't even exist. You wasted all that anguish on nothing. The beautiful belief that these were rare and valuable people was a complete illusion, something you invented. When you woke up it would melt into a puddle, like ice under the sun.

**That's very painful. It's easier to pretend you were ugly.**

But when you carry that error into adulthood, you walk around with a case of mistaken identity. You sacrifice your freedom of movement. You don't go dancing or swimming as much as people who don't feel ugly. You hesitate to walk in where you're not invited. You're not as friendly or generous as you'd like to be. And you tolerate mistreatment because you go looking for love in all the wrong places.

But imagine how you'd have lived your life if you'd known there was never anything wrong with you at all. Imagine growing up with ease and self-confidence, never avoiding any situation you wanted to be a part of, speaking up whenever you chose, to whomever you chose, trying out anything that interested you from singing to high diving without fear of looking like a jerk if you failed. Imagine loving people who loved you instead of people who didn't. And imagine never having spent a minute hating the way you looked or trying to find a way to be more beautiful because you thought that would make you more lovable.

When, in fact, you already were.

It was all for nothing.

**I'm not sure I want to know all this.**

After all, what's the point, right? You can't shake your fist at nature for caring only for the breeding competition and nothing for all the gallant young people whose beauty was inside them.

But you **can** see the heartless scam for what it was and refuse to give it any more of your precious time.

**Beautiful or plain, you should walk away from the whole scene as soon as you're able.**

Leave the beauty contest to the people who can't afford to leave it yet. Walk away and call yourself lucky.

What do I mean by that? Just quit caring about your looks, and you can do any damn thing you like. You'll do exactly that someday, when you're sixty or seventy or eighty. Why not do it now? It's high time to detach happiness from appearance. For one thing, it diminishes you. There's no way to become fully human when you're glued to the mirror. Give it up. Throw off your burden. It's the only way out of this time-gobbling sideshow.

*You're past the age of looking like food, so predators won't see you anyway.*

And if nobody's staring at you, you can relax and get a good look at the world around you. Being unnoticed is good for your brain.

Stop working so hard to look good. All that's really necessary is to look enough like everyone else to fit in at work and keep your neighbors off your back. Or doll up if you like, but only as long as it's fun. Otherwise let it go. *Don't be ugly. Don't be beautiful. Just be yourself.*

No matter what you think you look like, other people are always going to think whatever they want to anyway. They love you—or they don't—regardless of your opinion of yourself. *That's because your looks don't belong to you; they belong to the beholder.*

Give them over and walk away. You have better things to do.

Now, do you still want to be the object of predators?

**You probably said yes.**

Imagine a sheep that felt bad about looking unappetizing to a wolf. You know it's crazy, but if you're honest with yourself, you must confess the truth. It's not enough to know what's right and force yourself to do the right thing when your heart's not in it.

Sometimes you've got to listen to your heart even when you know it's lying to you, because there's nothing else to do.

If my words have fallen on deaf ears, it's not your fault. Nature is bigger than both of us. You can't give up worrying about your appearance just because your brain agrees with me. Test yourself: Try swimming in public in a tight bathing suit, and don't think about anything but how good the water feels. Not so easy, is it?

Well, don't worry. One day you just won't want to work for buns of steel and you'll prefer a good dinner to a good weigh-in. Even if you *never* prefer comfort to your own good looks, you won't have to summon up the courage to give youthful beauty away; it will be taken. You might look pretty good for an older person, but you'll never again look like a fertile young beauty, no matter what you do. One way or another, sooner or later, the outcome will be taken out of your hands.

Just remember not to grieve about it too much.

*Because it's the best thing that could possibly happen to you.* No one really walks out of the beauty game until they're thrown out. You'll hate it, and you'll complain loudly, maybe even throw a tantrum or two. But after a while you'll wake up and look around and you'll realize you're free to live your own life at last. And you'll wonder why you fought so hard to hang on to beauty in the first place.

But there's one last thing you should know about beauty because it might snap you out of the illusion sooner.

**The last person on earth who knows what it feels like to look at you . . . is you.**

You have no idea how you look; you never did, and you never will. People see us in action, alive and dynamic. We never see ourselves that way. Certainly not in the mirror and hardly even in videos or home movies.

But that's not the only reason we don't know how we look to others. Everyone looks at us through a screen of their own biases and memories or our resemblance to their favorite family members. People see you very differently from any way you will ever understand. Not only do you have no control over how you look to others, but *they don't either*. It doesn't matter what any of you do.

Take a look at the makeovers on TV talk shows. Perfectly normal-looking people are painted and stuffed into tight, sequined outfits and displayed under the lights. Does someone in the audience think they look better? I suppose so. But I can guarantee that many others liked them better "before" than "after."

The same is true of you.

Remember that when you're working too hard to look good to people. You don't have the power to control how they will see you.

If it's fun for you to dress up, go ahead. But if you're trying to influence people with your appearance, give it up. Someone who loves you will think you look great whether you think so or not.

Don't you just hate that? Here you are heading for the fat farm or the gym, for the plastic surgeon or the hair replacement salon. You're willing to put in your time to dazzle the public, and in fact, it makes no difference.

But one of these days you're going to be willing to march out into the world disguised as no one but yourself. You'll understand when you idealize beautiful people that nobody ever lived an ideal life. And you'll be grateful you outgrew that illusion. Because something remarkable will take its place.

**Developing a rich inner life**

To be constantly preoccupied by comparing your appearance with someone else's is to be trapped in a world where you can't have an inner life. If you don't change that as soon as possible, the years will turn you into a very bored—and boring—person. But if you use your brain and your gifts to develop a delightful mission of your own, it will drive away self-consciousness like the summer drives away the cold.

Because when you have a rich inner life, you're far more interested in how the world looks to you than how you look to the world. And you put beauty right where it belongs: in front of your eyes, where you can see it.

"I walk the same paths now that I walked twenty-five years ago, but now I am not aware of the figure I am cutting. I neither expect nor hope to be noticed. I am hoping only to *take in* what is happening around me even on the bleakest winter day, the blood-warm glow of the upturned clods in the ploughland, the robin's greedy whistle, the glitter of the stubble against a dark sky. I want to be open to this, to be agog, spellbound."*

When narcissism goes, you get the whole beautiful world in return.

**You get your real self, too.**

If you don't believe me, just imagine for a moment you somehow were incapable of understanding the concept of beauty. Imagine you went about your life, walked down the street, walked into gatherings of people—even when you hoped to meet someone new—but at no time had any consciousness at all about your own attractiveness.

What would be different?

Here are some answers I got from clients.

"I'd be comfortable."

"I'd be concerned with what I wanted, not with who wanted me."

"I'd belong to myself."

Try it out. Just get your clothes on straight, and then don't look in another mirror for the rest of the day. Forget how you look. The results might astonish you. Because one of these days

---

* Germaine Greer, *The Change: Women, Aging and Menopause*, 1991.

you're likely to realize something amazing: You've stopped being a thing and have turned into a person.

**"I don't look like myself,"** a forty-eight-year-old woman told me.

No, and she wouldn't even if she'd miraculously stayed young-looking. Neither will you. You'll never *look* like yourself again. *Because your self will never again be your surface.*

Sometime around midlife you're led (or thrown) off the auction block. You lose your value as an art object. What the world sees and who you really are have come to a permanent parting of the ways. And just as if you were an animal whose shell became too small, the restrictions of appearance fall away so you can continue to grow. The real you remains inside, getting richer and more exciting every day, and unlike beauty, this will never wear out until the day you die. You're in for a wonderful time after all the illusions fall away because for the first time since you were eight years old, you're going to belong to yourself.

Wouldn't you love to step into that wonderful world right now? Just thumb your nose at nature and vanity and youth and walk away from beauty? Well, you're almost there. You just have a few more illusions to get rid of first. But you can check in now and then and see how the process is going.

"Hey, heart, are you ready to quit the beauty contest? I'd like time off to do something more entertaining."

One day it will say yes.

## EXERCISE 12

### Here's your beauty quiz.

1. When did strangers of the opposite sex stop eyeing you? How did that make you feel?

2. Why do you want to hang on to your youthful appearance? Whom would you impress? What would the bene-

fits be? Write as many answers as you can, and then check off the ones that no longer look like good reasons.

3. Name people you know who have made extreme or radical attempts to look and stay young. How do you feel about what they've done?

4. If you had to choose between having a pretty face or a happy life, which would you choose? Was the choice difficult?

5. At this point in your life, if you had to go out and find someone new to love, what attributes would you be looking for? How high on the list would you put beauty?

6. If someone offered you a pill that would make you forever unaware of beauty or plainness, yours or anyone else's, would you take it?

Write down your answers, and hang on to them. You'll know how you're progressing through your midlife crisis by how they change. Beauty will always be nice, that's not at issue here. What is at issue is its importance in your life. When it stops being important, the crisis is over. You're home safe.

# 6
# Love

"The sun it shines so cold, so cold, when there are no
eyes to look love on me . . ."

George Eliot

"We were in a cult all right. So we didn't shave our
heads and go out begging for money. We bleached our
hair and went out begging for love. What's the
difference?"

A client

"Sure, I'd rather be in jail than in love again."

*Hear My Song*

*Teenagers. Remember how childish they used to look to you and how silly their heartache-love pop music sounded? Well, something inside you is changing. They don't look so childish these days, and that music is starting to sound good. Almost as if you just realized you'd forgotten something, you're picking up your head and asking questions about love that you haven't asked in a long time: Like, where's yours?*

*You're not a child first discovering love; you've got some experience and you've learned a lot. But you're growing unhappy with what you've found so far. Either you have a sturdy relationship that lacks the excitement of romantic love, or you've been in and out of intensely romantic relationships that left you shipwrecked. Why hasn't romantic love lasted? Why hasn't lasting love been more romantic? The middle years feel like Love's Last Stand. You've got maybe one or two more*

119

shots at best. Are you going to find true love before it becomes too late for you?

That depends on what kind of love you're talking about.

If you're looking for lasting passion, your chances of finding it are just about as good as winning the lottery. Not just because you're looking for love in all the wrong places, but because you're looking for the wrong kind of love, anyplace. The kind of love that lasts isn't romantic; the kind of love that's romantic doesn't last. Don't go running to the history books to show me stories of lasting passion. The very few times in history that both parties in a couple have maintained an equally intense erotic relationship over many decades, either they've lived apart under painful conditions or they've badly neglected the rest of their lives, including their children.

You may think you're looking for something very real and very simple, something healthy and normal, something all people need if they want to be happy. But biology has its eye on you. It knows you're becoming a senior breeder and are about to walk out the fertility door. As we've already pointed out, natural selection favors creatures who have a late surge of desire and produce extra babies before they become infertile. Of course you might not be in the market for a baby at all, just looking for someone to love.

But the forties are the crisis period. When midlife hits, you get a surge of longing for a great passion. Nature is still calling your lines out to you from behind the curtain and will continue to create longing in your heart.

I wouldn't trust it if I were you.

Everlasting romantic love is part of the big lie of youth, and youth is the only place where this lie can live. You're crossing into an era where you don't really like lies anymore, but you hate to admit that romantic love was nothing but hunger, hormones, and illusion. However, if you don't admit it, you have to forget everything you've learned in the last twenty years. Because the real problem with love at midlife isn't that you're too old to compete with a twenty-two-year-old. The real problem is that you know too much. You're too sophisticated *to fall for illusion, but you're not past wanting it all the same. Right here in the middle of being a grown-up, your heart has launched an all-out war with your brain. You're watching both sides, trying to do the right thing, but you can't help wanting your heart to win. You're hoping against hope that you'll be able to salvage some of the dream. Because without that dream, the future looks so bleak.*

*What you can't see yet is that it's never too late to find authentic love. But if you're still looking for the great romance, it was always too late. When you don't understand this, you're in trouble, because romantic love is a fake. The feeling that goes with love songs is not merely elusive; you can search the rest of your life and never find it. In fact, until you stop longing for it, you'll never get real love.*

*But a day is coming when you will honestly want no more part of love ballads, and when that day comes, illusion will pull back like the curtain in a play and reveal something you couldn't see before: so much love you won't be able to walk two steps without tripping over it.*

*In this chapter we're going to take a hard look at the difference between real love and fake love. Because once you understand what love really is, not only will you find it, but you won't be able to avoid it.*

*It will be everywhere.*

----

**Your desire to resurrect romantic love is based on two myths.** First, the widespread notion that romantic love is the same as real love, healthy, normal, and necessary, the stuff of happiness, which everyone wants and has a right to. Second, that without romantic love in your life, a dark future stretches ahead of you, sad, lonely, and empty. If such thoughts float around your mind, it's time to take a close look at those assumptions one at a time.

**Romance versus love.**

Let's come up with a definition of romantic love. I call romantic love the longing to be wanted—wanted for the beauty of your soul. Oh, and with hot sex thrown in. The kind of love that makes the whole world seem beautiful, where you fly down the street with wings on your feet. You know it exists because you've felt it in the past, but because of unforeseen problems, it never lasted. You're sure you've seen it now and then in some couples, but then they tragically got divorced. You certainly without doubt have had many authentic sightings at the movies. Anyway, it's advertised all the time, so it must be for sale somewhere!

Now read the following quote and see if it too sounds familiar:

"I lay in the arms of young men who loved me and felt less bliss than I do now. What I felt then was hope, fear, jealousy, desire, passion, a mixture of real pain, and real and fake pleasure, a mash of conflicting feelings. . . . I needed my lovers too much to experience much joy in our travailed relationships. I was too much at their mercy to feel much in the way of tenderness."*

Oh, yeah, that stuff. You remember that too.

How can anything so heavenly turn into such hell?

Isn't it just that you picked the wrong person or something? Let's find out. Search your memory for the best romantic moments in your past. Think about them for a moment.

How did those relationships begin—that is, when did you know you were in love?

Allan: "We met on a plane, she was so lovely I fell completely under her spell."

Genie: "I didn't even like him. Then one day I was on the phone, fighting with some supplier, and I caught him looking at me with this knowing smile and this warm look in his eyes. And my heart jumped in my chest. He suddenly looked gorgeous!"

---

* Germaine Greer, *The Change*, 1991.

*What's the difference between who you are most of the time and who you are when you're in love?*

Mel: "I'm exhilarated. I feel like I could do anything, like I'm bigger than myself."

Carole: "I feel like I'm worth something. Like I'm walking on clouds. The whole world gets beautiful. I like everybody."

Jory: "I want to buy presents. Usually I hate shopping for anything. I think about her all the time and I resent the time we're apart. My friends aren't allowed to do anything but listen to me talk about her."

*Now, were there any painful moments?*

Genie: "Well, sure. Waiting for his calls, that was hell. And then he started acting strange, and I died a thousand deaths."

Allan: "When she was away, I had these awful thoughts about her and other guys."

Carole: "It bothered me when he looked at someone else, even for a moment. I used to joke about things like that, but when I was in love, it was like a punch in the stomach."

*What happened to those relationships?*

Jory: "One day the feeling just went away. I got more and more angry with her, and then I didn't feel anything at all."

Mel: "She started to gain weight. It wasn't much, now that I look back, but at the time it felt like she didn't love me or she wouldn't do that to me."

Carole: "He finally convinced me that he wasn't interested in anyone but me. And I believed him. And then everything changed. He seemed so dependent and so boring."

Genie: "He turned out to be a real rat."

Allan: "She didn't understand me. It was hopeless."

Sound familiar? Let's contrast these experiences with a different kind of love.

**Describe the best friendship you've ever had.**

Allan: "This great woman, I've known her since college, she

makes me laugh. We used to talk on the phone for hours about our latest romantic fiascos."

Genie: "My best girlfriend in high school. I was always happy to see her. We always had the best time, no matter what we did."

Carole: "Joseph was like my brother, always there, ever since we were kids. Always came through for me."

In your friendship, did you feel you came alive with the same intensity as in a love affair? Did you get jealous when your friend looked at another person? Did you lose interest in the rest of your life?

Of course not. Because a real friendship may be very deep, but it's built on respect and affection and autonomy. There's a big difference between the love you feel for a friend and the love you feel for a lover.

*But maybe there shouldn't be.*

Just imagine liking your lover as much as you like your best friend. Imagine the comfort and companionship, the ease of communication, the congenial taking for granted, the freedom to be yourself.

"In sharp contrast to high school, I now possessed a large number of varied and decidedly wonderful friends, whom I valued immeasurably. Through them I discovered what it was to love people. There was an art to it, I discovered, which was not really all that different from the love that is necessary in the making of art. It required the effort of always seeing them for themselves and not as I wished them to be, of always striving to see the truth of them."*

Can't you have that and passion both?

No.

Why not?

---

* Lucy Grealy, *Autobiography of a Face*, 1994.

Because it's impossible. It's like wanting to be awake and asleep at the same time.

I know you don't think you're asking for anything exotic or rare, just the regular kind of perfect love everybody wants. You're beginning to resent the time you have to spend searching and the growing fear that you could actually get passed over and never, ever find it.

**But this isn't love; it's a setup.**

This all started in infancy, when all the rest of the triggers for romantic love are put in place. Somewhere deep inside we remember the sweet safety we felt as infants in our parents' arms and wish we had it back.

How do I know? Take a look our specifications for the perfect lover; they're exactly the same ones an infant would have for a perfect parent—with a little youth and sexiness added on.

If you don't believe me, ask yourself the following questions: What do men want from women? Someone sweet and adoring, playful, witty, and competent, but needy in the right ways. Someone who always has time for them but never bothers them when they're preoccupied. Someone who puts their wishes before her own. Someone who acts like the perfect mother but never comes to look like one. Sound familiar?

What do women want from men? Someone brave and wise and strong and kind and sensitive—and adoring. A man who understands and protects but doesn't suffocate them, who gets his greatest joy from their happiness, who has the resources and the desire to smooth their path and help them develop their potential. In other words, someone who is just like the perfect father—and one day *does* come to look like him!

Of course this time around we want to be the only child.

Now I know that's a vast generalization, but most of us will admit that more often than not, it's true in its broad outlines.

That's why romantic love is a contradiction in terms. Because it's always narcissistic. *It's not about the other person; it's about us.* We're always casting each other in our own private movies, so even when you want to be generous, you're more utilitarian and exploitative than you'd be comfortable admitting. That's why romance can never be love.

Experienced romantics struggle with the contradiction. They try to figure out how to transcend themselves and love someone totally without completely losing their own identities. They burn the midnight oil trying to make that impossible equation come out right so they can feel like responsible adults and still have romance.

*But there's no contradiction at all when love isn't romantic.* You transcend yourself without losing yourself every time you reach out to a friend in need or listen to a hurt child, or help a stranger on the street. Caring about someone else without fusing into them is no problem in these ordinary moments of helpfulness. Simple affection connects you and makes you happy.

But this is no solution to a romantic. It's far too dull. When romantics help their beloved, there's a high-drama rescue; they must pull each other from the jaws of hell into the arms of heaven. They must be rewarded with the acknowledgment that they are heroes. Now that's a different story altogether. Never mix it up with true generosity or concern or empathy because it's really just an erotic fantasy, as different from real love as cotton candy is from homemade bread.

The fatal flaw of this personal drama is that we never understand what the others really want or who they are. We may enjoy the feeling of indulging and adoring them so much that we forget to notice if they love us with equal unselfishness until we're already deeply attached. By that time we feel they owe us the same kind of love in return. Or perhaps *we* start out as recipients of this indulgence, happy that our ship has come in, when suddenly the generous hero in this wonderful movie stops being happy with the arrangement and expects *us* to start doing the giving!

Wait a minute! Promises were made—or at least implied.

This person we loved has turned out to be a fraud! Feeling self-righteously betrayed, neither of us is very nice when our costars don't follow our script, and another great passion comes to an unpleasant end.

**Romantic love at midlife is the most expensive of all the illusions.**

You probably already know what I'm about to say, but it bears repeating. *You've been here a few times before, and you should know more about love by now.* But no one ever seems to get it. We keep trying for the same fantasy.

Of course, if you're prepared to have nothing more than a short, intense fling, there's a reasonable chance you can have it. The problem is, it might be very costly if you're already attached or if you're unwise in your choice of this new partner. You could ruin a good marriage, jeopardize reputations, and break a few hearts big time (including but by no means limited to your own). But that's something you'll have to assess for yourself. Some people find the gamble exhilarating.

But when pure, sexy romance is the motivation for breaking off one marriage and starting another, you could live to regret it. I've been told the following many times in my private practice.

"Here I am at fifty-five with kids in college, and suddenly I've got a new wife and a new set of children in private school. Now I'll never get to quit working."

"My first husband was a nice guy. Sometimes I miss him."

"I love my kids a lot, but my second wife is starting to make my first wife look pretty good. What was I thinking of?"

Probably something like this:

"I've never been in love like this before. I love my wife, I hate to hurt her, but I can't turn my back on this wonderful woman I've met. Sure, she's younger than I am, but she's so incredibly wise that she's teaching me what love really is. I don't care about the cost. I'm not going to live forever. She makes me feel young again."

"Ron was a good man, but the sizzle was gone for me. I wanted a new kind of relationship, with fireworks that wouldn't ever fade."

But if you're in a terrible relationship, shouldn't you leave? *Yes, at any time in your life.* If there's no respect, and no way to work together, if the relationship is toxic or destructive, of course you should leave, but not just because you've got a crush on someone and not just at midlife. I don't believe the institution of marriage is more important than the people in it, but like any important relationship, you've got to take it seriously, not be frivolous or irresponsible. The tragedy comes when you leave a durable, friendly marriage because you miss excitement.

That's a real shame, because if you really like your mate, you're swapping the chance for the best love of your life for an illusion.

Romance is an expensive illusion for another reason: it's hard on your system. Unlike real love, romances come to an end with predictable frequency. When you were young, you hadn't put that fact together yet. Every love was the real one and would never end. But now, after having experienced a few such loves, you can never quite forget the truth. Unfortunately that doesn't make the breakups any easier, because if your heart breaks, it's the huge, irrational, wild, and primitive heart of the infant inside you that breaks. "Every time I break up, I break down," said one man. "I wish I didn't want this anymore."

So should you. Because the most costly element of romance hasn't even been mentioned yet.

**Romantic love actually prevents real love.**

Worst and most telling of all to anyone who wants real love: Romantic love not only won't give it to you, it will actually keep the real thing away. Why? Because when you crave intensity, you can't even see the people who don't offer it, and those are the people you really need. They can't see you either because they're in a different world and not interested in people who give away their brains for romance. You're shopping for different things. You want to be swept away by the perfume of fusion while they want somebody to talk to.

Romance also drives away the comfort real love offers. Even when we have romantic love, we're always on the alert to keep from losing it. We feel we must be able to sustain whatever brought us the love in the first place: our looks, our goodness, our generosity, sometimes even our aloofness. We become overly sensitive to any change in our lovers' feelings toward us.

Liking someone is an essential of real love, but it's not possible to like anyone you're madly in love with. Don't believe me? Ask yourself if you've ever had a passion for someone you liked so much that you'd have stayed even if there were no passion at all. Or ask yourself this: Which would you choose if you could choose only one? A sunny life, with or without someone to love, or an intense love, however sunny or cloudy your life would be? If you felt a twinge of conflict, you've got problems. Because you don't want to gain the world; you want to lose your self.

**America's favorite sweetheart—sex.**

"*On Golden Pond*—that's love. *Driving Miss Daisy*—that's love. *Romeo and Juliet*—that's sex." Said Ray, forty-three-year-old, happily married father of three.

After forty you will likely feel, with some validity, that you have been nature's love slave and just got dumped. You're feeling robbed, cruelly displaced, and it's simply not right. Ask anyone, and you'll find that we all believe in the inalienable, God-given right to nonending good sex until we die of very old age. We believe—men and women alike—that life without passionate sex is simply not worth living, and anyone who has to survive without it is pathetic.

It's time for a little correction in this bull market—with some help from Petrarch: "Do not listen to those dismal old men who weep that they have been released from the toils of evil lusts, while they should have wept when they were bound."

And Plato: "Socrates, do you still have intercourse with women?"

"Hush, man! Most joyfully did I escape it, as though I had run away from a sort of frenzied and savage master."

To make sex too important is like making anything else too important: food, money, or cars. But don't say that at a party. It's considered downright unhealthy to question sex in America.

Now, everyone is different, and each of us has to deal with who we are and what we need, but let's put an end to the Holy Grail aspect of sex. It can be a real inconvenience to be driven by an overpowering sexuality. Not only does it pull you off any course you're on, it makes you accept people in your life you wouldn't even talk to otherwise, because in a highly sexed person, sexual deprivation can result in terrible feelings of loss and abandonment. All the same, while you must eat and have shelter from the elements, sex is not required for the survival of the individual. It's optional. Instead of worshiping it, it might be wiser to check out what you really want and decide what *you* want to do about it. Don't listen to anyone else, because they don't know you at all.

*I don't care what they say, I won't stay in a world without romantic love.*

Then you'd better buy your ticket to Mars because you can't have love until the meaning changes for you. If you think love means "Win the desirable creature" and "Give me what I need, make me feel loved," you've got some work ahead of you. Because love isn't about winning someone or getting what you need.

**Love is about seeing.**

To love is not to possess something; it's simply to see it. But *really* see it.

To experience real love is to understand that a unique creature, separate and different from you, is standing in front of you. When you can see another human that way, you can't help loving him. To do that, however, you need a stable identity, a sense of knowing who you are, and no desperation in your heart. No small order, but at midlife you could be on your way.

And when you experience that kind of seeing, you'll be astonished. You can get a very brief glimpse of what I mean if you try this experiment. Sometime when you're out in the world, take a look at an ordinary stranger: a bus driver, or someone sitting near you on a train or in a restaurant. Spend a few seconds looking at him. Then imagine you just got a message from the future and found out he was going to die the next day.

Suddenly that person looks different. In an instant his value becomes clear to you and you see how unusual and unique he is. It's only a trick you've played on your senses, but it gives you an idea of how miraculous people will look to you one day, once you've learned how to see without the fog of self-interest.

That's love. The real thing. To see someone else clearly, not to look into the mirror of your own desire or to dress up the beloved with the scrim of your favorite fantasy, or to reinvent him for your own uses. What do I mean by reinvent? If you've been in love, you've done it: When you wanted your lover to be smart or good or funny or in love with you, you simply chose to see those traits in him. You invented your beloved as carefully as a set designer creates a set, and then you were astonished at how perfect it was. What you didn't realize is that the glow came from your spotlight. That's why no one else could see it.

Loving what is *actually* in front of you can come only when you've outgrown illusions of perfection—yours or anyone else's— and when you keep the freedom to build your life at the same time as respecting the other's right to do the same.

Nothing could be less romantic.

**Real love will drive romantic love away, too.**

When you finally learn how to differentiate between real love and narcissistic fantasy, you'll look around and wonder where your romantic illusions went. Because nothing kills romance as fast as real love. Grand illusions look silly in the presence of a first-rate reality. Life is an amazing gift after all, and at least some of it is supposed to be fun, not wondering when the phone will ring or waiting for someone else to make you feel alive. Real love is comfortable, sane, and affectionate. Next to it, romantic love looks masochistic and as weird as a Dracula movie.

Ask any happily married parent of a teenager; when you've got the real thing, it becomes very clear that romantic love is a fake. It's not attractive; it's bizarre.

Real lovers don't want to die in each other's arms; they want to live. In the real world. Just as they always have. They know that the only time you're supposed to miss someone with a primeval ache that makes the world go gray and lifeless is when they've died, not when they live across town in perfect health. To a real lover, a romantic's desire for the hermetic privacy of fantasy looks like an illness. Possessiveness looks pathetic.

And although you don't need them as much—or *because* you don't need them as much—relationships can actually become more available.

"For the first time, every man I look at isn't a potential mate or rescuer. When this first happened to me, everybody seemed boring. If men weren't potential mates, they weren't interesting. But after a while these same men started emerging as individuals, real characters, much more interesting than before. I actually like men now, although they're very different from what I had thought. Instead of being hurt or angry because they don't fit my fantasies, I either enjoy them as they are or tell them to 'shape up or ship out.' I'm not trying to win a popularity contest, so I'm not afraid of disapproval anymore. I'm more direct, and I don't say anything unless I mean it. And I won't spend time with someone I don't like. I'd rather be alone," a friend told me.

No romantic can say that because when she's alone, the whole universe feels empty. You, on the other hand, will start seeing people who were invisible before. You won't have one set of standards for good friends and another for lovers. You wouldn't consider loving someone you wouldn't have as a best friend. And when you do find a love relationship, you might be surprised by not even wanting to use the word *love* because what you feel is so unlike what you thought love would be.

"We don't know if we love each other. We sure don't think the other one is perfect or the ideal we had in mind. It's just that I know I was put here to take care of her and she knows she was put here to take care of me. I don't have a word for that."

**"I love you."**

Interesting phrase. I've come to think that the important words in it are *I* and *you*, not *love*. Fantasize for a moment actually saying that to someone: "I. You." Gives you an interesting feeling to be aware of yourself and someone else at the same moment, doesn't it? As if both of you had suddenly materialized out of nowhere. Now try another sentence, a bit less intense: Imagine saying, "I like you," the way a child might say it, with simple sincerity.

Both phrases have more authentic love in them than a dozen romantic "I love you's."

Maybe the biggest surprise of all is erotic love. It may take a little time to kick in because loneliness used to be your aphrodisiac; however, when loneliness goes, sex becomes a real whopper: funny, warm, satisfying, cozy, and friendly. Sometimes mind-boggling. When no fantasies stand between you and the person in your arms, your heart is connected to your body, and you're in for experiences you never had before.

"I never used to feel this way with sex. Before, I just went away inside myself. Now it opens a door to incredible closeness."

"He's such a good man; when we make love, I just want to hold him so close he'll never die."

**And that's just one part of what authentic love brings.**

When you open up your heart beyond the narrow and predatory longings of the young hunter, love stops being about just one special person and includes your whole environment, as if your heart had become a camera with a wide-angle lens. You get more out of every moment that isn't tied up with conflict or heartache. When your senses wake up, your experience enlarges over a wide arc. You have more room inside and can take in more, feel more, stand more amazed. The smallest details become intensely visible for the first time.

Authentic love puts you in a completely new relationship with everything in the world that is *not you*, like landscapes and languages, colors and textures, and especially the profound foreignness of the people who are closest to you. It's what you feel when you witness the powerful consciousness in people who know they're dying. It's in those moments you look into the eyes of an animal or a child and see them looking back at you.

And then love becomes the wonderful way you feel when you go for a walk early on a winter morning or laugh on the phone with a friend or read an exciting book or come up with a brand-new idea. It's what you feel when you're taking a hot shower on a cold day, or a cool shower on a hot day, or you have a whole day all to yourself so you can bury yourself in your work without interruption. It's the kick you get out of someone else's happiness. It's your respect for other people's battles.

"You get access to states you used to take drugs for," a friend told me. "I'll see something, springtime in the backyard, and say, 'Wow! Look at that!' If I were younger, I'd have noticed it but I'd have been too busy worrying about some guy that didn't call me back. But now, even in the middle of a hard year, I feel that way. It gets bigger all the time. I notice it's happening, and it's astonishing."

When you can love like that, you're never afraid of being alone. And you probably won't be.

You'd never tolerate a bad relationship if your world were that full because you'd have too much to lose. When you love like that, you're able to enjoy friendship, interaction, and ideas. You like to do things, to learn, to build, to read, and to think.

You've got lots of affection stored up and can do without for a long time if you have to, but like an animal that can graze almost anywhere, you don't have to worry too much about being hungry for long.

You'll be one of those people you've always envied, obviously contented, interested in the world, unselfconscious, and confident. And driven by choice rather than necessity. Compare that with how you felt when you badly needed someone to love, when you had to fake that confidence, and sincerity was impossible.

If you had a magic wand and could get rid of the longing for romantic love this very minute, everything good we've discussed above would fall into your lap. Love would be everywhere.

**It's not easy at first.**

When you first let go of your notions of romance, it can be a little scary. You're sure to feel a short period of emptiness. Not the huge, horrible kind, just a lack of electricity in your life. When you were younger, that absence of excitement might have sunk you into depression, but after midlife you'll be surprised to find that you stay well afloat. It's like giving up salt in your food; at first everything lacks flavor, but soon it has twice as much. That's what to expect in your future if you can give up the spice of pain and loneliness.

Wow, where do you sign up, right? Unfortunately you can't hurry this enviable state. Like everything else we've spoken of so far in this book, it will come in its own good time. In the meantime, be on your guard. Your attempts to listen for its arrival might be drowned out on every side. Why? Because a whole lot of folks want very much to delay your transition into sanity. Especially at midlife. Let me list a few:

**1. The economy just loves lovesickness.**

You can't turn on the TV or walk down the street or listen to your headset without being hammered by messages that coax you to remember the love that sweeps you up and never drops you. Maybe the economy didn't invent romantic love, but it knows a good thing when it sees one. Enterprising and ingenious, it sells you romantic movies to satisfy your love hunger and increase it at the same time. Like any good salesman, it wakes up a need and then offers to fill it.

If you're seeking romantic love, you're going to be driven to spend money like a reckless teenager—but lots and lots more this time around. For one thing, you have more money to spend. For another, no one can stop you. You're like a high school kid in your endless desire to buy more clothes and makeup and hair care products, but midlifers buy big-ticket items: gym equipment, dinners, memberships, hot cars, and vacations. Instead of romance with the right cigarette, it's romance in the right car or the right Caribbean resort. The economy is willing to work hard to make you feel like you're starving in the midst of plenty because you're the biggest spender in town.

**2. Beware of opportunists on the lookout for lonely hearts.**

Besides the economy, at midlife you look pretty good to parasites too. These people are not just Cary Grant–style jewel thieves; they include heroes who sweep you off your feet, people who want to own you so they'll never be alone, even fragile-looking souls who know how to make you take care of them because they're unwilling or unable to take care of themselves— anyone with a hidden agenda that doesn't include real love, and has developed a lot of determination and charm.

**These are the professionals of fake love. What do they know that you don't?**

*That all romantic love is a form of addiction.* Just like any other addiction, it has the pain that is healed only by the presence of the loved one and awakened again by his or her withdrawal. A moment of love feels like a cure, but it's just a mask. The emptiness always returns with full force as soon as the medicine runs out. Masters of fake love know that if you want someone to fall in love with you, it's important to keep their pain alive; you must launch "hurt and rescue" missions—hurt their feelings, and then proceed to console them—over and over. After a short time, they'll become dependent on you, needy and selfless.

"Criticism intensifies the relationship because it stirs a man's emotions. . . . Praise him first, to make sure he is emotionally strong enough to withstand the criticism you'll be handing out later. . . . Surely you've figured out what areas he may feel sensitive about. . . . 'Ben, you're a little short but very darling. I imagine you sometimes wish you were taller?' . . . learn not to show your emotions. . . ." says author Margaret Kent.*

**3. Other midlifers will also be very happy to encourage your romantic side.**

Because they need company for their own shaky romantic enterprises, all your friends going through their own midlife crises will encourage your impulse to find passionate love. They too are panicked and resentful at not being madly in love with anyone. Their urgent need for narcissistic love is just like yours, and just like you, they really know too much about life to believe in it. But they're happy to sit around a table and help you rework these impulses into more respectable language. "Is a romantic immature, or just someone who insists on feeling completely alive?" pleads a writer.†

Completely alive; that's pretty hard to walk away from. That's what I call good selling, even if the only buyer is himself.

**4. Of course, your most powerful opponent is nature.**

Nature is like Iago: real love irritates it. Why is that? Plain and simple, contentment doesn't make as many babies as pain and yearning do. Contented people make love, of course, but they don't lose their heads. They can decide to be faithful to their

---

* Margaret Kent, *How to Marry the Man of Your Choice*, 1984, called by one reviewer "How to Mangle the Man of Your Choice."
† *Psychology Today*, April–May 1997.

spouses even if other people look attractive. They're able to take precautions when they don't want babies because they don't worry about "ruining the mood."

Nature's main task is to fill you with nameless longings that only erotic love can fulfill. If you're someone who has never developed a rich inner life, you'll be easy to catch. But biology isn't fooling around. It will trip you up no matter who you are, by causing a hormonal depression in you and making romantic sex the only antidepressant that will fix it. You won't even insist on happiness. The true romantic will always choose miserable love over no love at all.

**Surrounded by these influences, it's not easy to break free or even want to. So what are your chances?**

If you're under forty, it's practically hopeless. Nature doesn't mess around with its most fertile. She'll fire up your hormones, reactivate your infant heartbreak, melt any sense of self you developed, and leave you lonely.

*But after midlife, little by little, and without your noticing, the heat will begin to calm down, and you will be handed your first chance to break free.* Nature isn't going to work very hard to make you miserable once you're safely into your second life. You'll find yourself having more choice in matters of romance.

"I don't know what I expected was going to happen after forty. I didn't make any plans at all. I thought I'd be happily married with kids and wouldn't ever have to think about it again. But that hadn't happened. I was pretty depressed, feeling like a reject and mad at men, like it was their fault life was passing me by," a client told me.

"Then on my forty-fourth birthday I went to dinner with a fifty-plus friend of mine, who has no kids and a job she hates, and she was doing her usual complaining about her life, about putting ads in personals columns and dating men who never turn out to be any good. So bitter and discontented. And a light went on in my head. She looked exactly like the Ghost of Christmas Future looked to Scrooge, *like that's where I was heading in ten years!* For her to be single with no responsibilities and not doing what she wants is crazy. Maybe I don't have any control over my love life, but I can do something about the rest. Right then and there I quit being depressed and swung into action."

This may go against popular opinion, but I think women are luckier than men because they can break free sooner. Women may lose years at the beginning—they often stop developing intellectually at adolescence, while men are more able to go for both love and individuality—and they often feel cheated at mid-life because they lose their sexual value earlier than men. But the fact is they have more time to recover and still build full second lives. Men aren't motivated to leave the mating game as early because they stay fertile much longer and don't get junked until much later when recovery is tougher and the time shorter.

But a slight natural cooling begins inside everyone at mid-life. If you're not paying attention, or if you fear and resent any slackening of desire, you'll continue to be the prey of influences all around you. The noise they make will drown out an amazing new thing: the silence that appears when nature finally quits goading you. If you aren't aware of that silence, you won't know it's time to break free.

Before this time you didn't know any better. Now you do. So keep a sharp ear open and listen for the absence of nature's demands.

**Until then do the best you can.**

If you're still in your forties and early fifties, it's going to be touch-and-go. You might have to live with these longings for a while longer. You won't always be able to resist the lure of romance and you might fall, but forgive yourself. If, on the other hand, romance doesn't cross your path, I hope you will no longer feel cheated or bitter. Remember, romance is like a case of the flu, which sometimes you catch and sometimes you don't. Don't glorify it or rewrite your life for it. See it for what it is, and wait for it to pass.

One day soon, if you start getting "that old feeling," maybe you'll remember how you felt last time you fell. One of the benefits of experience is that it's harder to be ignorant. When you can clearly remember the outcome at the same time as you're lured by the promise, you have stepped over the line into consciousness. Conscious people don't have to live by impulse; they can make choices. When that time comes for you, absolutely everything will change. You'll be like a new person walking in a new world.

Until then try your best not to create a home for romantic love. Boredom and emptiness are like a standing invitation for the romance sickness, because whatever else I say about it, romance is rarely boring. Give it a little competition by widening your love base and enriching your inner life. Don't go to the tanning salon; go to school. Don't get pampered at a spa; go to a disaster area, and help people out after a hurricane or a flood. Don't be shallow; become deep. Don't put your worth in your ability to attract someone you don't even know; put it in your excellent mind and your compassionate heart.

But never get cocky. Always maintain your respect for biology. An odd little ghost of mystery passion will lurk and make you look at strangers from time to time. Treat it the way an ex-smoker treats a cigarette or a gamekeeper treats a rhinoceros: Note it with respect, circle it with care, and tiptoe away.

**Because there is life after romantic illusions melt.**

There may even be real love.

"Love is not breathlessness. . . . That is just being 'in love,' which any fool can do. Love itself is what is left over when being in love has burned away, and this is both an art and a fortunate accident. Your mother and I had it, we had roots that grew towards each other underground, and when all the pretty blossoms had fallen from our branches we found that we were one tree and not two."*

Now, even if you should fall like a fool in love again, at least you'll understand what's happening, and maybe you won't break too many things. Maybe you'll even let romantic love serve its one useful purpose, to tie you to someone until you know them. And when it fades, if you're lucky, you too may find that your roots have grown together.

## EXERCISE 13

### *Love quiz*

1. What did you think true love would be when you were in your teens? Twenties? Thirties? What did you think it would do for you?
2. How does it seem now? How has your thinking changed?
3. Which movies do you think define true love? Have you ever seen this in real life?
4. Think over all the good, long-term marriages you know. How did those relationships begin, in passion or in friendship? If you could wake up tomorrow in one of those marriages, would you do it?
5. Do you know a couple in their seventies or eighties that typifies true love? How do you think they attained it? Could you do that?
6. How would you describe the difference between your love for romantic partners and your love of your friends? Or your children? Or your parents and siblings?

---

* Louis de Bernières, *Corelli's Mandolin*, 1994.

# 7
# What's Your Score?

"We wholly overlook the essential fact that the
achievements which society rewards are won at the cost
of diminution of personality. Many—far too many—
aspects of life which should also have been experienced
lie in the lumber room among dusty memories."

Carl Jung

"It's a small but interesting group, who are making
voluntary decisions about what kind of relationship they
want to have with the working world. . . . Many of
these people are forty-plus. They've put a lot of time and
effort into their careers and are realizing, 'Hey, I don't
see this paying off down the line.'"

James Portwood*

"I was part of that strange race of people aptly described
as spending their lives doing things they detest to make
money they don't want to buy things they don't need to
impress people they dislike."

Emile Henry Gauvreau

"Trouble with the rat race is that even if you win, you're
still a rat."

Lily Tomlin

*H*ow have you done so far in your life? That is, how do you rank
with your peers? Does your mother brag about you to her
friends? Or does she say you're still finding yourself? And how about
fun? Are you having fun yet? Or did you put off the fun part, buckle
down, and do the right thing? Or maybe life was a lot more fun in the
past when you were on your way than it is now that you've arrived.

Are you as excited about the future as you used to be? Do you

---

* Quoted in John Grossman, "In Pursuit of a Simpler Life," *U.S. Air Magazine*,
March 1996.

want to keep running your life the same way? Or are you ready for something new, but don't know what? Or do you have an idea, but it doesn't look feasible?

Do you agree that "He who has the most things when he dies wins"? Did you ever? Or do you long for a new way of winning, with no sense of competition or display of material gain?

You've been pounding away all these years to make a goal, and at midlife you lift your head for a moment to see where you are. But when you look around, you don't see anything clearly. Only more questions.

If you don't feel successful yet, you might be thinking, "Will I ever make it? Should I cut my losses and give up?" If you've achieved some of your goals, you might be wondering, "Have I made it yet?" And if you feel you have achieved success, you still sometimes think, "Is this it?"

The same worries rise in the hearts of both successful and unsuccessful people. What have you achieved, what did it add up to, and where do you go from here? Did you choose the right life? What on earth can you do about it now?

Devastating questions. If they've stopped you dead in your tracks and you're unwilling to make another move until they're answered, let me congratulate you on your wisdom. The rules for success changed when you weren't looking, and you're wise to want the new ones before you take another step.

What's the problem? You can't tell the difference between what you want and what the world wants from you. Here at midlife they're starting to diverge from each other, and that's the source of the dissatisfaction. You see, you want to be a winner. Everyone does. You want to be recognized and/or rich and/or established. You don't intend to rethink those values. Who could doubt that the "real" you wants them? But the real you is also starting to want other things: to travel, to have time for your family, to create something original, to try out those sides of yourself there's been no time for. But you can't pay the *rent that way, right? You'd look like a fool if you gave up your success path. But should you dare anyway? The inner conflict is excruciating.*

*Right off the bat, let me reassure you that you couldn't possibly have made a mistake up until now, whether you became a million-dollar-a-year corporate lawyer or a beach bum. Why? Because until now you were under a spell, pushed by forces that had little to do with you, driven by impulses you didn't understand. This chapter is going to describe some of the forces that have been working on you. You're going to be shocked at how completely you were surrounded and will see that you must forgive yourself completely because you had no choice but to surrender.*

*But no matter which direction you take from now on, nothing you've done was wasted. Every path you've chosen until now, even the "mistakes," will be so useful in the future that one day it will almost look like directed research. Once the light falls on how you came to this place in your life, you'll understand far better where you are and what to do next. Because all these conflicts signal your entrance into a new era of your life. For the first time you can—and must—pay attention to what you're doing. This is your second life. This one counts.*

---

**Most human beings are raised to know exactly what a winner is:** someone who achieves what he or she is supposed to achieve, whatever that may be. And achieving success isn't only about earning lots of money or winning trophies, it's about holding a certain position in society and winning the approval of your family, friends, and relatives. Who decides what a winner is, and how do you know what you're supposed to do and achieve? Every society defines that for its members, and approval and disapproval are its tools.

Approval means everything to you when you're young. If you can remember your childhood, you'll recall that approval was glorious and disapproval was agony. That makes it the most potent teaching tool for the age at which youngsters have the most to learn. As any parent knows, a receptive learner, one motivated enough to internalize what you want to teach her, yearns for approval and is pained by disapproval. This curbs your natural curiosity, which might otherwise send you off on your own explorations and put you in danger. But being restrained to this world of approval and disapproval focuses you more on rewards and punishments than on your own interests.

Unfortunately, this need for approval can be endless because instead of providing you with a permanent sense of well-being, it has a way of disappearing down the well of self-doubt, which was originally dug by disapproval. That's a basic dynamic behind the desire for success, and it's part of the early training of every child.

That may have been a very good thing in the formative years, but as you got older, approval simply stopped being good enough. At one time you'd have done anything to get high marks from a teacher, but now you couldn't care less. Not too long ago you eagerly worked half the night for the boss in exchange for a warm pat on the head, but now you just go home feeling ripped off. You're a veteran now, and you understand the game so much better than you used to. When they play the trumpets and hoist the flag, you can no longer be trusted to run happily into battle without a second thought.

You may not want to lose your job, but you are indisputably losing your drive to impress people. Maybe you've figured out that the carrot dangled in front of your nose kept moving out of reach. Or maybe you took a few nibbles and found out it was nothing but a carrot.

*Anytime you won a prize and it felt empty, as though something essential was missing or some promise to you wasn't kept, it's because the game went on so long that you outgrew the prize.* The child who really needed it isn't there anymore to accept it.

"By the time my father finally gave me his approval, I had

already stopped looking for it. The critic had lost his authority," said Matthew, a restaurant manager.

The result of your growing lack of interest in approval is creating a shift of values inside you, and it's jamming up your success drive.

*You may not know it yet, but your desire to have both a good life and a high score are on a collision course.*

You still want success, maybe more than ever. And you want enough achievement, money, and status to gain respect, even admiration. But suddenly, with a desire more intense than you ever experienced before, you want a lot more than that. You want a satisfying personal life, too. You want a chance to go after dreams that have nothing to do with success. The natural curiosity that was curbed in your childhood came from an inner self that is starting to show its presence, a self that wants more than its elders wanted for it, and this self doesn't intend to be restrained anymore.

*This is becoming a serious conflict, and there can't be two winners.*

You're confronting the "world versus self" choice that one so often faces at midlife: Which is more important to happiness, how you rank in the tribe or how you feel inside? They're almost impossible to combine. You can't rank yourself. When you're working on something you love, your focus isn't on approval, it's on your work. "How'm I doing?" is an appropriate question only when you're winning hearts.

How can you resolve the conflict? Well, first you have to understand the drama you've written.

**The hidden drama, the secret mission.**

Underneath every effort you've ever made to succeed, there's been a hidden drama with a beginning, middle, and end. In the beginning you assessed the challenge, in the middle you fought the forces against you with all your might, and in the final scene you were either supposed to rise to triumph or go down in defeat. And that final scene was supposed to take place by midlife.

If it wasn't for that drama and those values, you wouldn't feel disappointed or defeated now. It's the drama that prepared you for triumph and glory and joy; it was behind your drive to make something of yourself and your hope of a fulfilling payoff.

"I was supposed to be famous by now," an actress said. "I'm getting plenty of small parts and lots of high praise, but that's not enough for my age. I'm terrified even to say this, but it looks like I didn't make it."

"My business is doing all right, some people would think it's better than all right, but I'm still a one-man shop, and the industry is changing. I see trouble in the future. It's possible I'll have to start all over. This is not supposed to happen now," said the owner of an electronic parts warehouse.

*Where did we get this timetable, and who gave us our definitions of success?*

Our ideas of success and failure came from a variety of sources. Biology, family situation, peers, even the country you were raised in are sitting in the judges' box at the Success Olympics in your mind. Let's look at each of these influences, one by one.

**Biology and Success.**

We may no longer live in a world in which males have physical battles for the possession of females, in which females disdain all but the winning males, in which only the healthiest can survive, and only the strongest get enough food, but never underestimate the role biology still plays in the desire for success. Ideas and technology may change fast, but biology always drags far behind. The muscle is still in us: the desire for action, a sense of intensity, of high stakes. We're ready to fight to gain something as soon as we figure out what it is. Nature pumps us full of drive, setting the stage for the drama we'll perform. All we need is our lines.

The family we're born into provides the script.

**Family and Success.**

"My mother worked too hard to put me through good schools. I could never disappoint her. To her, a lawyer is the be-all and end-all," said a very unhappy lawyer to me recently. What did he really love? Other cultures, backpacking, teaching, and writing.

Well, what if he were successful in some career that involved what he loved? What if he built a wonderful career with his own business involving backpacking all over the world, getting contracts to teach cultural awareness to multinational corporations, writing books?

"She'd say it was too bohemian," he answered.

Every life goal is a delicate balance between you—your desires, your abilities, even your need to resist outside pressure—and the family you grew up with. You've designed your goals to affect somebody: a parent, probably, who could be won over, saved, or at least proved wrong about your worth.

Sometimes families let you know exactly what is expected of you. Depending on their values, they might tell you to go to the right schools and meet the right people—or get good grades, or be good at sports—so you can make a proper marriage and get a respectable career, so you can make money and send your kids to the right schools to do the same thing. Sometimes the goal is clear, but your family neglects to explain how you're supposed to achieve it. They might say, "Get rich!" or, "Be a doctor or a lawyer!" but since they don't know how to do that themselves, they're not clear on how you should do it. Other times the goal is undefined, but just as clear. "My family told me to 'Be somebody!' It didn't matter exactly in what field, but I was supposed to rise to the top, get somewhere."

And sometimes you can't figure out what they want because they're so conflicted they sincerely encourage you to succeed but when you do, they become threatened and try to pull you down.

Some families aren't concerned with your happiness at all, even intermittently. They demand that you forget yourself and give them whatever they want for themselves. When that happens, you grudgingly acquiesce, dragging your feet, and ultimately give your family a halfhearted effort, so hurt by their selfishness that you're willing to punish yourself in order to punish them.

And in some families you come to understand that the only way you can actually give satisfaction is to fail because nothing else will make them content.

In every case, you enter life in the middle of your family's story and try to fix something that went on in an earlier scene, one you might know nothing about. Maybe your father longed to prove something to his scornful older brother but wasn't able to. You sense his failure, although you may not understand its source, and try to succeed for him. Or your mother put her dreams on your back because no one else would give them to her. Perhaps your parents were so successful you've never known how to match them or so unhappy you were unconsciously afraid to surpass them.

What you sensed them longing for was based on how they were raised, when they grew up, and what dreams, disappointments, and dangers they experienced with their parents. As a small child you absorbed those values without question. But usually you grew into an adult in an environment different from the one your family was familiar with, and you acquired some values—and longings—of your own. Still, consciously or unconsciously, you did your best to make the whole thing work.

The lawyer I mentioned earlier knows the real facts all too well. Being a lawyer isn't the great career it used to be. Not only are there fewer jobs, but even employed lawyers are walking out on their careers in droves. Turnover caused by dissatisfaction in law is among the highest of any profession. But the lawyer's mother remembers when law was the profession that gave the most status and security, and she wants a lawyer son. He knows she's wrong, but he simply can't bring himself to walk away from what she needs. It's more common than you think: the blind leading the guilty.

**I refuse to play.**

If you think you can simply ignore the whole setup, good luck. Go your own way, and you'll be labeled not "independent" but "loser." When you're still developing your identity, this is more than you can take. You're driven to do well in your family's terms because their acceptance gives you your worth. No one has the option of staying neutral when they're growing up. Nor does it makes a difference if you announce loudly that you disapprove of your family's crazy values or even laugh at them. Their drama got inside you before you had the sense to protest. You made lifetime decisions based on that drama when you were a tiny child.

**Your peers and success.**

Your friends provide another essential element to make you strive for success: competition. Whenever you're in the mood to beat yourself up, all you have to do is look at the most "successful" people you went to school with. You can be jolted by comparisons at any time: If a friend's promotion is mentioned by your father, or if you get a birthday card or baby announcement from a schoolmate, you rank yourself against them automatically. Did you do better? Or did they do better?

That's why reunions are such hell. Theoretically you're there for affectionate reasons: to see familiar faces, rehash fond memories, and catch up on one another's lives.

So why do you sweat so much about your weight, your hair loss, your successful marriage or lack of it, your career performance?

You can't help ranking yourself against who you were when you were still in school. If you were a beauty, you want everyone to see you haven't lost your looks. If you had the most romantic relationship, you cringe if it's gone. If you got straight A's, you feel like a loser if you're not at the top of your profession now. You're afraid that your schoolmates will say, "C'mon, you went to top schools. You worked at top firms. You could be doing better than this!" If they sympathize with your unhappiness and say, "You should quit and become a photographer if that's what you want," the final truth comes from the way they choose to live. After all, why don't they quit, too?

And if you know you've done wonderfully well and you walk into the party proud of yourself, you'll soon realize that you're causing them pain, making them feel bad about themselves when all you wanted to do was be friends and equals.

But if somebody wins, somebody loses. That's the point system.

Your peers had a huge effect on your definition of success even if you were an outcast with no chance of entry into the inner circle. If you were made fun of and never accepted, your schoolmates were your enemies. They hurt and humiliated you and made you long for the kind of success that smashes your tormentors to the ground. The magnitude of your success fantasy indicates the amount of early pain you suffered.

"One of these days I'll be so successful and famous they'll read about me and eat their hearts out. And when they call to renew old acquaintances, or if they need something, I'll tell them I don't remember who they are."

In other words, the big win. That's the one America loves the best.

**America and Success.**

The unique history of the country you're raised in has everything to do with how success is measured—or if it's measured at all. Individual success for the average person is a rather new concept in history, and an argument could be made that the United States was the first to bring it onto the world scene.

Unlike the countries that your ancestors emigrated from, America was blessed with abundant natural resources, an absence of enemies on its borders, and the largest group in history of the most resourceful, independent, and active immigrants ever seen.

Those immigrants came from worlds where much of life was established and hard to change. You knew who you were and who your children would be, because moving up or down the social or financial ladder was almost impossible. Even when times were good, no clerk could become a prince, and very few chimney sweeps could become clerks. Some people accepted the status quo more easily than others and continued their lives in their countries of origin for as long as they were allowed to. But those who couldn't stand it, who were willing to swap certainty for opportunity, came to this country.

It was like a dream come true: in the countryside endless amounts of land available for ordinary people to own. In the cities, if you had the guts and were willing to work hard, you could improve your life and your children's lives. Europe has no tradition of ordinary people becoming successful. America has little else.

It can be a heavy burden to carry. In theory, you can be a winner here no matter what your beginning point, so hope is high. If you're poor in Europe or Asia, you're unfortunate. But if you don't become a winner in America it's your own fault; you blew your opportunities.

As a result, we've come to idolize competition like no other country before us. We worship the monster winner in sports or business, the one giant that makes all the others small. We invented the notion of the winning business team, the football model, where the boss is the coach and we want to win for him. More than any country our grandparents came from, we worship the warrior, the athlete, the high roller.

You see the language all around you in the self-improvement sections of any bookstore: how to win at love, money, life. How to conquer fear and self-doubt. How to be the one who winds up on top.

**The cult of "the best."**

It might be cynical or manipulative: Show enough pictures of Michael Jordan in your brand of shoes, and kids who want to feel like winners will buy them. But even if advertisers were sincerely trying to show people how far they can go if they try, they're making a mistake by holding up giants as models.

Because our cult of "top dog," and our insistence on making success an issue of competition, we ignore real talent and leave out enormous riches by picking one winner and calling everyone else a damning second best. If a thousand people were equally good at something, we'd have to pick the best on some arbitrary basis and forget the rest. A frightening waste of talent.

Not only that, but giants make lousy role models. For one thing, megastars usually fall into two categories: Either they are normal humans capable of full lives, who are restricted from leading those full lives because they're on public display, or they're absolute monsters of mindless drive who couldn't live normal lives if they tried. Their single-minded laser-focused energy is how they got to the top and explains why they can tolerate staying there.

So before you waste too much time longing for their brilliant successes, you might want to think about what they've really got. It's not what it appears to be.

**The alleged benefits of being famous.**

All around us, in films, on TV, and on the covers of magazines are the faces of the rich and famous. When you look at these icons of success, do they have an aura of glamour and self-confidence about them? Do they look comfortable and happy? Of course they do. Nobody famous ever frowns on the cover of a magazine. They're our icons, and they have shining auras.

"If I were the president or a movie star, I'd be happy, sure of myself, rich, and adored. Everyone would treat me with respect wherever I went." At the distance where glamour is undisturbed by reality, where mystery creates longing, celebrities are as beautiful and admirable as those giants we adored when we were tiny infants: our parents. But just as closeness and familiarity made us see what flawed creatures our parents actually were, closeness and familiarity with celebrities blow illusions about them right out of the water.

If fame feels so good, why do you suppose film stars become irritated when you approach them in public? *Because they want what you have: the freedom of anonymity.* You get more respect on the street than any celebrity can hope for. People don't feel they have the right to intrude on your privacy. Unlike celebrities, you are free to walk the streets, doing your own thing, thinking your own thoughts. No one will run up to you unexpectedly to ask for an autograph just when you were having a private moment with your child. You don't have to smile at anyone. You don't need to be accompanied by a staff or a bodyguard.

They're not having as much fun as you think either. Their audience has all the pleasure of someone who's in love and doesn't have to worry about being rejected. Their sensitivity and artistry or their commanding presence are the inventions of hero-hungry fans; the artists don't experience them at all. While working performers may get deep rewards from performing their craft (something you can also have), when they step away from that craft and join other adored celebrities, they must be like a magician who does magic tricks for an audience. They don't get to believe that the rabbit really came out of that hat. The only ones having a good time are the people in the audience as they sit in the dark, believing the magic and wishing they were stars too.

"For years I envied the brokers who were the stars of the company, watching them walk self-confidently through the office in their expensive suits. One day it hit me: I was measuring my insides against their outsides," a client said to me.

Larry did very well in his own business, but his friends did better. He got invited to all their parties but never really felt he fit in. And he couldn't stop comparing himself especially to his friends whose performances were so spectacular that they'd become celebrities. But to him, they always acted faintly superior and condescending.

"I always wondered how they got so sure of themselves," he wrote me. "What did they have that I didn't have? I knew that even if I got richer, I wouldn't be like them. And then one day my wife said, 'Why do they invite you if they're so far above you?'

" 'Oh, I guess they want me around because I'm the only one who talks about anything interesting. They just mouth the same things over and over, how much they spend on things, how well they're doing,' I told her.

" 'Maybe they need somebody who looks up to them,' she said.

"But why would they need that? I thought she must be wrong, but it got me thinking. And then I realized that I've often had this sense that they're working too hard to look good. I mean, once you get there, you should relax, right? That was the day I realized something I'd always known underneath: They don't *feel* as good as they *look*."

So, whenever you start wishing you were someone else, a famous actor, or an athlete, or a local celebrity, you might want to try out a reality test by measuring your insides against their *insides*. Because outsides are constructions. Anybody can build them. People show up on the covers of magazines because they hire promotional experts to get them there. It's part of their business.

**A high score versus true greatness.**

But what about all the unknown people of intelligence, spirit, kindness, and ingenuity, whom you never see on the covers of magazines? Those are the people we most desperately need to read about, but they're not on public display because they can't be bothered to get there.

Many of them are magnificent. You can find them closer to home, in your neighborhood, at work, or in your family. They are involved in their work or dedicated to creating something that matters. *They should be our beacons; we should be watching them.* Working in happy privacy, the outstanding teachers or gardeners or writers are allowed to develop their gifts at their own speed, to walk among us without being pointed at, to have lives with more in them than just one passion. And to be oblivious to their "score."

We need to know about people like the woman who started her own school in Chicago and teaches the classics to underprivileged kids and gets them into college. The man who left the city and started a small farm in the country. The student who studies history on her own simply because she's interested and the school doesn't teach it. The nun who went to Africa by herself because no one would give her permission, then sat under a tree until the children brought her food and villagers got to know her, and taught them to read and write and ultimately built twenty schools. The covers of magazines should dump those tiresome pictures of celebrities whose faces we've seen too often and who can't teach us anything about how to live, and show the faces of people who have followed personal dreams, the people whom agents and managers and promotion people never try to reach on the phone. We need to see what they look like, what they care about, how they made their choices, how they got started if we're ever going to learn what we need as individuals. Because only from their example can we hope to touch our own potential for greatness.

But the point system was never designed to give us that. It was designed to get something from us.

**What has the point system done to the individual?**

It may have made you perform like a star quarterback at work, but the point system may also have leaked into the rest of your life and eroded it entirely.

Say you're a woman who doesn't want to be held back in a man's world; you fight your way to the top and handle a family at the same time. You suffer a lot of loneliness and don't get to spend as much time with your children as you want to. But you hope your daughter will gain from your pioneering efforts by having more career opportunities. Instead your daughter wants a husband who will support her so she can stay home with their children.

"I saw how hard my mother worked, how little time she had for friends, or lovers, or us. I don't want that."

Or you're a father who wants only the best for your wife and kids: the biggest house, the best schools and clothes and cars, and never a worry. You wind up with a wife you can't talk to about business and kids who don't know how to take care of themselves and have been insulated from any other kinds of people. You love them, but they seem oddly shallow to you, self-centered and materialistic. Worse, they seem dissatisfied and have trouble finding goals.

Or you've got a great business head. You see where the most money is being made. You go to that place and fight like a devil for your share. You win. You wind up with more money than you can ever spend, lots of shiny toys, a trophy love partner acquired partly as a reward for your performance and partly to create envy in others, and a grudging entrée into the world of the big boys. But you never feel you can turn your back on such people because you know the rules: Lose your money, and you lose them too. So you end up like a poor little rich kid, lonely and with lots of toys.

**Life is not a spectator sport: true or false?**

It's been said that "life is not a spectator sport," implying that you've got to play to win.

*But life isn't any kind of sport at all.*

A sport has certain requirements. Your value is only as a player. What is wanted is not *your* best, but *the* best. There's always an opponent. If you win, somebody has to lose. To do well is what counts, and the audience gives you your score. This is what sports are about, but it isn't what life is about.

If you don't believe me, take a look at a few of life's everyday activities. Imagine that you do them for the love of it and then that you do them to score points. Pay attention to the richness of the experience in each case.

1. Exercising for health versus for the best muscles in the gym.
2. Sex for desire versus sex for a score.
3. Dancing or playing piano for pleasure versus competition.
4. Learning because you're interested versus for a high grade.
5. Talking to friends to hear new ideas versus winning a debate.
6. Traveling out of curiosity versus looking more cosmopolitan than your neighbors.
7. Building a house you love versus the best on the block.

See the difference?

In personal matters, winning is the lonely choice. Treating life as a sport is unaffectionate and dehumanizing, and it creates a poverty of experience. When survival is at stake, of course no one has a choice. You work as hard as you have to and pay whatever price you must. But winning to prove a point, no matter how honorable the motives, may have too high a cost in quality of life.

**But successful people have a lot of money. Don't pretend that's not a wonderful thing.**

I'm afraid I'm going to do exactly that, folks. After reading some articles about the misery that descended on most lottery winners, my suspicions were confirmed. Almost all of them became divorced or alienated from angry friends and family. One of them wound up in jail for robbery, because he had overspent his prize and needed money! Too much money can actually make you more miserable than not having enough.

Having been a very broke, worried, and overworked single parent, I put great store in having "enough" money. Enough to me means not having to work myself to death to make ends meet, not waking up at dawn clutched by fear that I can't afford a doctor for my kids or a carburetor for my car. *But I put no store in having to work myself to death for too much money or waking in fear that I'll lose my sailboat or have to pawn my diamonds.* When I ask people who ache to make the big hit, to be very rich, why they want that, here's what they say—and what I answer.

**1. Money gives you safety.**

You don't need great wealth for that. If you have enough money to meet your bills and take care of illness or other normal problems, you have as much of a sense of safety as a human can have. Any high-paying job can disappear. Big investments can founder. And those with fortunes so great they're in no danger of losing them need bodyguards.

The amount of money you need—above bare necessities— depends on your viewpoint. I know someone who scratched by on almost nothing but managed to travel the world year after year. I know people who feel rich on twenty-five thousand dollars a year, and a surprising number who earn twenty times that much but live in terror of poverty.

**2. You could do such interesting things if you were rich.**

Like what? Travel to exotic places? Go to Outer Mongolia? But that's impossible without a lot of money.

Don't be so sure. Lots of ordinary people manage to save their pennies and travel all over the world. Sometimes having less money results in a fuller experience.

"You can stay at a five-star hotel in Italy if you want to, but you won't meet any real Italians. And chandeliers and linen napkins get boring after a while," a friend told me recently. "Every time I visit a foreign country and stay in smaller places, or at the homes of friends, I come away with a much more powerful sense of where I've been."

But most rich people can't really stay in the inexpensive pensions favored by traveling Europeans, because they've lost their tolerance for inconvenience, which author Judith Viorst calls "the mother of adventure."*

**Money lets you help people.**

Some people say they want lots and lots of money because they could do so much good. "I'd give a lot of it away," they say.

Look again. How many millionaires actually do give it away? Usually something else gets priority. And how many actually have the day-to-day experience of getting out there and being in the presence of the people they want to aid? Their job is to manage all that money and hire someone else to run a foundation.

If you really long to help the world, you can do it right now. Join Earthwatch or the Peace Corps, or get a job in a foundation and hand out grants, or find a way to help a neighbor, or a kid, or some aging or ill person who isn't being taken care of by the system. That's just as gratifying and may do even more good.

**4. But you can start fun businesses if you have money. That's interesting, isn't it?**

A small business is fun, I agree. But the bigger it gets, the less fun it is. When you have to hire someone to set up your life and collect and distribute your money, you've lost the hands-on excitement. A friend who owns a few apartment buildings says that two million dollars' worth of real estate is better than ten million. With two million, he says, you visit your property, you check it out, you talk to your tenants, you improve the landscape. With ten million, you just deal with twenty money managers.

**Those are some myths about money. I hope I've debunked them for you.**

Because the key question isn't What's your score? The key question is, What do you need?

You may be surprised at your answer.

---

* *Modern Maturity*, January–February 1996.

You might want a chance to go after dreams that have nothing to do with wealth or fame. Many exciting lives fall below the radar of huge success. I know a woman who works with chimpanzees in Borneo and a man who works in a music store, teaching blues guitar to customers. They both love what they do every day of their lives, but you'll never read about them in the newspapers.

A neighbor I knew as a secretary recently showed up at a friend's wedding, standing behind a tableful of elegant French pastries that she had baked.

"I went to school in Paris to be a pastry chef," she said, smiling. "But I don't want to do it as a profession. I prefer being a secretary."

A friend of mine lives in a small village in Turkey, buying empty, run-down houses, restoring them and returning them to the village. A forty-six-year-old lawyer recently discovered the letters her great-grandmother, a missionary and traveler, sent from Asia to her family in Boston before the turn of the century. She's hired a writing teacher and gathered together a small group of people who also want to write the stories of their families. They work together every Saturday, writing and reading their material, helping one another solve research problems. They're even considering starting a tiny publishing company of their own. Will they ever get rich and successful, hit the magazines with a business success story?

"I don't think so," the lawyer said. "None of us wants to bother with that. We just want to publish our own books for the few people who might want to read them."

Such small potatoes. Too small for you. How would your father explain your lack of ambition to his friends?

And truth be known, you're a bit worried yourself. Fantasies of satisfying work could ruin your chances to make it in this world. Your growing desire for personal satisfaction could be sabotaging your old dreams of high achievement. Look out. You could be a failure if you're not careful.

## FAILURE

Let's take a look at what you were taught to fear most: the F word. Failure. First, let me define the word itself. Failure can be seen as the distance between what you expected and what you got—if and only if you define your worth by the opinions of others.

If you go after a dream and fall on your face, that alone isn't enough to make you feel like a failure. The first time you try anything, you're always astonished at how hard it is to succeed. While that may be sobering, it's part of the learning process and will only get you ready for a more educated try later. But what injures your self-esteem is your sensitivity to how successful you seem to others. If that's what's on your mind, you carry a heavy load.

"I had so much early promise and everyone expected so much. Then I went to college and became just another person. I never got over the shock. I think I gave up after that."

"I just realized that all my life I've been obsessed with trying to prove I was worthy to my father. I stay longer than anyone else at work, I do such a good job everyone is amazed, but it never feels like enough. I always feel like a failure."

That's failure. The first person has failed to be the genius everyone expected her to be and can't move on. The second has failed to win approval from a critical parent and can't stop overcompensating. You know what would help them both? To see these failures for what they really are: the keys that open the jailhouse doors and can set them free.

**The truth about failure; what's good about it.**

Failure sets you free from the rat race.

When you lose the game, the invisible audience disappears, and you get the calm focus you need to design a life that fits you. So you didn't get the points and you're out of the game. Good riddance. Now you can relax because you have nothing to lose. No longer are you the warrior or hockey player struggling to convince yourself you can't possibly fail. *You know damned well you can—because you did.* And you lived through it.

Now you can start saying no to things you don't want and start looking for what you *do.*

You've got to fail a few times to understand the terrain; you've got to know the pitfalls before you can decide where to put your next effort. Because failure makes you thoughtful and attentive, it's like having a wise old guru inside your head, advising and warning you but still pushing you to go for your dreams. Striving for a dream is essential, but success is never guaranteed, and your resources aren't endless. You have to be smart to handle that equation with finesse.

I've come to see this through my own experience with failure. As I mentioned, some years ago my one-woman business failed, my income disappeared, my kids got jobs to help pay for their school, and no knight on horseback showed up to help me. I just sat there in the rubble unable to see the future. I was still alive, of course. I hadn't gone up in a puff of smoke, but I was forty-three and figured it was all over.

Then I published my first book, *Wishcraft*. At forty-four! Amazed, I waited for success. But it was five years before anyone noticed the book, and it got issued in paperback only by a fluke. After that it slowly gathered momentum and still hasn't stopped selling. *Wishcraft* didn't make me rich. I struggled for another ten years at counseling, and things slowly got better until I published my second book, *Teamworks!*, at fifty-four.

Again, I was very enthusiastic. But what looked like a new chance at success bombed and went out of print. I wasn't just failing, I was making a career out of it.

Then my third book, *I Could Do Anything if I Only Knew What It Was*—published when I was fifty-nine—hit the best-seller lists all over the country and is still doing well years later. That has been a very satisfying experience, but don't think for a minute it's the end of the story. My fourth book, *Live the Life You*

*Love*, won the first-ever Books for a Better Life Award in self-improvement, yet it's selling like my first one did at the beginning: No one notices it's there. The book you're now reading is due to come out when I'm sixty-two. I hope it does well, but I'm through with predictions. That's what failure has taught me. I just keep plugging along because I like to write, and I'm very happy when my publisher wants another book from me.

**It must take a lot of character to persist through all that disappointment.**

*It didn't take any.* Because it never once occurred to me that this was what I was doing. I had no career goal after my first business failure except for surviving and taking care of my kids. As far as I was concerned, I had lost the battle for success and developed a lot of respect for the unpredictability of fortune. After that, I did my part and forgot about the rest. That's a very relaxing way to live. It gave and still gives me an unending supply of daily energy. No coach, boss, or general wants you thinking this way, of course. You can't blame them; after all, they're not in the business of making you happy.

But you *are* in that business. After survival itself, that's your only business.

**But anything's possible if you only believe it, right?**

"Believe it and you can achieve it!" I can't tell you how many times I hear that exhortation and others like it: "You create your own reality" or "The only limits are the limits of your imagination." Catchy phrases, but if you fall for them, you're back in a narrow narcissistic focus where you care nothing for fate, weather, or the stock market, much less your own emotional needs. When you've sold yourself that bill of goods, you lose your respect for reality and become intoxicated with the illusion of your own potential.

Rather than deafen your fears with drums and trumpets to go after your goals, you'll be better off discovering what's real. Instead of hiding your uncertainty by shouting out your own grandiosity, relax and begin to listen to what you have learned: Reality is bigger than you are. And that's the way it is. Nothing to sulk about. In fact, only now can you become receptive, respectful, even curious. Only now can you really begin to learn.

As any mountain climber will tell you, your chances for success increase when you respect your obstacles.

**Free at last.**

Looks like I've trashed success pretty thoroughly, doesn't it? Look again. If you can stop wanting what you were taught to want and start searching for your own goals, if you can stop fearing failure and start to see it as nothing but an institution of higher learning, you will find something amazing: *Right now, right here, in the middle of your life, you are poised to do something extraordinary based on who you really are.*

That's the kind of success that's never been open to you until now. It's also the only sustainable success you can ever have, sustainable because you enjoy it, and successful because it will use your original vision to create something no one else could possibly create. That original vision will never go away; it will become stronger and clearer with use.

But you'll have to reacquaint yourself with a whole range of emotions and tastes you might not have seen in years. They're the only compass you will have now, because you're in new terrain. If you really have pursued traditional success most of your life, you've never had a chance to try out many of your gifts. You've been using all your natural instincts for so long to figure out the success game that you hardly remember how to use them to figure out who you are and what you should be doing.

Can your work still get acclaim? It probably will. You're always brilliant at what you really love to do because love is the banner of genius. But the irony is that you can't do your best work until you stop caring about acclaim. And later when you finally get it, you'll be surprised at how little it matters. If you're someone who wants to love your life or your work for its own

166

sake, applause feels like a distant roar outside a closed window, and not a very interesting roar at that.

When Albert Einstein and Charlie Chaplin, at that time two of the most famous people in the world, pulled up in their car to an opening of Chaplin's latest film, the fans went wild. They clawed at the windows and climbed over one another to stare inside. Bewildered, Einstein said to Chaplin, "What does this mean?"

Chaplin replied, "It means nothing. Absolutely nothing."

Early success rarely lasts anyway. The composer Giuseppe Verdi felt that was fortunate: "When an artist allows himself to have two or three successes while young . . . he can be sure that the public will then grow tired of him . . . if the artist has the strength to stand up to this turn of the tide and go ahead on his own path, he'll be safe by the time he's forty."*

So let the cheerleaders and the marching bands pass you by. Let them rouse someone greener than you. You're a grown-up now, and you have something more important to do.

**Wake up to what really defines you.**

What's first-rate about you? Not what does the world *think* is first-rate, not what is useful, not what gets you the success your family would brag about, but what makes you different from anyone else? If you met a person exactly like you, what would you value most about him or her? Imagine seeing yourself across a room, and try to answer those questions. They're not easy to answer, but from now on it's very important to keep them in mind. Not so you can love yourself or praise yourself; this has nothing to do with self-appreciation. You simply need to know who you are and what you have to work with. You have to re-identify a self that's been off course so long you're not sure what it is. Like losing old measuring sticks and having to find new ones,

---

* Letter to Countess Maffei, 1876, from *Oxford Book of Aging*, p. 84.

this is a worthwhile endeavor but not a grandiose one. You've simply got to get in the habit of noticing what you gravitate toward, what makes your hands happy, what your mind loves to think about. Only then can you break free of the success lockstep.

Even though you have promises to keep—to your family or your boss or your community—you'll keep them like a free person, not a slave to approval. One of the best things about growing up and going through years of dubious success and interesting failure is that your inner satisfaction becomes more important than status or praise. That means that you *choose* to do a good job and keep promises. And you can afford to be generous because since it doesn't deprive you of what you need, giving is no longer a form of self-sacrifice.

**So what's your score?**

Who knows? It's only halftime. Everything can turn around in the next half. Of course, unlike a baseball or football game, at midlife you get to change the rules. And if people won't let you, you can walk off the field entirely and find something you like better.

Test the waters a bit. Have some fun defanging your worst critics. Tell them—true or false—that you screwed up just like they expected you to, and smile happily while they say, "I told you so." When you quit trying to avoid their scorn, you take away all their power.

"You really screwed up," your father says sternly.

"Ain't it awful, Dad?" you respond with a sweet smile. "Can I have more mashed potatoes?"

So, go ahead and disappoint someone who had high expectations of you, make your enemies crow with satisfaction, go to your school reunions happy and fat. And if anyone asks, "Did you make it?" use Mel Brooks's answer: "Make it? Make what? Who cares?"

You may not be comfortable doing that yet, of course. The carrot may have lost its value, but the stick still hurts. Being called a loser will still sting deeply. That's because you're living with leftover meanings. But just wait until the day you realize that these labels don't even bother you. *When you stop wanting the carrot and the stick no longer hurts, you're going to turn into a donkey with an opinion.*

And the point system will have had its day.

## EXERCISE 14

### *Score yourself.*

1. What did success mean in your neighborhood? Did your family have it? Did they aspire to it? What role did you play in their ideas of success?

2. When you attend a gathering, do you compare yourself with others? What are your criteria for "most successful"?

3. Do you ever think about how well you're doing compared with others in your age group?

4. Does it feel like it's too late to be a winner? Are winners only those who succeeded when they were young?

5. What material things did you want in your twenties? Thirties? Forties? What do you think about those things now?

6. What career goals did you have in your twenties? Thirties? Did you attain them? Did they make you happy?

7. What life goals (marriage, children) did you have? Did you attain them? How were they different from what you expected?

8. Where do you want to live when you "retire"?

9. What would you like to do that a lack of money keeps you from doing? How could you do it without money?

10. Name the people you admired at different ages in your life, from childhood on. What were your criteria (kindness, humor, money, admired by others, etc.)?

11. Given the choice between a successful man (a catch) and

a good man you loved, or between a trophy wife and a wife you loved spending time with, would you have a problem choosing?

12. What if you had no sense of your score, if it meant absolutely nothing to you, what would you do different? What would you stop doing?

# 8
# Escape to Freedom

"I wanted to keep my barbarian awe . . . I would run
off into the wide open spaces. Forget buses and trains; it
would be a pilgrimage. I'd travel on foot to Istanbul. I'd
wield a staff and carry a knapsack and have the feeling
of the open road underfoot. It was an electrifying
image. . . . Under huge skies trod a figure with wild
hair, great pockets stuffed with crusts and a gourd slung
over his back. He was grown-up but it didn't matter. He
was a vagabond."
Jason Goodwin, *On Foot to the Golden Horn*

"I think the reason I want to run away from home is
that the person who lives there is turning forty."
Client

*W*hy *is it when midlifers talk of fulfilling their lifelong dreams
before they're too old to do them, they're never talking about
dreams like publishing a book or singing at the Met? They're always
talking about escape dreams: adventure, romance, running away to
sea.*

*Now why would someone at midlife suddenly get serious about
running away to sea? Or running away to anywhere? Why do people's
dreams at forty involve escape at all? And why can you always sense a
huge longing behind the wish and such desperation underneath?*

*Because of another illusion from your first life: Youth is free; age
is trapped.*

*Of course it doesn't look much like an illusion from where you
stand. If you're forty or over, you probably haven't felt free for years.
If you're on your own, you're preoccupied with the unending and*

worrisome burden of building your career, finding the right place to live, the right person to live with, all before it's too late. If you've got a family to take care of, your job, home, and huge responsibilities have you in harness. All your thoughts are directed toward managing your responsibilities. It's not that you don't love these sides of your life. Part of you always wanted to settle down and build a life of your own. But you never intended to exchange the free feeling you once had for unending attention to survival trivia or an exciting life for a deadening daily routine.

You promised yourself you'd never let this happen to you. You weren't going to be owned by your possessions or turned into an automaton. You were determined always to be the captain of your ship, always in charge of your life. And if you played your cards right and made a lot of money, maybe you'd even be able to quit working before you were forty and set your soul free again.

But that's not what happened. Your possessions and your commitments and your habits do own you, and your responsibilities keep growing. Thirty-nine came and went, you haven't arrived where you expected to be, and there's no end of your workload in sight.

If something radical doesn't happen soon, you might never get out of here.

Almost every day you fantasize jumping off your treadmill and making a fresh start someplace where life will be different. Everyone, especially your family, can sense your restlessness. But it's not that you want to leave them. On the contrary, you're probably trying to sell them on running away with you. You'd love to be with them in a place far beyond the reach of civilization where everything is fun again. The kids may even love your ideas, but the other grown-up in the house keeps suggesting you take a vacation instead. When there's time, of course.

But you know very well that no vacation could possibly satisfy this urge inside you. You need something far more radical, a permanent change, cutting ties, jolting yourself awake, going far away, and making a fresh start. Anything smaller feels like a compromise and can never pull you free, because you're like Gulliver, tied down with a thousand threads, unable to move.

Sometimes you wonder what exactly it is that you long for and feel a twinge of fear that maybe there is nothing out there at all, that you dreamed up this whole notion and it doesn't even exist. Maybe everyone's right and you're simply having a bad case of midlife crisis, and when it passes, you'll become resigned to your life like a grown-up should be.

But other times you know in your heart that you're right to fight against what your life has become, and even though you can't quite name what it is, you know you have lost something fantastic that you must have and you're desperate to get it back before it's too late. These once-vague complaints are rising to a crescendo pitch. You've simply got to find a way to escape to freedom.

Before you abandon your life to hit the road, I'd like you to take a look at some issues you may not have considered before. Because although your feeling of being trapped is real enough, it's not coming from where you think. You're right to want a life full of excitement and freshness, but swapping the one you have for a Winnebago or a sailboat probably won't get it for you. You need a more lasting solution, and being impulsive right now could be the biggest decision you'll ever regret.

Let's establish one thing right at the beginning: Your desire to escape is not just the impulse of an immature, irresponsible child who resents pulling an adult load. Your sense that growing up has stolen something of enormous value from you is right on target. But before you make a move, you need to find out exactly what it is you're searching for. Once you've got that elusive feeling clearly in view, you can turn those longings into real freedom, the grown-up kind that will last you a lifetime.

------

**The lure of faraway places and a different kind of life.**
Who hasn't felt it? The desire to run away, to do something

fresh and grand and totally new with your life. Some call it "road fever." You've got it when you dream of chucking it all, buying a sailboat and pitting yourself against the elements on the high seas, or taking off on foot (or motorcycle) to travel around the world. Or when you have the vision of living simply, by your own hands up in the mountains in a cabin you built yourself for next to nothing, free from the traps of the materialistic, soul-crushing rat race down in the flatlands. Road fever is what drives you to move your whole family to New Zealand because it's beautiful and safe or to a wild piece of property you bought for a song in Central America because it's loaded with adventure and a person's work counts for something there. Or road fever may be a bridge burning that's supposed to propel you in a new direction, like marrying the baby-sitter and moving a mile away. But whatever the details, road fever always includes some change of location and a pilgrimage to a new life.

**There are many varieties, but they have a few things in common.**

You can spot the markings. The project is always radical, never gradual. There's never a debate, pro and con, weighing the cost against the benefits. And there's never a plan for afterward because that could jinx the whole thing; it's too negative, like expecting to fail. If you're going to a monastery in Tibet or a shack in Patagonia or just "heading out," you must fly out the window like a seagull. Putting your winter things in storage and making sure the retirement fund is wisely invested are the same as dragging along the very traps you're trying to escape.

But in truth, you're afraid that cautious reflection would make you lose courage. As Lucan said, "Bold actions hide great fears," and you've got more than a few fears you want to hide. For instance, what will you do when the adventure is over, live in a trailer park? Could you sell a used Winnebago and buy back your house? And what will you do for an income?

"If I'm honest, I have to admit I have these terrible nightmares. The house has been sold and my wife and I have quit our jobs and we throw the kids into this RV and drive off. And we scrounge to make it last as long as we can, refusing to buy ice-cream cones for the kids or go to the movies. Then in a year or two it's gone, and we run out of gas in a truck stop town and we all go to work at McDonald's."

Maybe you should just rent out your house and take a two-month leave of absence.

But such caution is hateful to you. That kind of thinking got you into this mess in the first place. Those are the questions of boring, frightened old people, and you want no part of them.

"Hesitate and all is lost," you tell yourself. You feel you must put away reflection because only action will free you. You make a list of supplies and shop for sleeping bags and put the house up for sale and buy books and maps so you can spend the evenings reading about sea-lanes or mountain ranges. You mark a date on the calendar, the day you lock your door and walk away from this life, never to look back. What a thrilling launch that will be! The preparation alone is better than any antidepressant ever developed.

"Wait a minute," you might protest, "this isn't just a pill. It *is* possible to move to a mountaintop and have a great life after the newness disappears," and I would agree. Just as it's possible to have a great day-to-day marriage after the intoxication of romance disappears.

*The problem is, when you have road fever you don't want to think of newness turning into day-to-day anything. Never-ending novelty is the whole point.* The hope that nothing will ever again be "day to day" is as seductive as the destination. Radical impulsiveness is an essential. That's why two weeks in Hawaii won't do the trick.

Anyway, you're not sure you ever want to come back at all.

"The way I'd do it would be to head out on the sea-lanes and never settle down anywhere for long. Just stop in one paradise for a few months or years, and then go to another," a friend told me with a faraway look in his eyes.

"Would you ever come back?" I asked.

"Maybe someday," he answered vaguely.

"Maybe someday." That's a perfect road fever phrase because it pries open the trap of a commitment to a specific date. It evokes an unhampered expanse of future in the same way a fairy tale evokes the past with "Once upon a time." When my friend says, "Maybe someday," he's really saying, "I refuse to make promises that don't take my wishes into account, and I will no longer be guided by schedules that don't suit who I am."

**You might think you're not quite that reckless.**

Perhaps you've created a variation on the "Farewell, maybe forever," kind of road fever. You've thought ahead and know you'll have to come back someday, and you've created some kind of fallback plan for survival after the dream is complete. You're realistic enough to know that on your return, life will be no better than what you have now, but you tell yourself that if you can just live your big dream to the limit, just once while you're still young enough to enjoy it, then you'll be willing to come home and continue your dreary, dreamless routine once again.

This looks so much more responsible: Sail away while you're robust and full of adventure and still a bit sexy and courageous. Have yourself a magnificent blast of adventure and then come back and face your inevitable decline into stodgy old age with no more adventure in it consoled by a treasure chest full of photographs sitting in your rocker and dreaming of the good times in your past.

*But there's nothing realistic about that plan at all.* For all its responsible-looking details, it's just as big an illusion as the first form of road fever. Look closely, and you'll see the negotiations of an unhappy child, bargaining a swap he'll never be able to deliver: "Just let me go to the circus this one time and I promise I'll never ask for anything again."

What *is* the truth?

That you'll never consent to be miserable when you come back, and you're not going to decline into old age either. You're just going to sit down on that rocker, still exactly as robust, full of adventure, sexy, and courageous, as you are right now, and wonder what to do with the next forty years of your life.

*Anyway, what you long for may not be out there at all. You could be looking in the wrong place.*

Whenever I meet people who have actually sailed around the world, I don't see the satisfaction I expect or the dreamy, reminiscent looks. Did they feel free on their trip? Often they say yes, they suppose they did. Did they have wonderful moments? Yes, certainly. Would they want to do it again? Usually the answer is that they have a boat for sale.

But their escape to freedom was supposed to fix their lives permanently. Why didn't that happen?

The problem is, none of us is sure what we mean by freedom. **What has freedom meant to you?**

Freedom has always mattered to you, but through your life it meant different things. When you were a kid in school, it meant the semester was over. A little later it meant you could stay out late, do what you wanted, not listen to your parents. If you were in a committed relationship, freedom was what single people had that allowed them to pursue sex with anyone they wanted. Then freedom came to mean not having to answer to a boss, like those lucky people who had their own businesses or didn't have to work at all. And now, at midlife, it has come to mean the freedom to escape the daunting superstructure and dulling routine you've constructed around yourself.

"All I do is worry about staying afloat. I feel like a galley slave, rowing and rowing, without any end in sight. And every day it's the same thing: get up, go to work, come home. I feel like a machine."

"I thought I wanted all of this, big house, two cars, private schools for the kids. But now it's suffocating me. And I don't know any way to get out. I've put up with it for a long time, but for God's sake, now I'm turning forty!"

*So is that it? All you mean by freedom is that you just want to run away from responsibility?*

Yes, that's exactly what you mean, but not because you're lazy. You're willing to work like an ox in every one of your escape fantasies. You'd build a cabin by hand, or stay up all night sailing, or go around the world on foot. It isn't hard work you hate. But the responsibilities you carry have done something far more damaging to your ability to love your life. They have focused all your thoughts on day-to-day survival. The dulling routine of your days has stolen away something precious that once made life worth living.

But is it the freedom to run away that was stolen? I'm not so sure.

Still, something of enormous value has disappeared, and you need to know what it is. So let's forget for a moment what you want to escape *from* and go looking for clues in what you want to escape *to*. Let's look at the destinations people set for themselves when they dream of escaping to freedom. I think we'll find some very telling clues there.

**Destinations that don't really exist.**

There is something very interesting about the destinations we pick when we have road fever. They're rarely places we're familiar with. If you've visited Honolulu a number of times before, you never say, "I'm going to chuck it all and run away to Honolulu." It may sound exotic to someone who's never been there, but you already know better.

You're much more likely to say, "Let's go live in the mountains," or, "All I want is to just get in the car and hit the highway," "Let's take off and go around the world," "I want to go to the South Seas."

What do these destinations have in common? Well, for one

thing, they aren't concrete. They don't have an airport. They're remote and hazily defined and unfamiliar. Don't believe me? Find a map and point to "the mountains" or "the highway." Or call your travel agent and ask her to book a ticket to "the South Seas." Indeed, the appeal of these destinations lies in their haziness. Something about the fact that they're mysterious and exotic and remote, even unreachable, is trying to tell us something. We're hot on the trail of something very important.

Let's track it by taking a little side trip into the very special world of travel literature. Travel writers are the specialists par excellence at waking up our deepest fantasies of escape. They know all about destinations that don't exist.

**Journey to remotest High Tartary.**

Look in any bookstore or library, and you'll see evidence of the latest upsurge in the popularity of travel literature. The number of books written by travelers about their journeys to distant places is surprisingly large, and new books appear regularly. Travel writers know how to spirit us away into remote worlds and often remote times as well. You might say novels do the same, but there's a telling difference: We accept travel literature as truth. It makes us believe we can march out today and buy a plane ticket to the place we're reading about. And how we long to do just that!

Rinsed of familiarity, distant places promise a new start. Shot through with all the romance, adventure, mystery, and glamour that faraway things have and nearby things lack, they draw us like a magnet. Listen to these names: Samarkand, Kathmandu, the Gobi Desert, Tibet. Or Polynesia, Tahiti, Fiji. Overtones ring out of those names that don't hover over the corner grocery store.

*But unlike travel guidebooks that direct you to museums, hotels, restaurants, and train stations, true travel literature is about places you can never quite reach.*

Although they aren't fiction, and we assume that the events described really happened, the haunting atmospheres described by travel writers, like their exotic-sounding place-names, are fantasies that by their nature can't exist. Because places aren't their names. Their names wake up our imaginations and we create our own world. Even if you can actually point to a romantic or mysterious-sounding place on any map, it won't be there when you arrive. Ask anyone who's taken the trip.

"What comes to mind when you remember Tahiti, Rich?" I asked a good friend who had been there.

"Four-dollar-a-pound bananas," he said sourly.

But unlike my honest friend, writers of travel literature are awful liars. Even when they try not to, they can't resist shooting the ordinary full of glamour. They'll present you with a faraway scene so beautiful it makes your heart ache. They'll even tell you about mosquitoes or near disasters in a way that makes them sound appealing. And you'll fall for it every time because you'd much rather hear their tales than the truth about bananas. Why? Because there's something in the feeling they awaken that reminds you of that nameless something you've lost.

Of course, there are wonderful locales that find their way into your heart and never let go. When you find such a place, you might want to visit it year after year, and the pleasure may never wear off. But when we talk of escape fantasies, we're talking about something far more elusive, something which grows only in an atmosphere of remoteness and unfamiliarity. This is the territory of the best travel writers. They know they're glamorizing reality and they sometimes even apologize for it.

Take Peter Fleming, for example, in the introduction to his 1935 book *News from Tartary*: "I have done my best . . . to describe the journey without . . . falsification, to tell what it felt like at the time, to give a true picture of a monotonous, unheroic, but strange existence. On paper it was a spectacular journey, but I have tried to reduce it to its true dimensions."

That's a very appealing admission, but don't trust him just

yet. Because an odd fact emerges when you notice the title of his book, *News from Tartary*. Where exactly is Tartary?

Well, actually it isn't anywhere. In 1935 there was no such place as Tartary. In fact, there's never been such a place. The name was coined in the West, and it meant "out there somewhere, where all the Tartars are," describing distant, unknown lands almost no one in the West had ever seen. Fleming adds a short afternote admitting that Tartary isn't strictly a geographical term and that ". . . it has come nowadays to be applied, if it is applied at all, chiefly to Sinkiang. . . ."

Then why didn't he call his book *News from Sinkiang*? Because Sinkiang is a real place and Tartary is an unreachable romance.

Travelers write books because they want to sell them, of course. But they aren't cynical opportunists. They know they can touch a special nerve in us because they have it in themselves; that's how they became travelers in the first place.

**What is that nerve they're touching?**

Here are some possibilities.

*1. Perhaps they touch a genetic longing for faraway places.*

The magic of distance and strangeness has held humans spellbound since stories were first told around hearth fires. It's possible that the yearning to see what's beyond the next hill results in mating with new people and new gene pools. It may help us discover better climates and new food sources. Maybe nature has placed a trigger in us, designed to go off when we've been in one place too long, and at such times we're unusually susceptible to tales of travel.

*2. Or maybe adventure is a gender issue.*

On our first thinking about it, memory tells us that most mountain climbers and Arctic explorers have been men, and we assume that most travel books are written by men as well, designed to appeal to the masculine love of adventure. Certainly many women will tell you that road fever is a man's issue because men appear to be wilder and more immature and hesitant to settle down. Men often agree. Garrison Keillor says that women should take over the world because they're so much better at making decisions, handling money, and running the country. Men, on the other hand, says Keillor, should be pirates. And it does seem that men feel more smothered by domesticity and are more likely to attempt pulling a home-loving woman into dangerous and uncomfortable adventures than the reverse.

But our impression is inaccurate. In front of me at this moment are books by women who traveled on foot to forbidden Tibet or into African jungles or the Rockies before there were any airplanes or automobiles, and by more contemporary American women writers who left the comfort and society of their city homes to live alone in shacks at the beach or in the woods for months or years at a time. And although I haven't counted, women authors of travel literature abound. The truth is that they always did.

No, the nerve that's being touched by travelers' tales isn't about gender.

*3. Possibly freedom is an American issue.*

Americans have a special feeling about freedom. Our ancestors originally came to this country so they would be free of oppression, and every generation since has inherited their indignation at any attempt to hamper personal freedom. Having a huge, open continent allowed them to continue to move somewhere else if their freedom was being restricted at home. Freedom is our heritage.

But that's not enough to explain road fever because Europeans, Australians, and others with no such heritage travel into foreign cultures far more than Americans do. Where an American college graduate might go overseas for a few months, they will often travel for years, come home for a while, and start all over again. Also, they habitually go to places that are far off the beaten track, especially to Americans, and they relocate permanently to foreign countries much more than we do.

Not only that, but our very wild and free American frontier films and commercials and billboard ads are copied all over the world from Greece to Japan, which shows the almost universal appeal of our tradition of refusing to take orders from anybody. The world sees our manly cowboys (their to-hell-with-danger cigarettes dangling from their lips) gallop on magnificent horses over hills that never saw a fence, free from rules, free to be wild, never control themselves or think about consequences. No, that kind of freedom isn't culturally based.

*But those ads give us a very strong clue.*

Look at them again. Heroic figures never taking orders, free to be wild and not control themselves and not think about consequences. What does that remind you of? Childhood? I think so. We were all like that once. And this may be the nerve that's being touched by our longing for distant places.

4. *We've never forgotten the special freedom of childhood, and we miss it, deeply.*

We'd love our bodies to be wild, our hearts to be carefree, our awareness of consequences to be nonexistent. As adults we're expected to tolerate ungratifying work, mortgages, and unreasonable bosses. But sometimes we feel just like a kid who doesn't want to behave itself, who wants to be wild and break free of controlling grown-ups.

The problem is, we are the grown-ups. And we already have that freedom. No one else really has any control over us. Don't believe me? You could take off every stitch of clothing and walk naked down the street right this moment, just like a little child, if you wanted to. But you probably won't. Because unlike a child, the adult inside you knows the consequences and doesn't want them. We want to forget consequences, but unfortunately we no longer can.

**Well, you're all grown up now, and that's that. Say good-bye to being a child and be sensible.**

Is that what you've been told or what you're telling yourself? *Well, nothing could be less sensible.* Of course, you can live with the fact that you can't run down the street naked. But there is something else you had when you were a child that has disappeared and this loss is something you *can't* live with.

This has nothing to do with narcissism or being the favorite. It's a completely different side of the child you once were; a side you can trust. Where your narcissistic side wants to hold you back from growing up, the adventurous, alive, curious child inside you will lead you straight into the promised land.

As Dorothy Sayers, the great mystery writer, says, " 'Except ye become as little children,' except you can wake on your fiftieth birthday with the same forward-looking excitement and interest in life that you enjoyed when you were five, 'ye cannot enter the kingdom of God.' "

You see, it wasn't simply freedom you wanted to regain, at least not the kind that lets you wander all over the world with a backpack, a toothbrush, and a candy bar.

**You long to feel the child's sense of wonder again.**

That's what travel writers know. That's why they lie to us, and that's why we love it, because they reawaken our lost sense of wonder like nothing else in the world. Names as mythical as Cathay and Tartary are just like our own phrases, *going away to sea* or *going on the road.* They wake up that delicious feeling we had when we were children and everything glistened with newness.

**But where did it go?**

From earliest infancy, when we were first gazing at this astonishing new world, we had an almost startling sense of wonder. Look at the eyes of any small child and you can see it. They're not thinking about something else; they're completely present. If they don't have something else to look at with rapt fascination, they'll look straight at you, often without the slightest self-consciousness. They are completely awake. Their feelings and their bodies are completely alive. Everything is new to them every minute. That's the way you once were.

But as you got older, the panorama of wonder narrowed down. Unless you had wonderful teachers, your natural curiosity was probably crushed under the pressure of cramming for exams and studying on a deadline. The stress of competition and the focus on being successful pulled your attention away from anything not obviously useful. And when you got a little older and had a settled pattern of living, responsibilities and routine took over the little scrap of wonder that remained.

*That's why you believe so deeply that youth is free and age is trapped.*

How free youth appears. Especially at this time in your life, younger people look so carefree. Of course, if you really remembered your own youth, you'd know perfectly well that you didn't actually feel free at all, but with hindsight you now assume that you were.

How trapped age appears. But if you think about it for a moment, reason will tell you that the responsibilities and goals that weigh you down today will probably diminish as you get older, and you'll have much more freedom.

All the same, there is enough truth in this illusion to make us pay attention.

Because although youth is shackled by its urgent drives and fears, young people often do have something quite exciting in their lives, and that is the constant feeling of possibility, the hopeful sense that something new lies ahead. And even though many older people report an unexpectedly new sensual awareness, they have often developed schedules, routines, and habits that appear rigid, even fussy to an outsider.

Unfortunately, if you have the ache to escape, chances are good that you've got the worst of both worlds. You've got youth's anxiety without its wonderful sense of possibility and you've got age's routine without its delicious sensual awareness. No wonder you want to run away to sea or try another sexual partner. You're afraid your ability to be amazed will soon be gone forever. And though you may not have known quite what to call it and can't remember when you lost it, you've been missing your joyous sense of wonder terribly. And wisely so. The longing to recover your capacity for wonder comes from the side of you that was born to learn and see, to explore and question and delight in the world around you.

**You can have it back. This is the right time.**

You see, your sense of wonder isn't gone at all. It got shoved very rudely into the background during your years of competition and drive. But it's still there, untarnished and without a sign of rust, patiently waiting for you to clear some space for it again.

**Your advanced case of Road Fever shows you're ready to do exactly that.**

Every time you ache to escape the mundane details of your grown-up life, every time you dream of faraway places, it's your hidden sense of wonder calling to you. You think that if you go somewhere remote and exotic, your senses will wake up and stay awake, and you'll never forget to smell the air and see the colors and feel the adventure of being alive. And you're convinced that the only place powerful enough to resist becoming dull and ordinary has to be so exotic and mysterious and remote that you can hardly point to an airport or a specific town.

Unfortunately, there is no place that will be endlessly new to you unless you have *already* recovered your capacity for wonder.

*But don't let that worry you.*

Running away from home may have looked like the only way to rescue yourself from dulling dailiness, but in fact, without pulling up any roots, you can recover all of your childhood sense of wonder.

Yes, I said all of it.

How? *By visiting the undiscovered countries in your own back-yard.*

Your childhood fascination with the world was strong because you were visiting a new place. You have to do that again. But you don't need to run away; you just need to stop and look around you. You don't need escape; you need to open up your senses. You need an adult-size dose of exciting thoughts, full-strength intellectual and creative stimulation. A permanent change of internal scenery.

*In other words, you need a new set of eyes.*

**You can start by taking care of unfinished business.**

You need to open up worlds of feeling and sensation you closed a long time ago, take a look at things you never dared to do, use sides of yourself you never thought to use. Your world is full of undiscovered countries, but you had to turn your back on them in order to grow up.

Now, you need to give your full support to the side of you that is rightly offended at the enormous price you paid to be a good member of society. Your restlessness is telling you that the time has come to reclaim your personality and your originality and your joy at simply being alive, to become an explorer once again, to take new paths into fresh knowledge, and to stretch your brain with new concepts and ideas and landscapes.

**You were right all along. You just had a few details wrong.**

You see, nothing could be smarter than demanding the return of your "barbarian awe." But you were trying to solve the wrong problem. You wanted to run away from home to avoid becoming "middle-aged" as if that would steal your sense of wonder. *In fact, being young had already stolen it, and your second life will allow you to get it back.* And the only way to get a new pair of eyes is to walk out of your first life and move boldly ahead into your second.

*Because the real trap is not the onset of middle age; it's the illusions of your youth.*

Those illusions drove you to focus so exclusively on what society calls the good life that you turned off your sense of beauty and wonder. (In the coming chapters I'll show you some powerful ways to recover it.) But only when you step into the real world as an individual willing to define the good life for yourself will you know what freedom is.

**So what is real freedom?**

Real freedom means the right to be who you really are. It's the freedom to go for your dreams, and to rediscover your original self that got buried under the seductions of achievement and family.

The freedom that counts is the freedom to live your life with your heart and mind and emotions wide open. The freedom to dare to keep learning. The freedom to respect and treasure your childlike sense of wonder. *This kind of freedom—and only this kind—will make you young again.*

When you have this kind of freedom, you'll find one day that you're in the middle of a fantastic adventure, and you'll realize you didn't have to go anywhere. That might require simplifying your life and lowering your expenses so you have more free time to spend with your loved ones. It might mean setting up a work-shop and becoming an inventor. Or traveling to new places wher-ever they are—on the other side of the world or in your head or in your relationships. Because real freedom is something that may not look bold to others, but to you it's a life-changing adventure. And since you are a unique individual, no one but you can say what that is.

*For one person that might mean waking up to his own feelings.*

"Feelings just weren't something I bothered with. I love my wife, and I'm often impatient with employees, but that's about it. Now I'm finding a huge range of emotions inside me, coming up more and more. I've realized that I felt incredibly alone as a kid and was too criticized, and sometimes that's why I get irritated so easily. Now I can feel that anger melting, and it's like I got my life back. And I'm laughing more; my wife could always make me smile because she's really funny, but now I crack up laughing."

*For another it might mean learning to listen to the people you love.*

"My wife and daughters always said the same thing, 'You never listen!' I never knew what they were talking about. So one day I came across a book about listening, if you can believe it, and I opened it up to a sentence that said 'Being listened to spells the difference between feeling accepted and feeling isolated.'* That's what they'd been saying over and over and I hadn't known what the hell they meant. It really killed me that I had done that to the people I love best in the world. So I went back to school in women's studies, and it has completely blown my mind. Talk about finding a new world that was right in front of you the whole time."

*And for another it might mean becoming athletic for the first time.*

"I jog around that path every morning, and on the third round I think, 'Is this really me? How did I get this strength? Was it here the whole time?' And now I'm looking at dancers, how they walk down the street. I used to think, 'Oh I could never do that,' but now I'm going to. I want to say to people, 'Love your body,' because every one of us walks around in an amazing and marvelous piece of equipment, and we forget it because we're shaped off the standard here or there. Now I think of those nerves and muscles and brain cells and joints and eyeballs, and those vocal cords and back muscles and rib cage, and I just want to say, 'Thank you, thank you, thank you.'"

*Or finding a group of creative friends.*

"It's great having these friends, always ready to show up at the last moment and bail me out of some project. So different from those proper types we used to socialize with. And it's great

---

* Michael P. Nichols, *The Lost Art of Listening*, N.Y., Guilford Press, 1995.

that they're creative, so I have to run in and help them out too. Reading the role of a murderer in a friend's screenplay, or driving a load of velvet to another friend's fashion show, or carrying cameras to some miserable location for my moviemaking friend (and getting coffee, and being an extra), or cheering from the audience as my singing friend takes her well-earned bows. It's like living in the dorm from heaven. At forty-eight!"

*Or waking up all five senses, and a few dozen more.*

You've got undiscovered universes in your own backyard.

"When I have been working late on a summer night, I like to go out and lie on the patch of grass in our back garden. This garden is a square of about twenty feet, so that to lie in it is like exposing oneself in an open box or tray. Not far below the topsoil is the London Clay, which, as Primrose Hill, humps up conspicuously at the end of the road. The humus, formed by the accumulations first of forest and then of meadow land must once have been fertile enough, but nearly a century in a back garden has exhausted it . . . the turf on which I lie is meagre and worn, quiet without buoyancy. I would not have it otherwise, for this hard ground presses against my bones and makes me agreeably conscious of my body. In bed I can sleep, here I can stay awake. . . ."*

"Instead of cooking dinner or watching TV, I went to sit by the lake. I forced myself to sit perfectly still for twenty minutes, just to see if I could do it. It was hard. I wanted to jump up every two minutes, but I didn't. And then I started hearing things! I heard a duck land in the water and a dog sniffing around the shore. And then I started seeing things! It was just getting dark, and tiny bugs started swarming just over the surface of the lake. And then everything started happening at once! Birds started swooping down for the bugs, and fish started jumping and splash-

---

* Jacquetta Hawkes, *A Land*, Boston: Beacon Press, 1951.

ing back into the water, and the wind picked up and the air got misty with little bits of water suspended, feeling so good on my face."

Does that sound familiar to you? Wide-awake, senses alive, learning and discovering how new this world is every waking moment. Full of barbarian awe.

*That's what you've been restless for.*

In the next chapters we'll discover how your load became so heavy in the first place and begin to find big chunks of time to do nothing but reawaken your sense of wonder. Nothing could be more important. In the meantime I'd like to suggest a few things you can do today to invite wonder back into your daily life. If your adult side resists, remember it was the adult who lost your sense of wonder in the first place, and put your faith in the wonder-filled child instead.

## EXERCISE 15

### *Reclaiming wonder.*

1. Today carry a sprig of fresh or dried spice like basil or rosemary in your pocket within easy reach. Whenever you hang up your phone after a business call, or look at your watch, or finish running for a train, reach into your pocket and squeeze the spice with your fingertips. Then smell its fragrance on your fingertips, and watch yourself snap back into the pleasure of wonder.

2. This moment take the palm of your hand and touch something near you, like the polished wood of your desk or the fabric of your sleeve, and pay complete attention to the sensation. See how many different surfaces you can touch without getting up from your chair. Imagine what this same experience must have been like when you were only one year old.

3. Discover how many senses respond to the atmosphere

outdoors. First sit somewhere outside or next to an open window, and close your eyes. Take in the warmth of a quiet summer day, or the bluster of winter, or the quickness of wind on a bright-cloudy day. Notice how much you know about this day without using your eyesight at all. Listen to leaves rattling or water lapping, and feel heat or cold or dampness on the skin of your arm and wind in your hair, and smell leaves burning or flowers blooming. And notice the extra awareness of quickness or calm or crispness, of hints of memory about days like this or the expectation of rain or snow or nightfall that comes from somewhere harder to name.

Once you've taken in all you can with your eyes closed, open them and look around you. Take special note of what shows you the kind of day it is; screen out other distractions. Note clouds moving, bright shadows or the absence of shadows, dawn or evening light, spring sweetness, autumn richness, winter purity.

All that belongs to you. That's what you lost and what you want back again. And now it rests in your hand. **Now you can travel the world if you like. Or you can stay home.**

When you've got your sense of wonder back, you won't let it go again. That means your whole life can be full of adventure from now on. Now you can travel to the roof of the world, or see the Great Barrier Reef, or the Antarctic if you really want to. Or you can travel through the unexplored caverns of your own soul. But you'll never have to run away from home again.

As Eric Hansen, author of *The Traveler: An American Odyssey in the Himalayas*, says, "The most precious gift to bring back from a journey is the ability to see the extraordinary in the everyday. . . ." But when you see the extraordinary in the everyday, you're always on a journey, no matter where you are.

So open those eyes of yours and look around you. You were

made for wonder. Your dreams of escape weren't a mistake. They were your initiation into becoming a world traveler, a great explorer. And turning forty wasn't just another birthday. It was the first step in your return to the wonder-filled child you really are.

Here's to many more.

## EXERCISE 16

### *Road Fever Pop Quiz*

1. What did "freedom" mean to you when you were younger? What does it mean to you now? Do you ever long for it?
2. Have you ever dreamed of running away to sea or taking to the open highway? What did you hope that would give you?
3. What would you want to take with you? What would you want to leave behind?
4. What do you imagine would change about you if you went to a new place?
5. When was the last time you felt as wide-awake to your environment as a small child does?
6. What would it take for your life to become an adventure?

# 9
# Power

"One reason I go at this pace is the challenge of it.
Every time I get through some huge pile of work,
I think 'Can I do more? Can I crank up the pace?
How good am I?' "
Richard, management consultant, forty-two years old

"Sometimes I feel so overwhelmed from this impossible
load that I could collapse. But other times, when I've
just pulled off something miraculous, I whisper Yes!
and feel like Wonder Woman!"
Isabel, advertising executive, single mother

". . . Busy, busy, busy we pass the days of our lives—
gone all too soon. Gone before we get to our dreams of
creative expression, self-fulfillment, nurturing."
Carol Orsborn, *Enough Is Enough*

"He who rides a tiger is afraid to dismount."
Chinese proverb

*Do you find yourself racing to put out fires, taking on new obligations when you can hardly handle the ones you have? You might have a lot of logical reasons for pulling such a heavy load, but there's a another force operating you might not be aware of, and reason has no part in it. I call this force the illusion of power. And as you're about to see, it shows up in places you'd never even suspect.*

*You may not have noticed, but everything we've been talking about so far in this book has been about the illusion of power. Each chapter has been about the shock midlife has dealt to your system and the threat it poses to the belief each of us secretly holds inside us: that we are special and shouldn't have to accept any limitations. We believe that truly special people can do anything they set their minds to. If they can't, they aren't special.*

*The campaigns we've launched—eating vitamins so we'll never* die, coloring our hair so we won't become old, testing to see if we're still desirable or fighting to hang on to high status—have all been power struggles with reality. Every one of us tries to control reality from the day we're born, and all the cultures on earth have been behind the effort every step of the way. That's the reason we have schools and oracles and psychics, kitchen and forest gods, car races and arm wrestling and speed contests. How strong are we? How much power do we have? What can we do to get more power? Can we make even the impossible come out our way if we're clever enough, if we throw a massive effort against the obstacle, believe in ourselves? You'd think that these illusions would have diminished year by year as we grew up and that we'd know better by now. But in fact, most of them are intact, saved and hidden away like treasures from the invasion of reality, ready to bring out and use whenever we need them.

Plain and simple, we can't bear to be reasonable about how much we can do.

Of course it's good to be strong, to be able to handle tough situations, to take care of ourselves and our families, and to get the most out of life. There's nothing wrong with that. But we never say, "Enough. That's all I can carry." Instead we throw our shoulders against impossible loads and brush away any creeping doubts about our strength as if they were enemies. The result: Rising to the next crisis has become our way of life.

But humans aren't designed to live in a constant state of emergency. It's like using an ambulance to haul rocks every day, and it will have the same result: One day the machinery is going to break down. It may take a disaster to prove it to you, or you may be lucky enough to wake up on your own, but one way or the other, sooner or later, reality strikes.

And then you'll see the truth: You are not a god, just a human who has created a life that is simply too big to handle.

But to actually change your pattern takes more than simply being aware of it. You won't be able to slow down until you go to the root of *your illusion of power and find out what actually drives you to keep testing yourself against the impossible. The cause is not at all obvious, but here's a clue: If you're like most of us, you're holding down some seemingly unrelated feelings with all your might, and it is these feelings that are secretly causing the alarm. You'll learn more about that in a moment.*

*Here's the good news: Once you see what's really driving you, it's not at all hard to change. And the payoff is simply huge. Your stress will melt, your head will become clear, and you'll become far more efficient. But the best part is that your days will become so unexpectedly delicious you'll never want to fall for the illusion of power again. When that happens, you'll find you've just stepped over the line into your second life.*

---

**Did you ever wonder why we're all so scared at interviews, auditions, first dates?** You might assume that we fear rejection, but if we were sure of rejection, we probably wouldn't be so scared. We'd give up and relax. No, the reason we're afraid is that we're sure that somewhere inside us we have the power to make really important things come out our way, but we're not sure how. We don't expect to have the kind of power Mussolini or Genghis Khan had, but we hang on to the conviction that if we paid attention and made all the right moves, we could make almost anything go our way.

While we need to give important things our best effort, we don't have that kind of power at all, and we never did. We can't make anyone like us, for example, in an audition or at an interview. We can be professional and agreeable, develop our talent, and show it to the fullest, but other people will base their decisions about us on all kinds of things, many of which are totally out of our hands. *They* can't even make themselves like us. A casting director might need a short blond and you're a tall brunette; an interviewer might want someone with different experience. No amount of talent and competence can affect that.

*We can't stand that kind of thinking.* When we want something badly enough, to be told we can't control the outcome is simply intolerable. So we try to influence fate. We cross our fingers or wear lucky pieces of clothing. We walk in the left door instead of the right. We check to see if Mercury is retrograde.

If we get what we want, it proves that we had the right formula, and our will has triumphed. We have the power to be fate's favorite after all. However, if we don't get what we want, it doesn't prove the opposite. We just decide we didn't use the right ritual, and we have to figure out how to get it right next time. As childish as this may seem, it's hard to let go of it completely, and for the most part that's all right. This kind of "primitive magic" makes us feel the world makes sense and can calm us down when we're too anxious.

Unfortunately, most of our magic creates more anxiety in us, not less, and can keep us from living good lives. You'd be surprised what form some of these magic charms take: positive thinking, perfectionism, blame, shame, even some forms of regret. They're all designed to tackle our feelings of being overwhelmed because we're convinced we should be able to do anything. One of my favorite examples of magic is that staple of modern existence, the to-do list, and we're going to do some interesting work with to-do lists later.

Of course, keeping a list of what you have to do is usually a great idea and, for most of us, necessary by the time we're forty. At this point most of us have so many responsibilities we need help keeping track of it all. Many people have what adds up to two or three full-time jobs, all the obligations of a family (sometimes two families!), and possibly aging parents to take care of as well. Even those who have no such responsibilities are working double time trying to stay in shape and look good, shopping and entertaining and socializing at the right places, spending many lunch and dinner dates trying to find good mates so they can get married and have children. And if their careers have been derailed, they're working hard to get them back on track. They don't dare stop putting in the endless effort those goals require, and they're driven by the constant sense that they could and should be doing even more.

If that's you, forget self-fulfillment. You'd be happy to get some sleep. (You might even have trouble sleeping because you have so much on your mind.) But you don't dare think for a moment that you won't be able to do everything you've committed to. It feels as if your survival is at stake if you can't continue to carry the load you've hoisted onto your shoulders.

**When did we develop the illusion of power?**

Think back to the earliest age you could possibly have felt overwhelmed or stressed out because you had to do things you didn't know how to do. You might find yourself going back further than you expected, to kindergarten or earlier, to the child's shock of first having to remember things everyone was telling you—never do this, always do that—or they'd be mad at you.

But maybe you don't have to go back that far at all. Just think back to your entrance into high school or college. After the first shock of suddenly having term papers and exam deadlines flying at you, you turned into a worried person. That's where those nightmares come from, the ones in which you're hiding behind a door because you forgot to wear clothes to school or you discover to your horror that you've got to take an exam for a class you forgot to attend.

Remember your first days at a job? You wanted to pitch right in, make a good impression, but you didn't understand exactly what you were supposed to do. Your anxiety and disorientation made it impossible to get your bearings. You felt like a fraud who would soon be exposed and humiliated.

Of course, you've outgrown all that by now, right? Don't be so sure.

How did you feel last month when a new boss came in? Or last week when you first sat in front of the phone at your own business, about to make a sales call? Or the day you realized it was going to take most of your waking hours just to earn your rent, and your beloved babies were going to demand *all* your time, apparently for the rest of your natural life?

In every stage of your life, before you had much time to think about it, you started moving fast to keep up with the new demands. Getting everything done became more and more a survival issue. You may even have considered it an exciting challenge, but it was an unending challenge because there was always more to do. Living under pressure became commonplace. Being overextended seemed normal and the only way to make the best use of your opportunities. After a while you even thought you were used to it.

*But in fact, most of us never get over the shock of having too many demands to fulfill. Sometimes it can even cause near paralysis.*

"I have to send out more résumés, read more books, make more calls than I'm making. There's got to be a way to make this business succeed. But I know I'm not giving it my best, because I'm tired before I start," said George L. at a class for entrepreneurs.

"I want this business to make it, and that means I have to set up sales calls, but some mornings I just can't move. The work sits on me like an elephant," said another member of the class.

"Anyway," said Bill J., who was starting a consulting business, "even if you force yourself to call, you just don't sound right. Nobody ever buys. It's like having to climb a mountain of sand with a tribe of cannibals chasing me and with a confident smile on my face."

When you move into paralysis state, even the things you love start to look like obligations. Whatever used to nourish you dries up. Your family just represents another demand and something else to feel guilty about. The fun you used to have, the things you longed to do all fall by the wayside. The quality of your work isn't what it could be either. You're forgetting things, not taking care of details.

The myth of endless personal power is beginning to show structural cracks.

**The need to believe in your power peaks at midlife.**

"At work you think of the children you have left at home. At home, you think of the work you left unfinished. Such a struggle is unleashed within yourself. Your heart is rent," said Golda Meir.

Never before have you felt the need for your illusion of power more than now. There are two reasons for this. One, as we discussed, is that little two-year-old narcissist inside you. Because midlife is when our illusions of power are under their greatest assault, it's staging its last campaign to hang on to them. The loss of the omnipotence is a calamity to its mission of regaining its throne.

But there's reality here too. You're carrying a heavier load than you ever have before, and you really do need to be superhuman or you'll never make it.

*What may not be so apparent is that these two causes are closely related.* If it weren't for the narcissist within, your expectations of yourself might be more modest. You'd accept your limits more easily. Instead, no matter how difficult your life may already be, you push even harder and add even more demands to your life.

"Well, if that's really the best school for our kid, we'll just have to find the money to send him," Jerry told me.

"Jerry," I said, "what if you just can't do it?"

"I'll find a way. I'll have to," he said. "This school will give my kids enormous opportunities. These connections are priceless."

In fact, Jerry doesn't like his job much. It exhausts him and keeps him working long hours under very high stress. But after all, that's what they pay him for, and Jerry needs every penny.

Does it sound familiar? Have you become expert at tearing through your work and swooping in for lots of hair-raising rescues? But do you sometimes secretly worry about what could happen if you start to lose speed? If you find yourself almost boasting one day about how you keep pulling off the impossible and then the next day complaining about how much you have to do, or flying off the handle when someone lets you down or puts too much pressure on you at the wrong time, *you're pushing too hard*.

And you're not doing it only because you think it's necessary. You're testing the fantasy to reassure yourself once again that you can do the impossible.

"Remember," you tell yourself, "you can handle this. So it gets a little rough sometimes. That's the price of admission for a good life."

Inspiring talk. Unfortunately, it won't fix anything for long. It might even do harm, by supporting the fantasy that you are superhuman. That's where the magic of the to-do list comes in.

**Magic and your ten-page to-do list.**

This exercise could also be called "How to abuse being well organized." Of course, it's not only possible but common to use to-do lists in a practical way. Properly used, they're terrifically helpful. But somewhere along the line overextended people start using them as a sort of magic spell.

Here's how it works: If you have too much to do, you simply write down everything you have to do on paper. If you're using the list as it was intended, you'll list only a manageable number of tasks on your list and plan to do them. No special feeling. But if you're using the list for magic, you'll write down everything that's worrying you. And you'll immediately feel better. Then, because that felt so good, you'll add a few more chores and maybe do a soul-cleansing sweep and write down every single thing you could possibly need to do.

When you're finished, you're as satisfied as if you'd already completed the tasks.

Unfortunately, the spell doesn't last long once you start actually *doing* what's on the list. You march out intending to pick up something, return something, and fix something, all in time to be somewhere else, but instead you find that doing the smallest task takes a frustrating amount of time. At some point in the day you face this awkward revelation and give up, maybe have a drink or flip on the television and try to forget the whole thing.

But the next day, as if you lost your memory, you write another new to-do list and start using magic all over again! And magic spells have a way of multiplying because when they're ineffective, we double them and double them again.

It never works, of course. But that doesn't stop us. We keep piling on more and try harder to be better organized. And we paint ourselves into a corner. But to stop would mean we can't have it all.

*"But I love everything I do. I don't want to give anything up."*

Maureen spends most of the week working late into the night at a high-powered, time-consuming job, so she wants to spend every waking moment with her husband and children on weekends. But what she doesn't remember is that her weekends are filled with so many other activities like cooking and entertaining—"Which I love to do!"—or shopping for wallpaper and light fixtures for the new addition to her summer cottage—"Which was my idea!"—and with other things that are "just for her," like tennis lessons and aerobics classes, that she doesn't have a spare minute to be with alone with her family.

"I'm exhausted, and practically in tears half the time. But I can't jeopardize my job. And I couldn't wait any longer to have children or I'd never have them. And I need something for myself, too. I love decorating, and I need exercise."

*What if she admitted something has to give, that she can't have it all?*

"I'd feel so deprived. I'd feel cheated."

If you assume you can *do* it all—and you have the exhaustion to show it—you believe you deserve to *have* it all. After all, you're capable of getting everything you want, and you're willing to work for it. Anything less wouldn't be fair, would it?

But this harnesses you to a wagon that gets heavier each year until either you can't pull it anymore, or worse, it collapses under its own weight.

## EXERCISE 17

### My *wishful-thinking magic to-do list.*

Find a quiet place where you can write, take a blank sheet of paper—one sheet only—and a finely sharpened pencil, and prepare to write very small.

Now, off the top of your head, write down everything you really should do this coming day. As soon as you're finished, add whatever tasks you'd *like* to do if you had the time. When you're finished, remember everything that has to be done sometime this week, like paying bills or changing the oil in the car. Then, if these aren't already on the list, add whatever other people want you to do for them. Next put down all the things you really *must* do one of these days, like organize your finances so you can afford to send the kids to school or find ways to pull in more money, or make projections of what you can expect to make in the future. Now add the things you ought to do, like understand the stock market and keep up with the financial news reports, learn business French, get in shape. And read more.

Is the paper getting full? Write smaller, and see if you can fit items in the spaces between other items or run up the side of the paper in the margins. But keep writing on the same sheet, because you're nowhere near through yet.

Now put down all the things you'd love to do for yourself one of these days, like play tennis, take that photography class, write poetry, or take a dance class or learn a new language. In addition, write in all the things a well-rounded person ought to do, like listen to music, read the newspapers, go to the theater. You probably should also study what all those vitamins really do for you, so you'll know which ones to take. Now write in all the things you believe a good person should do, like call on the needy, bake cakes for people's birthdays, volunteer for good causes.

You're not through. Write all the things you think you might like to do to have a perfectly beautiful home, like make your own holiday wreaths or cover your own furniture or learn how to bake. Add all the things you long to do, but haven't done for years, like pull out your telescope and watch the stars, write a science fiction story, restore a beautiful old car, raise orchids. Now write things you always meant to check out, like special courses for further education or unusual vacation opportunities.

Move around to the back of the paper if you need to, and write from memory a list of all the mail you intend to check out, such as credit card opportunities, frequent flier offers, insurance policies, magazines, and mail-order catalogs you don't want to throw out until you glance at them.

Did I leave anything out?

Had enough? I hope you're laughing instead of getting a splitting headache. I suggest you add anything else you can think of, then go to a copy center and have the sheet of paper enlarged as big as you can.

*Then mount this amazing work of art, frame it, and put it on your wall.*

Now let me tell you a story.

When my son was living in Italy, he had a friend named Pietro. One day Pietro was commenting on Americans and their to-do lists. He said, "You, Mateo, like all Americans, put down many things on your list, and all the day long you try very hard to do them, and you cross them off one by one. But at night, when you go to sleep, always there are some things left on your list, so you are a failure.

"I wake up, and I have only one thing on my list. Today I go to visit my friend Mateo. I take a shower and dress myself. I drink a cup of coffee. I buy a good bottle of wine and take the bus to the house of my friend. We spend a very good afternoon. We talk, perhaps we walk. At night I go home and cross this thing off my list, and when I go to sleep, I am a success."

What does Pietro know that we don't? *He knows how to live.*
**Why can't I do that?**

"Breathe deeply, start with your toes, and relax. Live in the moment. The past and future do not exist, forget them."

Good luck.

Sometime when you're in a real hurry, with deadlines hanging over your head like an executioner's ax, try sitting still for twenty minutes and meditating. Will that relax you? Well, it's supposed to, but more likely it will make you a nervous wreck. To concentrate on your breathing when you feel—correctly or not—that danger is advancing is one of the most peculiar demands on oneself I can think of. It goes against every animal instinct we have.

That's why, for most of us, stress reduction methods don't work. We can't float in an eternal present when we're worried. Our minds don't work like that. It's simply our nature to remember past losses and worry about future dangers. These responses are hardwired into us. The truth is, we've done reasonably well as a species because of worrying and remembering the past and rehearsing the future. We've been able to learn from one another things we've never experienced, to imagine events that we ourselves never saw, and to prepare ourselves for accidents that haven't happened yet. In the Stone Age, when our ancestors sat around the fire and told stories, they were teaching one another how to stay alive, where to go for the best forage, what kinds of animals—including other humans—were dangerous, and how to avoid or placate them. In this way, they built knowledge with every generation, gained strategies for survival that go far past instinct, and increased their power from generation to generation.

Of course, we're still not nearly as powerful as we wish we were.

Other events, other creatures still do as they like with us. Natural catastrophes still throw us to the ground at their whim. Floods, hurricanes, earthquakes, volcanoes, and avalanches are as powerful against us as they ever were. We call ourselves the rulers of the animal kingdom, but other creatures defeat us with stunning regularity. Which animals? Just note what's missing from any endangered species list, and you'll know what we're afraid of: viruses, microbes and germs, mosquitoes, scorpions, cockroaches, houseflies, and dangerous snakes. We'd be thrilled to endanger all of them. We've conquered lions and elephants and whales, so now we admire them enormously and want to save them, but the only people who worry about the disappearance of dangerous bears are those who live far away from them.

This history of our species translates directly to our experience as individuals. After four decades you've learned that any damn thing can happen. You've heard of people who got hit by falling rocks, caught incurable diseases, or made simple mistakes that ruined their lives. When you were a teenager, you were convinced nothing like that could ever happen to you, but as you got older, you began to see that in many ways you too were vulnerable as an infant.

Do you have private rituals, like using your left hand to open the door or refusing to give yourself some kind of treat? That's because the more helpless we feel, and the more vulnerable to danger we imagine ourselves to be, the more rituals we need to protect ourselves. It's all part of trying to control a universe that's starting to look as chancy as a roulette wheel.

But as you've seen, not everyone feels the danger all around them as we do, and that's a very interesting fact. My son's friend Pietro, for example, has only one thing on his to-do list. Why doesn't he see the world as we do, as a place where you must get control of many tasks or something bad is sure to happen? Maybe because his culture doesn't pressure him like ours does, and he doesn't want as much as we do.

*Maybe what's really got us running scared is not our fear of avalanches and microbes but our cultural training.*

Take a look at the struggles in your life. How many of them are against physical disaster? I think you'll find that what scares us day to day much more than physical disaster is the worry that our kids won't go to good enough schools, that we'll lose control of our financial balancing acts, that we'll never be as rich or power-ful as we imagined we'd be and we'll always have to struggle. Or that we won't be able to deliver what we promised our families, and we won't look good in the community or we won't look good to somebody who's important to us. And then there's the sad worry that we'll get lost in the fray and be cheated out of what we want while we struggle to avoid those dangers.

No wonder you want to pretend to yourself that you're in-vincible. If you can persuade yourself you'll somehow manage to get it all, you won't have to face what's really going on inside you.

**What's going on inside you?**

You're scared.

"That's no big discovery," you might say. "I'm scared I won't be able to do what has to be done. I'm scared I'll go broke and have to beg on the streets. Of course I'm scared."

But that's not what you're really scared of at all.

You're scared of the truth. All your life you've set your will against the world believing that if you made the right moves, you'd get everything you wanted. By midlife the truth is ines-capable: That's not how things work. Now you can see how naive you were and how little attention the universe pays to you per-sonally. You used to feel at least the *potential* for power, and now sometimes you don't even feel that anymore. *The side effect is the feeling that if the world isn't about you, it makes no sense at all. It doesn't matter how grown-up you feel, this is a very scary realization.*

You can see the fear clearly in people who need to blame somebody—the boss, the kids, the fool in the mailroom, the idiot next door—for anything that goes wrong. Why do they blame? Because if problems can be explained by someone else's screw-up, then you haven't lost all your power; everything still makes sense. You still have a chance of getting back in control. Even blaming yourself is better than feeling helpless.

"I'm so ashamed that I let my business fail," Julia, the ex-owner of a clothing business, told me.

"But your whole industry went under," I protested. "You were one of the last to close your doors. You must have been doing something right."

"Still, I should have been able to do more. A smarter person would have figured something out," she said.

"What would you have to feel if you didn't blame yourself?" I asked. "Imagine for a moment you didn't feel inadequate, didn't do anything wrong, and the business failed anyway. What would you feel?"

Her eyes widened, and tears came into them. She shuddered. "Ooh, I hate this. Scary!"

"Why?"

"I'd be totally helpless!"

"So the choice is that you're bad or you're helpless. And you'd rather choose bad, wouldn't you?"

"But why did the whole thing happen then?" she said.

"Whatever the reason, it probably didn't have much to do with you," I said.

And she started to cry sadly.

I wasn't surprised, and in fact, I was very glad for her. Because she had finally tapped into the grief that underlies all fears of helplessness.

**What you're *really* afraid might overwhelm you.**

"When I've got more to do than I can possibly handle, I feel so alone! Like I'm in trouble and someone should rescue me," said a working mother of two children.

"Sometimes I secretly feel like a lost kid, like I'm too little to do all this," said a successful businessman.

"I feel completely unprotected."

As I've found over and over when working with clients, the fear of being overwhelmed isn't about work, it's about buried emotional pain. Because when you've piled too much on your wagon and you're having trouble pulling it, you have a reaction that comes straight out of your past. Plain and simple, it's the feeling that no one wants to take care of you because no one cares enough.

That's not always obvious. It seems more logical that you're simply afraid no one will take care of you, not that someone doesn't *want* to. But imagine for a moment that you're feeling lost and someone very wise and kind puts his hand on your shoulder right now and says, "Don't worry. This isn't so bad. I'll help you out."

What did you feel?

"Tears almost came to my eyes," said Robert. "It felt like my dad was there, looking out for me."

"Did your dad always take care of you?"

"Only when I was very little. Then he couldn't do it anymore. I understand now that he was ill. At the time I thought I'd done something wrong and he didn't like me anymore."

"My father was always critical, always angry," said Julia, the woman who blamed herself for the failure of her business.

"No one ever put a hand on my shoulder and offered to help me like that. It never occurred to me until this minute that such a thing was possible. I figured I was on my own," said Lynn, a single parent of two teenagers.

*That's what you'll often find in people who make very high de-*

*mands on themselves: that they didn't feel taken care of as children.* Admitting helplessness wasn't an option; it was simply too terrifying when they were small. So they became as capable as they could at their age and made up the shortfall with fantasies of power.

That's not enough to cause the grief they're feeling, however. The grief comes from the feeling—correct or not—that no one *wanted* to take care of them. In children, that translates into the unspoken certainty that they don't deserve to be helped. True or not, when children aren't taken care of, they believe they're not loved. They don't feel merely alone; they feel unwanted and unworthy.

And at bottom, what overextended adults are really afraid will overwhelm them is a broken heart. They're afraid the pain will flood over them, and they'll drown in it.

*But that flood of pain can save them. In fact, nothing else will make stress disappear.*

**Fear isn't something you can bluff.**

You can't talk yourself out of fear; you have to go to its source and take away the danger. In this case the danger is this underlying feeling you're having, the child's feeling of grief. What's so dangerous about giving in to the feeling of grief? Well, nothing in reality, but we automatically shy away from emotional pain just as we avoid physical pain, because they feel equally threatening. But if you take some time and allow the sorrow to surface, you'll be pleasantly surprised by the outcome. You'll experience the hurt, but you won't drown or be overwhelmed at all because nothing is more natural than releasing feelings. Look at any baby, and you'll see the truth in that. And once expressed, the feeling will pass, leaving big changes in your viewpoint. Because no matter how realistically bad any situation seems, once you've let your feelings out, everything looks very different and far more manageable. You may feel the remnants of sadness for a little while, but almost immediately you'll feel calm and unafraid.

But you can't reach this calm fearlessness with adult logic. Just because you know you're more grown-up than you feel at that moment, there's no point in saying this is only a childhood feeling and can be ignored. Childhood feelings are huge, and if they're not dealt with, they can create enormous stress in you. If you try to reason yourself out of them, they'll stay as powerful as ever, and you'll have to fake self-confidence. Faking anything is exhausting.

So turn the job over to the real master of emotions, the child inside you who is having these feelings in the first place. She'll know exactly what to do.

**Let your inner kid show you how.**

Find a place where you can be alone and won't be interrupted. Then try this exercise and you'll see what I mean.

## EXERCISE 18

### *Reach in and touch a feeling.*

1. Bring on the anxiety.

Take a look at your checkbook and think about your expenses, or remember all that paper on your desk, or simply think about all the things you have to do, whichever makes you feel most overwhelmed or tense. Pay attention to what this anxiety feels like. Become conscious of its effect on you, and give it a name. Tell yourself that this is stress, this is what it feels like.

2. Now bring up the hurt.

For a few moments close your eyes and pretend you're very young and full of that same stressed feeling. Heave a deep sigh. Imagine you're a small child with responsibilities too great for you and no one to help you. Now let your feelings rise up and roll over you just as if you were a small child without inhibitions. Let your face express the feeling just as a three-year-old might. Search for the words that will bring up the most emotion: "I hurt," "I feel so unprotected," "Nobody wants to take care of me." Even "Ouch." Sigh again, and if a tear falls, all the better. It's a little scary at first, but releasing your feelings won't harm you. Remember, babies do it every day.

Keep your eyes closed for at least a full minute, and let the hurt feelings roll through you. You'll feel them rise inside you like a tide or a wave of heat. Take the palm of your hand, and press lightly on your upper chest just under your collarbone. If the hurt is centered there, a deep sigh will release it. Or touch your throat, and see if you want to let out a quiet groan. Or put your fingertips just below your eyes on either side of your nose, and if the feeling is there, you're moments away from feeling tears in your eyes.

Try to stay with any form of the hurt until it peaks and subsides. Then take in a deep breath and release it and open your eyes.

Now check out what you're feeling, paying special attention to your stress level. Has it changed?

"I don't feel the anxiety anymore. It's gone."

"I feel very calm. I'm still sad, but I don't feel worried."

"The noise in my head stopped. I didn't even know it was there, it was like water rushing by. Now it's quiet."

Now look once more at your checkbook or the pile of papers on your desk that gave you the anxiety in the first place. Does it look any different to you?

"The things on my list look like harmless facts, something to take care of, but not a threat to my life."

"I just noticed all the things on my desk that don't really need to be done. I didn't even see them before. I wasn't thinking straight."

That's right, he wasn't thinking because you can't think when you're running scared. That's why it's so important to let that hurt come out and float away.

**Are these immature adults speaking?**

Not at all. They're capable, responsible grown-ups who

pushed themselves so far that these buried childhood feelings of pain were triggered.

"I come from a worried family," Maureen said. "They always expected something terrible to happen, so they were very limited and controlled, and they got nuts if you wanted to do anything interesting. I got a scholarship to college, and they wouldn't let me go! They couldn't even explain why! The minute I was eighteen I flew out of that house and started grabbing at everything in sight: career, family, hobbies, travel, you name it. I've always been terrified that if I stopped or even slowed down, I'd be cheated again."

"I was on my own too young, I think. You just couldn't ask for help in my family. If you had a problem, their eyes glazed over, and they didn't want to hear it. Everything had to be all right," Jeff said.

"I couldn't ask for help either, because my family had it so tough I just felt sorry for them. All I could do was not be a burden and promise myself that when I grew up, I'd take care of them. Admitting I was lost would have given me a panic attack. I thought I was tough when I was five. I'm beginning to see I had to feel tough or I never would have stopped crying," Louise said.

**Those feelings must be allowed to surface.**

I wish everyone knew this, and knew how to let their feelings surface as you do now, but that's rarely the case. Instead we pack our rising feelings down with such determination you'd think they were trying to destroy us. In fact, being overwhelmed has triggered the child's emotional memories, and they're confusing the adult you now are. If they come out, they'll fly away like a summer storm and leave your reason more in charge. But in our culture people rarely see this.

"Hey, I'm a grown man," a CEO once protested to me.

"Good thing," I answered. "It takes guts to cry."

"Well, I'm not going to burst into tears in the stockroom," a saleswoman told me, almost defiantly. "Everyone will think I'm having a nervous breakdown."

The saleswoman has a point. If you start crying at work you can create any number of problems for yourself and everyone else. Instead just go into the bathroom and be alone for a minute or two. That's all it takes. You don't even have to cry; just let a wave of hurt go through you and let it subside. And heave that long sigh when you're finished.

It's a very practical thing to do. Remember it the next time you're stressed. Instead of pumping yourself up with positive thinking, or blaming someone (maybe yourself) for the mess you're in, or prioritizing your to-do list, stop for a minute and get in touch with what you're really feeling under all that hurry and worry. You'll find that it will save you an enormous amount of time in the long run by keeping you from tripping or losing your keys or forgetting something really important.

Just release your real feelings. Let them out, and watch yourself calm down. And open up too.

**Get ready for a small miracle.**

Look around you; your senses are awake. Colors are brighter, and you can hear surprisingly well.

"Every time I get emotions out and stop being scared, I can see colors and details I didn't notice before."

"I feel so serene and focused," said Ellen, a designer and dressmaker. "I could look through these fabrics forever."

*That kind of openness and focus will allow you to do the best work of your life.* And use half the energy to do it. That's not all. When you're not rushing to avoid danger, all your senses open up, and you're in touch with your environment. That increases your safety too. Your chance of having a life that runs smoothly can only increase if you're able to listen to it the way this woman listens to her family.

"When a long time passes and I hear nothing from my youngest son, that's a red flag. When I hear a lot from my oldest son, that's a cause for concern, since he is normally very self-reliant. When my husband keeps singing the same tune over and over, I know I have to confront him or our relationship will get out of whack."*

Not only that, but when you're not stressed, you'll notice immediately that your memory improves. As a result, it's not so hard to get organized, and things you dreaded doing begin to seem much more do-able.

"I felt a little better after I cried," my friend Jacques said. "Nothing radical, but the next day lots of things that seemed impossible were easy to do. Crying is powerful medicine!"

**Being calm completely changes your experience of time.**

Without anxiety driving you, all the time tangles you got caught in—the ones that made you feel rushed even when you were standing still—fall apart by themselves. You simply don't feel overwhelmed anymore, no matter what you're doing. In fact, you actually have less to do in any given moment because your mind isn't preoccupied with a sense of emergency. Whatever you're doing—walking, directing a project, or writing a report—*you have nothing to do but the task in front of you.* The clock stops acting like a terrorist and just slowly ticks away.

**You may not have found more time for yourself, but look what has happened.**

Maybe you can't cut back on your tasks yet, but when you're calm, you can simplify them, because you don't make things more complicated than they really are.

You can begin to cut your to-do list down to a realistic size. You can't make it go away yet because there's a lot to do, that's the reality. But the moment-to-moment experience of what

---

* Stephanie Allen and Carolyn A. Ziegler, *Doing It All Isn't Everything,* New Perspectives, 1993, p. 105.

you're doing changes completely because something amazing happens when your anxiety is gone.

*Every task you do feels exactly like what you should be doing.*

You start enjoying your work again. If you must drive to the store, you enjoy driving. You enjoy the weather too, whether it's rainy or cloudy, and whatever is playing on the radio. When you pick up the kids, you're not thinking about the other things you must rush to do; you enjoy their company. You don't need to control everything so tightly either.

"When I don't try so hard to control my kids, they relax and don't create trouble," a mother said.

Your senses wake up, and you actually begin to enjoy the details of what you're doing. If you're typing, you enjoy the click of the keys. If you're sewing, you have the patience to do the job right.

If you should stop feeling that calmness, it probably means you accidentally got too many things on your to-do list again and you're getting scared again. You need to tap into the sadness once again. Then you'll remember to cut your list back to a reasonable size, and when inevitable snags occur, you won't panic, you'll just stop and take the time to fix them.

*Because when the hurrying ends, time opens up.* You can hear your employees; you can hear your boss; you can even hear your own heart. And as you walk out the door on the way to another task, you can hear a child laugh, or a bird sing.

**The gift of limitations.**

The best surprise is that accepting your real limits gives you real power. Once you give up your struggle to be all-powerful, you'll have the most unexpected feeling.

Safety.

Why? Because by giving up your illusions of power and accepting your real limits, you admit that the universe is running on its axis without any help from you. It's all being taken care of. You're not a lonely, frightened, and overworked god; you're just one small, cozy piece of the whole huge dance. *That means you can quit tying up all your reserves of energy in self-protection and get on with your life*. You don't have all the power in the world, just the power you actually need.

Once you drop the burden of omnipotence, you stop being responsible for the universe, and you become responsible only for what you can actually do. You stop wasting energy on either panic or grandiosity. Now the great reserves of energy you had as a child can return to you and give the lie to any notion that getting older makes you tired.

*What makes you tired is trying to be omnipotent.*

So smile and say it right now, loud and clear: "I am only human."

Not too bad at all, is it?

**That could be the best piece of news you've ever gotten.**

At midlife, when we're most burdened, our illusions of power are becoming weaker and weaker. If we take this opportunity to admit that all our magic has failed, the harness finally falls off and we don't feel pulled anymore. And the stubborn, heartbroken child inside us finally gives up and lets us go.

All deals are off. You didn't become fate's favorite after all. Nothing turned out the way you expected. You have no explanations; nothing makes sense. But oddly enough, although there's an empty place where all the strategies used to be, you don't even feel depressed. Occasionally you feel pretty good. And being ignorant feels better than you ever could have expected.

Now you realize that while you can still sometimes comfort yourself with your magic rabbit's foot, you can't control the universe and you never really could. Something else will have to do the job—be it God or physics or the stars. But whatever force runs the show, you have to admit it's been running it for a long time without your help and will probably continue to do so.

"The more I realize the world is bigger than I am, the more I feel I belong in it," said a client of mine recently. "And the dumber I admit I am, the wiser I feel. Explain that."

It sounds like something I once heard of called wise innocence.

**Wise innocence, innocent wisdom.**

Wise innocence means you're willing to leave God's work to God and throw yourself completely into doing your own. It means you understand that setting a destination gives you only a sense of direction, not a guarantee of arriving. The wisdom of realizing you can't do everything gives you the delicious sensation that there is always enough time for anything that matters. Like curiosity, innocent wisdom gives you the humility to let the world be itself instead of forcing it into your mold. It means you live like an artist, trying to make something with a heart full of respect instead of conquest, listening while you're telling, being guided as much as leading. It means you accept the fact that you didn't invent this universe and will never be able to control it.

You're just going to have to settle for loving it.

**But does this mean you should give up on your dreams?**

If you don't really have the power to make things come out the way you want, does this mean you have to give up your big dream? Do you now settle for smaller ones? Not at all. It just means you go for dreams you truly love, not ones that are supposed to prove you're special. *It means you begin trying to be everything you can be and stop trying to be something else.*

Of course you *are* giving up the dream of having and doing it all, and that may have seemed like your big dream. But think for a moment about what you wanted. Was it to be happier moment to moment? Was it to love your family with an open and receptive heart and have the patience and comfort to show that love? Was your dream to show your children how a serene, creative adult lives his life so they'll be happy about growing up themselves?

Or did you just want to make sure they had the right schools, the right outfits, the right neighborhood, the right vacations, and a daily view of exhausted and worried parents working double time to provide all that? If that's your big dream, maybe you'd better take another look at it.

"But what about trying to help the world? Does this mean we should just give up fighting the good fight?"

Of course not. We always have to fight the greed and selfishness and shortsightedness and violence around us. But ask a seasoned gardener if weeds are inevitable, and he will tell you they are, absolutely. Does that mean he gives up? Of course not. Weeds come with the territory. Gardens are still wonderful. And you always give them your best effort, whatever the outcome.

**But why do your best if it's all a crapshoot?**

Lots of reasons. For one thing, because narcissism is diminishing, you see that there's no point in sulking just because you can't control an outcome. For another, doing less than your best isn't interesting for you. When you no longer pretend to have complete control over the outcome, your job becomes very clear: you must try your best to do 100 percent of your 50 percent—that is, your share before fate steps in—and take pleasure and pride in your work. The other 50 percent doesn't belong to you anyway.

Best of all, when you finally cut your losses and walk away from the bargaining table, the most delightful thing of all happens to you. No longer focused on dragging fate over to your corner, you fall in love. *And this time you fall in love as you never have before—with the world as it is, not as you wanted it to be.*

Because when you stop trying to be superhuman, you take the significant step over the line from the biologically programmed narcissism of your first life into the independence, consciousness, and individuality of your second life. You can compare it to stepping outside the gates of a military post with an honorable discharge tucked in your pocket. You see, once you make peace with the fact that the universe wasn't designed for you personally, you're not a good soldier in nature's army anymore. Why not? Because unlike a good soldier, you're going to choose your own battles. You can't be tricked into superhuman heroics for someone else's dream anymore. You won't want to give up the pleasure of being wide-awake and completely present ever again.

**This is the change I've been promising you from the beginning.**

Power is the final illusion of your first life. When you're ready to admit you are a human being and not a god, all the other illusions have nothing to prop them up. The narcissistic child inside you fought like a tiger but fortunately was defeated.

"Defeat strips away false values and makes you realize what you really want. It stops you from chasing butterflies and puts you to work digging gold," said William Moulton Marston.

The immortality, the eternal youth, the beauty that would bring you perfect love, and the glory of the winner's trophy were butterflies. Finally you can get down to digging gold.

Now a surprising and delightful new time is ahead. When you understand your human limitations, you're not in a hurry anymore. You're not suffering under the burden of so many responsibilities because when time slows down for you, you enjoy so many moments of each day. Now there's no desperate hurry to figure out what you want to do with that lovely life of yours because as soon as you jump off that speeding treadmill, you're already beginning to live it.

**A glimpse at your future.**

Take a moment to fantasize what your days would be like if you had absolutely no need to control every outcome. Think about it for a moment. Imagine you do your daily work to the best of your ability, but you have no intention whatever of doing more than is reasonable or of being responsible for making things come out right.

How would that feel? What would you do differently? And what would you stop doing?

Think about it for a while and enjoy the fantasy. Because one day in the not too distant future, that's the way it can be.

## EXERCISE 19

### *Power quiz*

1. Do you keep more than one to-do list (one for work, one for home, one for weekends, etc.)? Think about how many items you could cut from each list. Are there any lists you could eliminate altogether?

2. If you were only human and got tired or bored or stressed like an ordinary creature, which items would you take off your to-do lists?

3. Can you imagine living in a small village with nothing but time on your hands? Describe a fantasy day. Would you love it or get nervous?

4. Which tasks make you most anxious at work? What do you think is behind the anxiety? (Remember, anxiety is the same as fear. Go looking for the danger, real or imaginary, that's causing the anxiety.)

5. List two meetings you *don't* need to attend at work. Now come up with a speech to your superior about why you don't have to attend them. Have a junior person attend for you and take notes.

6. List two forms of self-improvement that you're not doing anyway and decide not to think about them until next year.

7. Take one of the things you'd love to do—like restore an old car or plant orchids—and schedule it for a weekend sometime in the next six weeks. Write in ink.

8. What would happen if you stopped doing your *least* favorite chores around the house? Would someone else jump in

and do them? Would the house fall apart? Would the neighbors talk?

9. Do you believe it's acceptable to be imperfect? Did you ever?

# BOOK TWO

Book Two: Reclaiming Your Original Self
Your Second Life

"To be nobody—but yourself—in a world which is doing its best, night and day, to make you everybody else—means to fight the hardest battle which any human being can fight, and never stop fighting."

e. e. cummings

"Despite psychology's reluctance to let individual fate into its field, psychology does admit that we each have our own makeup, that each of us is definitely, even defiantly, a unique individual."

James Hillman, *The Soul's Code: In Search of Character and Calling*

# 10
# The Courage to Live Your Life

"To assign unanswered letters their proper weight, to free
us from the expectations of others, to give us back to
ourselves—there lies the great, the singular power of self-
respect. Without it, one eventually discovers the final
turn of the screw: one runs away to find oneself, and
finds no one at home."
Joan Didion, "Self Respect" *Slouching Towards Bethlehem*

"I wanted all that: the time for exploration and
adventure, the passion for doing something I really cared
about, the appreciation of simpler things that contain so
much beauty."
Carol Orsborn, *Enough Is Enough*

"If you bring forth what is within you, what you bring
forth will save you. If you do not bring forth what is
within you, what you do not bring forth will destroy
you."
Jesus, according to the Gospel of Thomas

*Think for a moment. What could you do with, say, five completely
free hours a day—every day? Or three completely open days a
week, every week? Plus a few weeks or months here and there
throughout every year that were entirely yours? Imagine it: depend-
able, predictable, uninterrupted stretches of time that belong to no one
but you.*

*Did your eyes grow dreamy for a moment, like they sometimes do
when the TV screen fills up with commercials showing faraway
beaches, blue water, and palm trees? Ah, all that uncrowded space.
All that uncommitted time. Pure heaven, right? Leontyne Price agrees
when she says, "The ultimate of being successful is the luxury of giving
yourself the time to do what you want to do."*

*Of course few adults ever have that kind of time. If you're any-
where between thirty-five and sixty-five, chances are good you're so*

*overextended you'd be lucky to have one really free hour a day or one wide-open afternoon a week. Holidays and vacation time—if they exist at all—are probably spent catching up on work or family obligations. If, by a fluke, an empty afternoon or Saturday does come your way, you're probably so exhausted that you only want to rest.*

*Anyway, free time is so unusual you're not sure how to use it. You don't automatically pick up your favorite book and sit by a window, or take out your oil paints and easel, or stroll by the seashore the way people do in period movies from the turn of the century because leisure is something we hardly comprehend anymore.*

*But who you are is not a concept in the sky, and it's not a record of your accomplishments either. The most original and creative side of you can re-emerge only when you get some time of your own, free time, wide-open time, uncommitted time, time in which to go after dreams or do absolutely nothing if you choose.*

*Without it you can't have a self.*

*In theory, if you'd followed the lead of that creative brain of yours all along, you might never have lost yourself in the first place. You'd have given yourself all the time you needed, say, to write a biography of your favorite person in history, or learn Italian and live in Rome, or start your own jazz band. Or just try one thing or another, until you found out who you were. But you probably didn't do any of that because in your first forty years of life you had to choose between fulfilling your talents and fulfilling your needs, and like most people, you chose your needs.*

*But now you've turned a corner. You're ready to create your second life.*

*The time has come to reach out and take back the self that stepped aside to make room for the parent, the spouse, the wage earner, the maintenance man, the rescuer, the nurse, the warrior, and the rest of that long list of roles you took on over the years. You need to develop your own thoughts, reawaken your creativity, recover your originality, satisfy your curiosity and go after all the important things your spirit craved but you never had time for. You need to move your wishes to the top and let the wishes of a lot of other people drop down—or fall off entirely—your list of priorities.*

*That's going to take a lot of courage because if you're someone who habitually puts other people's needs before your own, you'd rather jump off a high diving board than say no to a request. But trust me, it won't be as hard as you expect, and it will get easier. As Emerson said, "The greater part of courage is having done it before."*

*And in the end, this courage is worth any discomfort because it's an investment in your own potential. With the time you gain, you'll be free to launch the top project of your second life: to become all you might have been.*

———

**"We've only got one night a week to be together, Grace. If you take that class, we'll never see each other," Jerry said.**

"But all you do is work or watch TV. We never talk about anything anyway," Grace answered.

"Oh, never mind. Do what you want," he answered angrily.

"I knew he'd make it hard," she said to me later. "But why does *he* get to do what *he* wants, and I'm some kind of monster when I do it? That's simply not fair. Why doesn't he give up something if he wants to be with me?

"I can go ahead and take the class," she continued, "but now I'll feel like such a heartless witch every time I go. Anyway, I'm not sure I really want to take that class at all. I really just wanted some time for myself. I'd like to go to a movie by myself or just sit in the backyard—all alone—and look at the sky. Forget asking for that! He'd think I was crazy."

Grace is right to be upset, but she's making a typical mistake. She's made Jerry the center of gravity, and she's trying to move around him. What would happen if she made herself the reference point? Instead of feeling controlled or guilty or smarting at injustice, what would happen if her only thought was, *What would*

229

*be the best thing for me?* No argument, no convincing, no push or pull, no blaming, no accommodation, and no rebellion. Just a simple assessment, as though she were shopping for a blouse, pulled one off the rack, held it up, and looked in a mirror to see if the color was right for her.

"Let me see. Would spending that evening with Jerry be good for me?"

The answer could be yes. If Jerry really misses her and wants to be closer, it's possible that staying home might be the best thing for her. On the other hand, if he's simply more concerned with his comfort than hers, it won't be good for either of them. In any case, she can't automatically give up her plans for his. She needs to stop being afraid of his moods.

But would that in fact make her a heartless witch? Quite the contrary. If she felt she really had the right to choose what was right for her, she'd stop complaining, stop blaming, and forget about injustice. She'd be kinder and less angry, more willing to listen with an open mind to Jerry's side of the discussion.

Of course, she'd also be much harder to manipulate.

But it's easier said than done.

Like most of us, Grace will lose the fight as soon as the bell goes off. Because if she decides to take the class, Jerry might honestly believe she is being unkind. Although he might well change his mind after a while, Grace feels so miserable the moment he starts to sulk that it's hardly worth starting the argument.

Sound familiar?

**Whose life is it anyway?**

Well, it's yours, in theory. You've got the right to live it as you choose, so long as you're not stepping on someone else's rights. But your rights don't mean much if you don't have the courage to claim them. For instance, do you always give in because it makes you feel selfish if you refuse to help someone? Do you have trouble speaking up as soon as something is unfair to you? Does conflict make you uncomfortable? Do you get a terrible feeling when someone's angry at you? Are you afraid people will dislike you if you're not cooperative?

If you said yes to any of those questions, one thing is obvious: You're trying to earn your right to exist. That means your life doesn't really belong to you at all.

You can forfeit your ownership of your life in many ways.

**Your life isn't yours if you're locked in conflict.**

Sometimes you're so preoccupied with a battle, real or imaginary, you can't even consider doing what you really want. Kevin is a salesman who hates his job. His real love is to study and write history, but he says his wife stands in the way because she's completely unsympathetic. Every time he opens a book, she reminds him that he should be out making sales calls. He gets so resentful he can't concentrate on his books even when she's not around. Of course she's partly right because he neglects his job out of the same resentment.

"If I put down my books and really try to make money, I feel like she wins!" he said.

Janice works with her second husband, Mark, organizing his office, but what she really wants is to start her own accounting business. Mark is a good man but often stressed and angry and quick to criticize. Janice is afraid to get her CPA certificate and go after her own clients because she knows he'll be very upset.

"I give him his way all the time because I don't want any problems," she said. "The hassle isn't worth it."

Janice isn't afraid of Mark's anger; she's afraid of her own. This is her second marriage, and she's afraid that if she gets angry, she'll want to leave it.

**Your life isn't yours if you waste it complaining.**

Complaining seems to have a life of its own, divorced from any intention of actual improvement. Most of the time it's more like a litany or a chant than any expectation of change.

"My husband plays golf all day on the weekends and just

leaves me there on my own. We work together during the week, but on the weekends he's got the right to do just whatever he wants. He sure treats himself well."

"You kids never help me when I ask you, but I always help you with your homework and everything else too."

"When I first came to work here, the assistant was in charge of all those details and I was in design. Now I'm here until ten at night working because somehow I'm doing all the details too. And the assistant takes a nice long lunch every day."

Empty talk. *The complaints are valid, of course, but nothing will come of them because chronic complaining is a substitute for action.* You may announce to the whole world how unfairly you're being treated, but since you can't bring yourself to do anything about it, your complaining never stops and nothing ever changes.

Sometimes it almost seems as if we're bragging about how much we tolerate. We say, "Look how hard my life is. See how much I work. Other people are bad to me," but what we really mean is *"I'm a good person."*

Don't believe me?

Check out your feelings carefully, and chances are you'll find that you're proud of being a better person than your exploiters.

"I would never treat anyone that way," you think. And you're probably right. Of course you shouldn't let anyone treat *you* that way either, but you're not working on being treated well; you're on a continuing mission to be the most unselfish person alive. When that's the case, some part of you gets satisfaction from the contrast between your behavior and theirs. You may even get pleasure out of giving in to the most outrageous demands. It legitimizes the pain you feel from their selfishness, by elevating you to the status of a saint or a martyr.

**Your life isn't your own if you fear free time.**

"There's no point in finding free time. I used to think I'd sit and relax and finally read all the books on my bookshelf and just be good to myself. But I get so antsy and lonely when I'm on my own, I don't do any of that. I wind up inventing chores and can't wait to get back to start work again," said Eileen, a bank officer.

"I've actually spent months on unemployment just so I'd have time to paint, and all I did was hate it. There it was, all the time I needed, but I couldn't paint. I'd walk around the apartment for a while and then just run out the door and do something, anything!" said Kelley, a gifted painter who rarely paints anymore. Free time is so uncomfortable for her that she's gone back to work and stays late every night. On weekends she's busy helping friends, deeply concerned with the slightest problems of people who aren't at all concerned about her desire to paint.

**Your life isn't yours if you accommodate selfish people.**

As infants we all start out as narcissists, but most of us eventually develop a sense of fairness and some concern for the rights of others. There's a class of people, however, who never grow up and who have no idea why they should. I call them "people who eat people."

They have no problem turning down requests for help because their first thought is "Why should I have to do that?" It never occurs to them they should give back as much as they take because they feel they're not like other people. Anyway, they have a hard time imagining that other people actually have feelings or needs or plans as valuable as their own. Like small children, they flatter and charm and make promises to get what they want and are outraged if they're not given their way. Their efforts on their own behalf are impressive: They'll create a complete philosophy to convince you (and themselves) that anyone who withholds anything from them is disloyal or dishonest or wants nothing but to injure them. When they have a problem, they sigh and look unhappy—where you can see them. Narcissists rarely waste time suffering in private.

They're people who have turned two-year-old self-centeredness into a profession.

*The fascinating thing, however, is not these childish tyrants; it's the people who become their caretakers.*

If you're someone who has trouble saying no, they can play you like a fiddle. You may know how unfair your situation is; you probably even protest from time to time, trying to make them understand the unfairness. If you do, their responses stun you with callousness. You complain to friends, not realizing that they usually see the setup far more clearly than you do and are horrified that you capitulate to such a person. Often they say as much. But you never listen to their advice because what you really want is for the selfish person to understand how bad he's making you feel.

What a strange thing to want from a narcissist! Unlike you, who care too much about the feelings of others, narcissists don't care enough. If you even consider arguing with them about fairness, you've already lost, because they see life as a war of survival, and they're always combat-ready. Expecting fairness from them is like expecting the opposing team in football to give you the ball out of the goodness of their hearts. The absurdity would be funny if it weren't so destructive to your life.

**Guess what? You just outgrew every one of those time wasters.**

If you identify with any of the people above, you're eating up your precious time, and the waste just became too extravagant. If you believe that you only live once, your "good person" badge is looking more and more like a booby prize every day because it takes you away from doing what really matters to you.

If you weren't tied up in these unproductive conflicts—both inside you and outside—and if you claimed the right to do what's best for you, some very big changes would happen in your life. For one, you might be relaxed enough to let your originality emerge and develop your unused talents. And then you might do something extraordinary.

But it takes time to develop talent. Where will you get that time?

**One way is just to take it. Outrageously.**

### EXERCISE 20

*Outrageous fantasies*

Here's a very easy exercise for you; all you need to do is read the following section and notice your reaction.

First, think about all your maintenance and social obligations, and find the ones that don't give you enormous pleasure every time. Now imagine you make announcements to all the people concerned—not apologetically, just blurting it out any old way—that you're going to stop doing all of them.

"I don't think I'll do any more ironing. Maybe I'll take up piano instead."

"I'd really like to help buy fences for the garden, Rick, but I think I'll use the money to go to Mongolia. I understand they're having a full eclipse there in the spring. Save your money, and you can come too, if you like."

"Gee, it's no fun for me to loan you my car. I'm sure you can understand."

If you really did it, you'd definitely get their attention. You might surprise them so much they'll be too stunned to respond. You could call it a preemptive strike. Picture this.

You calmly tell everyone that you've decided to stop all the dinners and parties and gift giving. "You know, it's just so time-consuming."

You're very serene about the whole thing because no one takes a shouter seriously. (If you ever want to startle anyone, say something outrageous in a calm, friendly voice.)

Now imagine you've moved it to the next level. You're talking with friends and you say, "Oh, thanks for the invitation, but I only go to weddings."

Or, "I never send thank-you notes anymore. I never really enjoyed doing that."

Or, "Mercy, I had no idea I was this opinionated."

Or, "Oh, I'm such a grouch you should just expect bad behavior from me."

And if anyone gasps, "You can't just do that!" you can always agree enthusiastically by saying, "I know. Since I turned forty, I just do any old thing. I'm really bad news."

That's the fantasy. Now, what did you feel?

If you typically have a hard time standing up for yourself, it should have made you laugh, and that's very good for you. But that laugh also reveals how hard you've been working to avoid being called a selfish or thoughtless person. That's why it should have been an interesting feeling to say something like "I know. I'm really bad news." Imagine throwing away all that goodness you've been clutching. Even fantasizing that kind of release can be a revelation.

It exposes the potential disaster for what it is: nothing. People will disapprove for a while, but you might discover that disapproval doesn't bother you as much as it used to.

Of course you should always remember that if fixing your home and making Thanksgiving dinners and visiting family and buying gifts give you your greatest pleasure, you are an artist at these things and shouldn't consider giving them up. But for most people, competitive celebrating and gift giving, like competitive dressing, housekeeping and cooking are for people under forty who still think they're immortal and have endless time to waste. You know better.

But you need some warm-up exercises and a little practice if you're going to change.

Here's a project I'd like to see you really put into action, not just in fantasy. It may seem extreme, but the purpose is to clear a wide area and then replace whatever is essential.

## EXERCISE 21

*Two-week unannounced strike in goods and services.*

Give up doing the following things for two weeks: answering the phone every time it rings instead of screening your calls, returning every message, answering every letter, buying gifts and going to most birthdays/weddings/bar mitzvahs/confirmations, doing favors you wish you could get out of, having houseguests, picking up cleaning, groceries, hardware parts, videos, or anything else that can be delivered or sent for, shopping for clothes, watching the news, reading the paper and everything else that comes in the mail, checking out the Internet every night in case you miss something, watching TV, fixing the screen door, organizing your photos.

That would give you a lot more time, wouldn't it?

You don't even need to make an announcement. Just stop doing anything you don't want to do. Become absentminded and unpredictable. Forget to pick up things you promised to get for people. Forget to bring gifts to birthday parties. Be a bad problem solver. Give lousy advice, and become inept at consoling people who are chronically unhappy.

People will grumble, then they'll worry (tell them you're pretty sure you're having a midlife crisis), and then they'll do the important stuff themselves—or find another sucker. You'll have a few weeks or a month to learn what will get you into trouble, and in the meantime you'll see which chores get picked up by someone else and which are totally irrelevant.

*Remember, you can always do what you really have to do. That's never the problem.* But you must sort it out from what you don't really have to do, and it's going to take a little while for you to understand the difference. But it could be one of the most important things you ever learn.

**Are you feeling sick to your stomach yet?**

"I'm having an anxiety attack," one woman laughed. "I'm certain someone will shoot me or carry me off to jail!"

"I'd be afraid everyone would hate me if I stopped helping them every time they asked, and they'd never call me anymore," confessed a kindly man.

"Even thinking that way makes me uneasy. I'd never actually have the nerve to do it!" said a woman. "Besides, what about other obligations, like reading the paper and keeping up with the news. You can't neglect them, can you?"

Sure you can, if you feel like it.

"But what if everyone did that?"

Don't worry, everyone won't. The question is, could you?

What about helping people? You don't want to stop that entirely, and I don't blame you. But there's a right way to do it.

**Be good only to the good people.**

People who think it's our duty to rescue selfish or unkind people might not go along with me on this one, but I happen to believe self-sacrifice is a sin and a waste of God-given gifts. *Wasting our gifts is one right I don't believe we have.* Not only that, but guilt is not the same as love. Don't fool yourself. It isn't even good for the other guy because when bad behavior has no bad consequences, selfish and unkind people learn nothing. Withholding generosity from selfish people and extending it to good people are acts of courage and integrity.

But if you really want to come through for someone deserving, you should do it. Not because you're interested in a good epitaph—"She was the nicest person who ever lived"—but because you enjoy helping people you respect and care for, and you like letting them know they can depend on you. Not only are they the ones who deserve it most (they're usually kind to others as well), but they typically get very little help *because they're not manipulators.*

"My friend was making a movie, all his own money, a great

unselfish guy, and talented too. And whenever he needed something, I got the biggest kick out of coming through for him. As a matter of fact, I even resented other people who let him down. Everybody should have helped him. You know why? He'd help other people in a minute. And he's no user. I wouldn't give a user the time of day," said a client.

And you shouldn't either. Ever again. Save your generosity for good people, and you'll save lots of time for yourself.

Now, where can we carve out some more free time for you? **What would happen if you handed off some of your work to someone else?**

Don't say, "Who else? There's only me to do all this." Just hire a part-time personal assistant.

*Yes, that's what I said.* Call the local school, and ask for the most responsible, well-organized student it can recommend and hire him. It's time you stopped wasting precious time on things someone else could do. Imagine having a box on a table with your assistant's name on it; you look through your mail and toss half in the box and the other half in the wastebasket and forget about it. Once you've lowered other people's expectations of you, you might need an assistant for only five hours a week.

"But it would cost a lot of money, and anyway, no one ever does it right, you always have to do everything yourself, and besides, my mother—or somebody's mother—would disapprove and think I was very lazy."

Yes, it would cost money. But less than you might imagine, and you might be able to cut out some other expense or even get a part-time job and give your money to a housekeeper, bookkeeper, or part-time personal assistant—anyone who can help you free up time.

"But that would use up the same amount of time!" you might say.

Believe me, in the end an assistant will save you more time than you can imagine.

"I started to notice how much time I used up *worrying* about what I had to do, aside from the time it actually took to do it!" said a working mother. "My mind was never free."

By having an untroubled mind, you gain a lot more time than the actual minutes or hours your chores would use up. Worry is an enormous waste of time: worry about dust balls under the bed, bills that need to be paid, broken toasters that should be returned.

But what if the following things were off your mind forever: cleaning house, doing the laundry, paying the bills, keeping the books, sending thank-you notes, going to the post office, answering mail and phone calls, arranging travel plans and appointments, telling people you're not at home, taking your name off junk mail lists, handling mistakes from the credit card companies and the phone companies and the insurance companies, waiting for repairmen to show up, sitting on hold on the telephone, returning things you bought, taking broken things to be repaired, even escorting out-of-town visitors around town.

*Now that would give you some time, wouldn't it?*

What if no one does it as well as you do? So what? Shop until you find someone who does it well enough, and then forget it. They're not perfect? So what? I hope for your sake that you aren't trying to be perfect either. Otherwise you're throwing away precious time you could be using a hundred times better.

## EXERCISE 22

### *Your "don't-do" list.*

Keep a notepad and pencil with you as you go through the next week or so, and every time you come to an activity that someone else could do—or that doesn't really need doing at all—write it down. If you're not good at deciding what's really essential—and you probably aren't—try imagining for a moment that you fell sick and could do only the most essential things. Or imagine you're a movie star or a millionaire and you just don't happen to feel like doing anything *because you don't have to.*

That will help you draw up your list of inessentials and have some outrageous fun just imagining them gone. But you won't actually have the courage to stop what's on that list, will you? No, not until you uncover what's hiding under all that guilt.

Let's bring it out into the daylight. Try this experiment.

## EXERCISE 23

*Make a six-week standing appointment with yourself.*

1. Get a pencil and small notebook, and on the inside front cover write down an amount of time, at least three hours long, that you intend to make your own for the next six weeks, such as "Wednesday evenings, 6 to 9:30 P.M."

2. Then, on the first sheet of blank paper, write down the names of people who need to know about your decision, and plan to tell them as soon as you can.

3. Pay careful attention to what you feel as you do these steps. Are you scared? Nervous? Guilty? Keep a log of your feelings.

4. Now, with notebook and pencil in hand, speak to everyone on your list. Talk to them one by one, and tell them that you'll be using that time for your own purposes and won't be available to help anyone. If you're on the phone, write down their responses as they speak. Otherwise wait until you're alone, and then write down what they said in your notebook. Follow it with a description of how the conversation made you feel.

5. *Now, for six weeks, take that time for yourself.* It doesn't matter how you use it except it must never be used to do any chores for yourself or anyone else, including your boss or your dog. You can go to the movies, but don't pick up the laundry on the way home. You can sit by a window

and listen to music, but turn off the phone. You're not on call for this period of time.

Pay careful attention to what happens as a result. Do events such as emergencies or unexpected occurrences conspire to take your time away? Or do other people think their desires are emergencies and try to make you help them?

Or do you prevent yourself from taking the time, sneaking in a few chores just because you have no other time to do them? Or because you're feeling selfish or bored?

*Remember, this isn't a test; it's pure research. You won't be graded on your success or your failure.* Your goal is simply to become conscious of any obstacles to taking free time. You're not really trained to actually take your own time yet; you're just checking out the territory.

Here's what most people found:

"I couldn't stand it! I felt so guilty and selfish!"

"I was as scared as if I'd stolen something!"

"I kept feeling like everything would fall apart without me."

What about you? Did you find something similar about yourself? If you're like most of us, you'll be amazed how hard it is to take time for yourself without any kind of justification.

**For some odd reason, not everyone has this problem.**

"What will people say?"

"Am I allowed to do that?"

"Who will do take care of everything if I don't?"

Common questions. But I can't imagine them being asked by Albert Einstein, James Joyce, Isaac Asimov, Dervla Murphy (who bicycled with her young daughter all over the world), Anaïs Nin, or Edith Wharton, can you?

"Well," you might say, "the first three are men: that explains that." Or does it? James Joyce often watched his small children and wrote while his wife went off to work. True, it's said he didn't run a shipshape household, but so what? He wrote *Ulysses*.

Yes, society usually encourages men to develop their abilities more than women, and studies show that from an early age they're encouraged to think more independently than women. But in the end most men end up answering to the authority of other men and using their time to work for the survival of themselves and their families just like women do. We may see inequities in the household and in the paycheck, but in fact, men rarely use their time to develop their talents either.

"All right," you may reply, "but look at how many of those famous, accomplished people were wealthy! Edith Wharton was surrounded by servants, for heaven's sake." Maybe so, but she still had to fight like a tiger to avoid the social chores that drown most wealthy society people. Georgia O'Keeffe and Anaïs Nin weren't wealthy. And Dervla Murphy managed to travel the world and find time to write books with money she earned herself.

Well, they were special, and special privileges are given to extraordinarily talented people like Einstein and James Joyce, right? Take another look, and you'll see that you might have it backwards. Not one of the people I mentioned was a child prodigy like Mozart, whose father cleared everything out of his path to open up every minute for his musical talent. Einstein was a patent clerk, and Joyce an underpaid teacher. But somewhere they got the notion that what they wanted was important. Somehow they felt they had the right to their own time. So they took it.

*And it was that time that allowed them to develop their talents and show the world they were special.*

**They had the right to their own time.**

It's said that Charles de Gaulle never answered the phone. "If I wanted to talk to someone, I would have called them," he said.

And there's a scene in a Mae West film where she comes into the office of a rude, cigar-smoking bully who's on a phone call. When he motions to her to sit down until he finishes, in perfect Mae West fashion she answers, "I'll sit *down* when I'm through standing *up*."

You might find these examples extreme and never expect to do them yourself, but outrageous people have cleared a huge space in which we can launch smaller rebellions. We can imitate them or not, as we choose, but we have to let ourselves grin when we think about their colossal nerve because that grin is the beginning of the cure for time bondage.

Annie Dillard put time priorities nicely: "I don't do housework. Life is too short. . . . If you want to take a year off to write a book, you have to *take* that year, or the year will take you by the hair and pull you toward the grave. Let the grass die. . . . There are all kinds of ways to live. You can take your choice. You can keep a tidy house, and when St. Peter asks you what you did with your life, you can say, I kept a tidy house. I made my own cheese balls."

Secretly afraid someone will think you're lazy? I challenge you to picture Margaret Thatcher or Madonna or Margaret Mead worrying about being called lazy. Can you do it? I can't.

*If they're so comfortable, why are you so guilty?*

There are various personal reasons, depending on your particular upbringing. Maybe you were taught that you always came second. If you had parents who were so self-centered that they felt you were born to give them attention, every time you neglected their wishes, you were, by definition, selfish. Or if you had an unhappy parent, for whatever reason, you might have felt, as most children do, that you'd done something wrong, and you've mistakenly been trying to make up for your guilt ever since.

But you have another reason for feeling guilty and bad, and this one is real.

**You're hiding anger.**

How does it make a person feel to have no rights, to consistently give more than she receives, to feel she needs to earn the right to exist over and over again?

*This makes a person very angry.* But good people like you aren't supposed to be angry; they're loving and generous and self-less. That's why you spend a lot of energy keeping that anger suppressed. You're ashamed because someone might guess it's there (often that someone is you!), and you're terrified that it would do terrible damage if you let it out.

You could be right. As Ambrose Bierce said, "Speak when you are angry and you will make the best speech you will ever regret."

That kind of anger, held down since childhood and constantly added to, makes a big explosion when it's suddenly released. The explosion is intimidating and coercive to others and can often be destructive. Because it's mixed with real hurt, it makes you as dangerous as a lion with a thorn in its paw. You can sense that in advance. In fact, the weaker you are, the more dangerous you feel. This shows itself by the odd feeling in the least aggressive people that if they speak up in their own behalf, they'll destroy someone.

It's even at the bottom of the feeling of cowardice we have when confronted by a bully. Weakness may be what you feel when someone pushes you around, but in fact, you might actually be afraid of losing control of your own rage. If you got all that backed-up anger down to a normal level, you'd be calmer and feel stronger. Bullies probably wouldn't bother with you in the first place.

Why don't we express our anger while it's still small, so it doesn't build up to such an unwieldy level? Because of an overwhelming dread of being hated, *a dread so huge and irrational you can be sure it came from your childhood.*

"I remember when I was around nine years old, we were supposed to stop playing and come in the house as soon as the streetlights went on. One time I saw they were on and told my friends I had to hurry home or I'd be in big trouble. One of them said, 'What's the big deal? So your folks will smack you, and it'll be over.' And I thought, 'Is that all he has to worry about? Just getting hit?' I was afraid of something so terrible I couldn't even figure out what it was," a woman told me. "Later I realized what the terrible thing was. It was the look of distaste, even disgust in my mother's eyes whenever I did something she didn't like. I couldn't bear that look. I could see how she felt about me, and it made me want to die."

"It was simply out of the question to have any feelings but positive ones in my house. It was simply not done," a client said.

"My brother was always sick, and my parents had it so hard I never felt I had the right to be angry at anything," another client told me.

"My family was so angry that if you showed a flicker of anger, World War Three would have started," said another.

You see, you have to feel very safe as a child to risk being angry. If you don't feel safe, you don't make demands, and you don't defend yourself. And when you grow up, that behavior simply continues.

**How to stop being afraid of that childhood injury.**

You can bring that anger level down in a way that causes no damage to your relationships at all. Here's a technique you can use to dispel that uncomfortable mix of anger, shame, and fear. I call it the silent scream.

## EXERCISE 24

### *The silent scream.*

Find a place where you can be alone without interruption for a few minutes. This technique works best if you're lying on your back, in your bed or on the floor, but it's just as useful if you're sitting or standing. Close your eyes and sit up straight, arching your back slightly and putting your shoulders and arms back to open up your chest. Now imagine you're standing on a mountaintop or somewhere else wide open, away from the ears of everyone.

Take a deep breath, and without making a sound, imagine you are letting out a long, long scream at the top of your lungs. You might want to open your mouth wide, as if you were taking a bite out of a huge sandwich. But be very careful not to strain your throat. Let the imaginary scream come out with as little throat restriction as possible, more like a blast of heat coming out of a furnace than a sound using vocal cords.

As soon as you run out of breath, take in another long, deep breath and let out another very long silent scream. Try to do this at least three or four times, preferably more. If you make sure to go to the end of your breath each time, at some point, there will be no strength behind the screams, and you'll stop.

*As you scream, pay attention to what feeling is coming out.*

You'll find a great feeling of relief and an immediate drop in tension as you release these silent screams, but you'll get even more out of the process if you know exactly what you're feeling. Your first few silent screams might be just a warm-up, a way of putting your toe in the water to see how cold it is. After all, you haven't screamed at the top of your lungs, even in your imagination, since you were a tiny infant. But after a few tries you could find yourself arching your back even more, putting your arms back, making fists, and hearing pure rage in those screams.

You often find that after a few such screams the anger changes into tears. Don't drop your energy; try to push that feeling into silent screams too, because grief needs just as big a release and is probably the root cause of this anger in the first place. Unwept tears often hide under rage. If you listen to the imaginary sounds you're making, you might now hear all the varieties of hurt you can hear in a small child, from howls to wails to sobs.

At some point, after around ten silent screams, you'll be finished and won't need to continue. You should feel comfortable, even relaxed. *And you won't be angry anymore.* Where did that anger go?

It came out, the way it was supposed to.

When we're very little, we don't hang on to feelings and let them grow; we process them immediately. But as we grow up, we're trained out of that behavior. Loud feelings upset everyone around us, so we hold them in. And they build up.

But using the silent scream can be a very good way to combine the infant's open expression with the adult's sense of responsibility, a very useful tool to release tension and discover what you're feeling, and express it.

**Once the rage is out, you'll find something amazing happens.**

You won't have any trouble saying no to anybody. Or looking calmly in someone's eyes while he says something that would ordinarily upset you.

"Mary, you're just going to have to do my work and stay late. I have to run," your coworker might say to you. But because you have no backed-up anger and no fear of being disliked, you'll calmly answer in the same tone you'd use if you were telling him what day of the week it was, "I wouldn't leave it if I were you, Jim, or it will still be here in the morning," and you'll put on your coat and leave without a trace of discomfort.

**There's another kind of anger you ought to know about.**

There isn't any pain under this anger, so you're never afraid you'll lose control and punch somebody, but most of us don't remember it exists. We should, however, because it's very healing in its own way.

It has various names. It can be called "identity anger" because what it's really saying is "What I want matters, too." The feeling ranges in size from a hearty "What the hell is going on here? No way! No more!" down to an astonished "Hello!" or "Are you kidding!" It's even been called "The Primal *What?*" It doesn't mean "You done me wrong." It means "I beg your *pardon?*" and "I don't think so."

It's worth your while getting this anger up and out. The problem is, since this is a robust, physical feeling, it's best when you can actually roar like a lion instead of only pretending. If you live near a subway, you can do it there, as Liza Minnelli did in *Cabaret*. Otherwise, see if you can't find a basement or a garage where you won't alarm anyone, stand up tall, raise your fists, and roar out some good old outrage, as if you'd just hit your thumb with a hammer. Do your best to let out as many roars as you can, until there seem to be none left.

You'll probably wind up laughing and then want to start over again, as more memories of past outrages surface. Go right ahead. But soon the laughter will take over again, and finally the anger will be gone. And if someone were to walk up to you at that moment and try to manipulate you into doing something you didn't want to do, you'd just smile with amusement and say, "I wouldn't waste my time if I were you."

**And then will I be cured?**

Sorry. Getting rid of whatever makes you say yes when you want to say no is a long, hard process, and a permanent cure might not even be possible. Anyway, no matter how "healthy" you are, you don't get cured of feelings any more than the weather gets cured of thunderstorms. New events will always cause new feelings. They're supposed to.

But look what you *will* have: Now you'll know what's happening when you feel your stomach twisting up, and you'll know how to stop being weak and uneasy and become strong and comfortable again. Just get in touch with your feelings, and let them pass like a summer storm. Every time you let yourself do that, it's so easy to be straightforward with people you'll find it will hardly take much courage at all.

No, you won't be transformed into another person. But you *will* get the courage to live your life the way you want to. That's not too shabby, is it?

**Courage. What is it, and how much do you need?**

We think we know what courage means because we've all been given the images of physical courage, men at war, women holding the fort against attack. But those stereotypes are misleading. Courage is different for everybody because fear is different for everybody. Some people can stare down anyone, no matter how formidable, but would rather die than give a speech.

*The only requirements for an action to be courageous are that you know it's the right thing to do and you wish it were easier.*

So what does this mean in real terms? It means you have to roll up your sleeves and do the right thing for yourself. No more excuses. The era of complaints and pleas for justice is over. You can't expect people to be fair just because you request it, especially when you've allowed them to get away with their behavior for such a long time.

You'll have to take what you need; that's why it takes courage.

That means you'll have to stand strong and allow people to disapprove and be upset. I don't mean you should abandon your family—you've made promises, and you won't have a clear mind if you don't keep them—but that doesn't mean that you must carry your dependents so high that their feet never touch the ground.

It also means that you can't *ask* people to see you as a person with rights; you have to *become* that person and let them see whatever they choose.

Chances are, the people who depend on you will be able to take care of themselves more often, which will give them a great gain in self-confidence, competence, and self-esteem. You might even ask them to help you once in a while.

"If only my kids would just stop needing me to help them with their homework. I'm in school too! All I ask is to be free of demands for just a few hours so I can study for exams," said forty-six-year-old Susan, who had returned to graduate school.

*Why is that all she asks?*

I think she should ask for a whole lot more. I think she should ask them to help with her homework.

Now there's a thought for you.

If she manages to pull it off, she'll have kids who feel useful and valuable and smart and loving. She'll stop being a martyr, while they'll stop feeling secretly ashamed of themselves for taking advantage of her. Everybody's going to do a lot more laughing. And she's going to have one exceptionally great family.

All it takes is the courage to make it happen.

Once you decide to start using all the unused sides of you to the fullest—which is what your second life is for—you're going to need courage more than ever before. Deciding to really live your life and become everything you're capable of can be a frightening enterprise. That's what Nelson Mandela meant when he said, "Our deepest fear is not that we are inadequate. . . . It is our light, not our darkness, that most frightens us. We ask ourselves, who am I to be brilliant, gorgeous, talented, and fabulous? Actually, who are you not to be?"

But to act on these words, you need to belong to yourself. That takes the courage to do many things you might not be doing right now.

**The courage to say no.**

And never to have to come up with a good reason for it, either. Just to say, "I'm not comfortable with that. I don't think it's a good idea for me," and not to explain why. If pushed, to say, "I'd like you to respect my feelings, if you don't mind."

To refuse to answer mail or phone calls you never wanted to receive in the first place, to use your time for yourself, like Picasso or Georgia O'Keeffe. To quit complaining and take care of business, so your life helps instead of hindering you. To quit catering to manipulators and to retrain people you've allowed (or encouraged) to become dependent on you.

The courage to act on your own behalf. To say to others, "That doesn't work for me. It will have to be changed," and to yourself, "I don't need permission. I won't die if they're mad at me. I don't intend to feel guilty."

The courage to say, "I'm sorry, but I've changed my mind. Hope I haven't inconvenienced you."

The courage to do the right thing, but always to define that for yourself. The courage to refuse to give in when you know you're right.

**The courage to live your life your way.**

When Alicia's kids went to college, she decided to redecorate. "I was alone. No husband, no kids, no dog. So I had a wonderful time. The living room became pink and romantic with overstuffed couches and chairs at a time when no one had anything but white and cream walls and modern furniture. Then I turned one small room into a replica of a Greek peasant cottage, rough white walls, lace curtains, a blue door. I eat breakfast there every morning. And then I turned a bedroom into a Moroccan movie set. I painted the walls glossy apple green, put shiny gold wallpaper on the ceiling, inexpensive red oriental carpets and futons on the floor, and beads on the windows. I still love it. I can never wait to get home.

"But a number of visitors who saw it said I was very brave to decorate my house that way. Brave! Isn't that sad?" she told me. "We're talking about *decorating*, not rescuing people from a burning building! But there was a time I'd have cared more about what people thought than what made me happy."

When convention smothers individuality, it must be ignored. That takes courage.

**The courage to be everything you can be.**

Lil, a corporate manager, writes, "I put a note to myself on that report. It said 'Lil, are you willing to be as smart as you can be in this presentation?' It made me smile because I'd forgotten I put it there. A reminder was all I needed because holding back is a habit, and I forget I'm doing it. So I pulled out all the stops, and I just dazzled them. I didn't care if I was being proper; I let myself get enthusiastic. And I didn't care if they understood me; I just said the most exciting things that came into my mind. It was a real high. I still don't know what will come of it, but two partners who never talked to me before came up and started making conversation, and I think they were actually trying to impress me!"

Being everything you can be requires the courage to honor your interests with the deepest respect. To pick up that flute you haven't touched in years, or to start to play the piano, or to learn something of no practical value and know for certain that there's nothing frivolous about it. To go back to school if you want to, without a good excuse.

Being everything you can be also requires the courage to learn something new and be lousy at the beginning, to walk into a gym when you look like hell, to refuse to blame yourself for your ineptness. And the courage to accept your limits if they're real, to refuse if they're not. To go as far as you can, or to quit, as long as you decide it's the right thing to do. *And to change your decision if you change your mind and never bother yourself with how that looks.*

And if anyone should say, "When are you ever going to make up your mind?" to answer thoughtfully, "Beats me." Not because you're insolent but because that's the truth.

**The courage to feel your feelings.**

The courage to be sorry for something you've done. The courage to apologize, but never to hide from the truth, to understand that you may have done harm that can't be undone. The courage to forgive others and to be compassionate, but never to use it as an excuse to be weak or let them take advantage of you. The courage to change your ways and feel the fear and hurt and anger that change often brings.

**The courage to ignore your critics.**

The courage never to let anyone else tell you who you are. To remember that if people think you're a fool, or a bad person, or even a *good* person, that doesn't mean you have to be one. The courage to admit it if your friends really are cruel or manipulative or unkind and to quit pretending they're your friends. And to befriend anyone you think is a good person, no matter what anyone else thinks. The courage to develop insensitivity to destructive criticism and never to let anyone make you doubt your ability. *The courage to admit it if you have foes and the courage to enjoy yourself getting the best kind of revenge, the kind they'll really hate: to have a great life and become genuinely happy.*

**The courage to earn less money.**

This means you say, "I'm not going to the lake for our vacation this year. I want to stay here and paint." Or, "There's no money for summer camp for the kids this year. We'll have to come up with something better." The courage to quit copying what other people do, to rethink activities like Little League. To initiate something that's interesting to you, like starting a kids' newspaper or a kids' radio show or making a video documentary of the neighborhood pets or of the merchants in the closest shopping center. Or starting a summer theater group with the other tenants in your building.

Of course the neighbors will talk.

"Poor Bob, no money to send the kids off to camp. And when is he going to get a new car?"

If that kind of talk makes you nervous, take a lesson from a smart little girl.

My friend Jean, an art teacher, told me this story: "A very talented boy in the class had been sadly talking about how everyone laughed at a sculpture he'd made in the schoolyard, and this little girl stood up straight as an arrow, put her finger in the air, and announced to him, 'Pull up your collar, put on a smile, look your critics in the eye, and get going!' He burst into laughter, and we all cheered!"

**Remember that feeling.**

Whenever you're under assault, pull up your collar and do just as that little girl said. Whenever people are trying to manipulate you, always ask, "What do I really want at this moment?" and, "Will this be good for me?" and hang on to those questions like a cross when you're facing a vampire.

*That's courage. It will give you self-respect the moment you begin to use it.*

**It will be worth all the trouble it costs you.**

Look what you might get! In the next few years you could become a motivational speaker—if you didn't choose to do your own laundry or your own bookkeeping. You could explore hidden canyons in faraway countries and compare notes with other naturalists or you could photograph the Silk Road that Marco Polo took through Asia in the fourteenth century—if you didn't have to spend every vacation with relatives. You could learn to ice-skate or become the dancer you always longed to be if you didn't have to work late so often. You could develop a new species of orchid or create an exhibit of antique dollhouses or rebuild an old motorcycle if you didn't volunteer so much. You could take the family on a canoe trek down a beautiful river if you didn't need a new kitchen. You could write and produce your own play or start a small nonprofit organization to fund local artists (including yourself!) or run for office or teach the children in an African village to read and write. You could give a love relationship some time to blossom, or take up the study of medieval history, or start your own home business if you had the time.

**Success stories.**

Caroline is a successful TV executive who never felt she had the right to hire people to do her chores. Now she's given up cleaning her own house and handling her own finances, and started moonlighting as a set stylist on television commercials, which has always been a secret dream. She's in charge of making sure the furniture is the right color and well placed, that the actor is carrying the right kind of accessories, that the set has the right mood for the product's image.

"They say I have a genius for space and color. What do you think of that? I'm starting to make nearly as much money as I do with my day job. What's amazing is that even with two jobs I have more time and fewer worries than I had before."

Lillian, an ex-homemaker, stopped volunteering for things she didn't enjoy and started directing children's theater about four years ago. She is getting results with the actors that no one has ever gotten before. She's planning to write and illustrate a children's book next year.

Maureen, the busy career mom who wanted it all and couldn't stop rushing, doesn't do any shopping anymore. She gave up tennis too. Now she spends her weekends sitting outside in her yard reading and playing with her kids and talking with her husband. "I'm not putting in a garden. I'm not adding a room. I'll do that when the kids grow up."

Kelley is beginning to paint after work because now she leaves at five-thirty. "I told my boss I'd be thrilled to work later, but I wanted overtime. Now he tells me to go home on time!" She's also stopped rescuing all her friends. "That was harder. I just got bad at answering calls, and finally they gave up."

Corinne liked so many things that her husband called her a Jack-of-all-trades, master of none. She tried to narrow her focus for years but didn't enjoy herself. Now she's designed a T-shirt with a cartoon of Leonardo da Vinci on the front, and she has written under it, "Jack-of-all-trades. *Master*," and does whatever she loves.

Kevin, the salesman who argued with his wife, decided to bite the bullet and let her win. "I know we need the money," he admitted. Once he started bringing home more money, she became quite cheerful and even brings him tea when he studies!

And Janice won't have to divorce her second husband to start her own business. "I just went ahead and did it and let him make a lot of noise. Whenever I walked past him, I put my fingers in my ears, and after a while he started smiling at how funny we both were. We're the best of friends again," she said.

**What will your success story be?**

You weren't put on this earth to sacrifice yourself to someone else's success story. While I believe deeply that friends and family have the responsibility as well as the joy of helping one another flower into their own potential, *we all have the right to take care of our own needs too.* Not only the right but the obligation. Giving yourself the chance to reach your full emotional, intellectual, and creative height is the right thing to do. Being careless with these things is simply wrong.

Your needs might be very simple at first—I need some sleep, I need a good laugh, I need some time to think—but if they don't take top priority, you could create a bigger tragedy than you ever imagined. You see, if somebody else always comes before you, you'll never grow into who you really are.

**And one day it actually <u>will</u> become too late to be all you might have been.**

Think about that for a moment.

*Scare tactic! No fair!*

If you think that last sentence was a scare tactic, you're right. But I know how frightening it is to change, so I thought I'd remind you how frightening it could be to stay the same. Chances are you'll have a lot of time ahead of you to create your own success story. But I'd get moving as soon as possible anyway. As my grandmother used to say, you should never play it too safe.

## EXERCISE 25

### *Your thirty-year plan.*

Here's a project that will keep you from forgetting what your life is really for. Take a large, blank sheet of paper, and pin it to your wall. On the top write this quote from Tennyson (which is also a scare tactic): "How dull it is to pause,/to make an end/to rust unburnished, not to shine in use."*

Now make a grid by drawing five lines down the paper and

---

* Alfred, Lord Tennyson, "Ulysses."

six lines across. That will give you thirty squares. Once the grid is complete, start entering, in any order, all the things you might do if your time belonged to you and if you were completely unafraid. Don't be too literal about where they go; just start writing them into the boxes, blocking out a month or a year for each, *for the next thirty years*. In the next chapter, you'll be looking for your dreams and adding to these entries, so don't worry if you can't think of too many right now. What's important is that this thirty-year calendar exists and that you put it up somewhere you can see it every day.

You're not used to thinking of the coming years as a time for one dream after another to come true, but that's exactly what it should be. And this thirty-year calendar, no matter how fanciful or casually done, will serve one crucial purpose: It will remind you that you can have an exciting future and give you more courage to fight for your right to create it.

If it doesn't, just scare yourself a little by reading the words by Tennyson that you wrote at the top of the calendar. Or write it again in the thirtieth square: "How dull it is to pause, to make an end/to rust unburnished, not to shine in use."

Or rewrite it for yourself in bright red ink, like a promise: "Never to become dull, always to shine from use."

That's what courage is for.

## EXERCISE 26

*Test your courage.*

1. In how many ways do you forfeit your right to your life? Through conflict, or fear of other people's anger, complaining instead of acting, etc.?

2. Do you ever hear yourself saying, "Oh, my [husband, wife, kids, boss] would never let me do that"?

3. Do you cave in to other people's tantrums because they make you feel so bad?

4. How did your childhood family feel about expressing emotions?

5. Which tasks do you enjoy the most? Which do you enjoy the least? Why do you think you feel that way?

6. Do you have people in your life who take advantage of you? Can you figure out why you let them do it?

7. What do you really think of people who give themselves what they need? What did your childhood family think of such people?

8. Are you actually going to try the exercises in this chapter? Do you think you'll really get an assistant? If not, write down all your excuses, and post them where you can see them every day.

9. Can you find a picture of Charles de Gaulle or Mae West to put over your telephone?

10. Imagine you had all the time you needed without feeling pulled by any obligations, your mind free of guilt or inner conflict, totally untroubled. What would you be doing with that time? Do you think you might use it to go after your dreams?

# 11
# Turning Dreams into Goals

"We grow great by dreams. All big men are dreamers.
They see things in the soft haze of a spring day or in the
red fire of a long winter's evening. Some of us let great
dreams die, but others nourish and protect them, nurse
them through bad days till they bring them to the
sunshine and light which always comes to those who
sincerely hope their dreams will come true."

Woodrow Wilson

Now you're ready to go forward.
 You've seen through the illusions biology and culture were
using to dazzle you, and you've begun to take back at least a part of
your life to use as you please. Now what?

Simple. You're going after your dreams. Now.

Does that scare you? It scares a lot of people your age. Dreaming
at this stage of your life can feel very odd to someone who thought forty
was an ending point.

After all, how can you go after a dream now? You've made your
decisions, now you have to live with them, right? Anyway, you probably let your chances pass you by, didn't you? And you have commitments; you can't turn on a dime like you used to. You're torn between
wanting a whole lot more out of life and feeling grateful that you have a
job.

*Or maybe you're like someone I know who is freer than she ever expected to be at forty-two, unmarried, no kids, having spent too many years in an "interim" career, who says, "I don't know what I thought was supposed to happen after forty. It never occurred to me to make a plan."*

*But you can sense you're changing. You're getting bolder than you've ever been because you found out that time is not endless. Parts of your life that you've been tolerating for years have lately become intolerable. You're not clear what lies ahead, but you definitely do not want business as usual, so you're scanning the horizon and trying to figure out what move to make.*

*Before you take any steps, however, you should look over all your dreams. This time around, what you love has got to be part of the plan.*

*Right now your dreams are as disorganized as a kid's closet. In the back are boxes whose contents you can't remember anymore, and in front are all the dreams that were based on first-life illusions, now in terrific disarray because your identity is changing. There's a new person emerging in you, and this person isn't desperate for love and approval anymore. She wants to be happy more than she wants to win the gold medal. That means all your dreams have to be reevaluated.*

*The first question that has to be asked is, Who did the dreaming?*

*Was it the lovesick young person you used to be? Or were you trying to fulfill someone else's dreams? Were your dreams designed to right some wrong that is no longer important? Are they the leftover, uninformed dreams of someone who didn't know the ropes?*

*Or do they come from deep inside you, do they originate in your heart? Do they fit the creature you really always were, not the one you tried to be? Are they made of visions that make you happy when you think of them? If so, they're gold. Because these dreams are the messages sent by your gifts. They are the only kinds of dreams that can come along to your second life. They are the finest life-building material you'll ever find.*

*So let's sort through your dreams, old and new—even some you never dared dream—so you can begin to create the second life you always would have wanted, if you'd known it was possible.*

*Have you ever had one of those sleep dreams in which you open a closet door in your home and find, to your delighted surprise, that an entire suite of rooms was hiding behind it all this time, and it belongs to you? Your first thought is of all the wonderful things you can do now that you never had room for before—you could have a studio here, and a music room there, and a library back there—but then you wake up, disappointed, to find it wasn't true.*

*Well, I have some very good news for you: That dream was true. And discovering this new life is what it was all about.*

———

**Have you ever wanted to take an acting class? Or teach one?** Do you have a secret wish to go walking on a glacier? Do you ever fantasize yourself writing at a worn wooden table in a cottage in Wales, looking out over green hills, and walking by the sea to the village store for your bread and eggs? Or being a minister and having your own congregation? Do you sometimes think of studying anthropology and going into the rain forests to meet fascinating native people? Do you ever wish you had become a doctor or a painter or a scholar when you still had the chance?

"Yeah, but you can't really go out and *do* those things, can you—without trashing your whole present life?"

You bet you can.

There's a very good chance that you should.

Because there's nothing frivolous about a dream that comes from your real self.

It's your heart calling to you like one of your own children, trying to tell you what it needs. Your dreams must be respected the way the people you love must be respected. Treated right, they can give you a life so satisfying that one day you'll say, like so many others: "I never imagined I'd be so happy at this age. How long has this been going on?"

When you've been living the wrong life—that is, the one you were "supposed" to live—you have a very peculiar feeling. "Sometimes I think I'm living a life from some book of rules," a recently divorced, forty-three-year-old woman said, "like a book of manners that tells you how to behave."

"I feel like I'm a slave to my skills set," a computer programmer complained. "I'm trapped in the body of a computer programmer, but that's not who I am."

"Whose life am I living?" an optometrist said to me recently. "I'm helping my wife and kids become artists, but I think I was supposed to be an artist myself!"

Midlife is the first time you have the luxury—or the desire—to go after the dreams of the unusual, one-of-a-kind person you really are. The unique side of you has always been on the scene, of course, but as you went through the social and biological stages of life, the illusions of youth crowded it aside. You were the beautiful one, or the plain one, or the successful one, or the lonely one. You were the fast-track professional or the one who didn't make it. Your wishes and dreams came from that identity. But for the last few years that's started to change. Behind the scenes, when you weren't looking, your individuality kept developing, and the singular person inside began to appear on the scene.

Now your dreams need to make the same transformation. **Exploring a new country, your brain.**

> "Originality does not consist in saying what
> no one has ever said before, but in saying
> exactly what you think yourself."
> —James Stephen

*Do you have any idea how unusual you are?*
What's inside you is brand new. You're a combination of talents and abilities and unique experiences. You have an amazing way of taking in the world around you, a way no one else

would think of. All that combines to create an inner yearning to exercise your creative muscles and a direction so original that if you took it, you'd create something as unusual as you are. Even your dreams, the real ones, are original at their core.

Every now and then a voice from the audience of one of my speaking engagements contradicts me on this idea. "How can you say everyone is original? Don't you think most people are ordinary and very much like each other?"

But how could that be so? "Look around you," I say. "In this roomful of people not one of your faces could be mistaken for another. Not one nose or eyebrow looks like another. If you have unusually good eyesight, and the person next to you has physical strength, and that one has a special way with animals, how is it possible that your brains aren't equally distinctive?"

Of course it isn't possible at all.

The way your brain works, the paths it takes, the odd things you're sensitive to that no one else notices, these are as unique and innate to you as your way of walking or the timbre of your voice. Like them, your thinking identifies you. Take a good, long look at who you really are. You're not what you do. You're not a banker or a gardener or a housekeeper or a mom or an astronaut, for that matter; you're an original and important thinker.

You probably weren't raised to feel much like an original or important thinker. Because your brain has been evaluated for years by a world that didn't—and, for the most part, still doesn't—have the tools to measure it, you have no real sense of its astonishing uniqueness. Until your middle years most of your thinking was in the service of conformity. To succeed meant watching what others were doing and doing the same thing, hopefully better. No one says this more clearly than Lucy Grealy, author of *Autobiography of a Face*, when she writes, "Society is no help. It tells us again and again that we can most be ourselves by acting and looking like someone else. . . ."

As a result, the most original parts of you were rarely called into use.

The results weren't all bad. You may have accomplished a lot and learned useful skills; maybe you became a more disciplined worker than you would have been otherwise. But these days the originality that was never allowed to surface is beginning to make you uncomfortable.

"Something is itching, but I don't know where to scratch," said a forty-four-year-old graphic artist.

"I still like what I do, but it isn't enough anymore," said a fifty-one-year-old nurse. "I'm not sure what would change that."

*If you're feeling like they are, it's because conformity has lost its charm.* You're getting ready to do your own thing and be your own person. The problem is, it's hard after all these years to figure out who that person might be. You could take up a hobby, but in your heart you know you want far more than that. You want something new to learn, something that rings in your soul and makes you forget the time, something you could be brilliant at.

And whenever you suddenly remember that your time isn't endless, that wish turns into a three-alarm fire, fraught with urgency. You yearn for a passion; you're not ready to leave this earth without doing something that feels truly important.

If you're like most people who feel that way, embarrassment might stop you before you even start. After all, it's foolish to entertain such grandiose thoughts, especially when you're over forty, right?

*But there's nothing grandiose about it.* There's someone remarkable inside you, someone with a major role to play in the drama of your life, trying to tell you she hasn't been on the scene yet. She's got the dreams that reflect the unused creativity, untapped brilliance, thwarted adventurousness of your one-of-a-kind brain, and chances are that the environment you grew up in didn't spend much energy pointing that out to you.

You can get a sense of whether that's true or not by trying this exercise.

### EXERCISE 27:

*The highlights of my life.*

**1. According to me.**

Take a blank sheet of paper, and label it "The highlights of my life according to me." Now, starting as early in your life as you can, write down the biggest things that happened to you, as you experienced them. Try to remember how they felt. Include your biggest insights and discoveries, your most wonderful moments, anything that had a memorable impact on you.

When you've put down everything that comes easily to mind, take another sheet of paper and put this heading on it:

**2. The highlights of my life according to others.**

Write down what other people saw as the highlights of your life. You can guess if you like because even when their values were unstated, you had a sense of what everyone really cared about. Write down what your parents and siblings and friends probably saw as the highlights of your life.

Were they the same or different? What does that tell you?

Rosalie was surprised at the contrast between the two pages. "My biggest moments started with going to school for the first time. It was like magic to me. And then moving across country. That was good and bad, but it was big, I never forgot the journey and the new place, how different my new life was. There was a tree in my backyard, and I used to climb it and hide up there for hours, dreaming; that was a special thing for me. And I had a friend, such a wonderful friend, for about five years. When she moved away, I was heartbroken for a long time.

"Then going away to college was very big for me, another life changer, just huge. And when I got my first article published, my first time in print.

267

"But you know what I think my family and even most of my friends would have written? A beauty contest I won when I was seven, and nothing else until my wedding day!"

Others noticed similar patterns. Families saw nothing important in childhood, only the milestones of adult life: marriage, children, and successes. Personally experienced moments usually went right past them.

There you can see clearly the difference between the self *you* experienced and the self your world saw. If no one pointed out your distinctiveness to you, it's possible that no matter how much they loved you, they never really saw it or thought about it very much. But all through your life your real self has been present; the original self never went away completely. It showed up in moments that mattered to you and no one else.

And every moment indicated a unique way of being in the world. You're not like anyone else who ever lived.

**What's the point of finding this out now?**

"I've made all the wrong turns, and too many mistakes. I think my big moment came and went. I've wasted a lot of time on the wrong things."

*No, you haven't. Mistakes were what your first life was for!*

Most of us are raised to believe that if we're ever going to have our dreams, the foundation has to be in place well before the age of forty. Perhaps when life expectancy was shorter, that might have been true. But it isn't true anymore. In fact, your first four decades of experiences, good and bad, have been essential *for their errors.*

A young interviewer asked an elder statesman the secret to his success.

"My secret? Good judgment," said the elder statesman.

"Yes, but how do you get that?"

"Experience," he answered.

"But how do you get that experience?" the interviewer persisted.

"Bad judgment."

You see, nothing is wasted. Everything that's happened to you has been laid out like a landscape in your mind, molded and transformed by your unique thought processes.

And now you need to launch an expedition into a land hardly visited by mass education, social rules, or biological imperatives and certainly never, ever by IQ tests. It's the core of your originality, and it's so unusual and unknown that you can spend the rest of your life trying to map it and never be finished. *Remember, your wishes are the messages your talent keeps sending you.* No one else can tell you what that originality is made of or where it can lead you because no one else can dream your dreams. No one but you.

**Gathering your dreams together.**

To begin the search for the dreams that are really yours, you need to locate and bring together as many of your dreams as you can find. Then you can take a good look at what you've got. Get your pencil and a few sheets of blank paper, so you can write a list. Now let's cast a wide net, because there are many kinds of dreams. There are the dreams you almost forgot, the ones you know you don't want anymore, and the ones you think you can't have anymore. There are even some you never dreamed at all because you didn't have the vocabulary for them, but they've got to be found because they could be the most important of all.

**Wait a minute. What about hard reality?**

I know it's not an easy thing to march out, dream in hand, and make it come true. And, if you're a grown-up, you've already found that a lot of your dreams didn't come true at all.

"Good luck about finding a dream job. Maybe you'd better face the fact that the world doesn't pay you to follow your dreams," I overheard a woman say recently.

That may or may not be true. Some dreams pay very well; others don't. What looks impossible may be easier to attain than you ever imagined, and what looks easy may turn out to be more trouble than it's worth. There's no way to know yet, and it doesn't matter at this stage of the game.

*But it is always possible to get what you love into your life.*

In a big way too. A way that makes you come alive. Further on in this chapter, you'll read about lots of ways that people have already done that for themselves, and you'll learn how to do it too.

But it isn't yet time to worry about whether a dream is possible or not. Right now you need to see them all in front of you. What you're about to do is write the longest list of wishes you can come up with. Only after you look at the dreams that made the final cut, can you deal with the obstacles to attaining them.

But just in case some obstinate voice keeps pushing aside dreams that seem absolutely impossible, I want you to keep some scraps of notepaper nearby as you work through this chapter and place an open box on the floor beside your chair. You can label it "Why this dream is impossible" if you like. Then, every time you imagine something wonderful you'd love to do, and the voice says, "Ridiculous!" just write down all the reasons you can't do it and toss the scrap of paper into the box for later.

*And then add that "ridiculous" dream to your list.* You can even pretend this is a contest and the winner is the one with the longest list. But no cheating. Only the dreams you really care about will count.

## EXERCISE 28

### *Okay, start dreaming.*

For a warm-up, go looking into your past for the dreams you once dreamed. Write some ages from childhood on, down the left side of a sheet of paper, leaving a number of lines between each entry. Continue onto another page if necessary. Then start writing down dreams next to the approximate age you dreamed them, starting as early as you can. Write without thinking too much just to get yourself in the mood, but try to enter some kind of dream at least every four or five years, even if you have to do some guessing. You'll be adding to this list later, so be sure to leave room for more entries. Here's an example.

**Your dream history.**

At three, I dreamed of having my own puppy.

At seven, I dreamed I had lots of good friends.

At eleven, I dreamed I was beautiful and popular, and a movie star.

At fifteen, I dreamed of boys, of being sure of myself.

At seventeen, I dreamed of a college full of wise teachers who loved to help students.

At twenty, I dreamed of being a photographer or an anthropologist.

At twenty-five, I dreamed of moving to New York City.

At twenty-nine, I dreamed of going to graduate school and getting a Ph.D. in history and teaching in a small New England college.

At thirty, I dreamed of breaking free from an unhappy marriage.

At thirty-three, I dreamed of having enough money to pay the bills.

At thirty-seven, I dreamed of walking away from a toxic work atmosphere and working at home where I could be with my kids.

At forty, I dreamed of starting a business and being successful.

At forty-one, I dreamed of writing a novel.

At forty-four, I dreamed of moving to an island in Greece.

Now you try it.

When you're finished, look over your list and think for a moment. Can you find anything else? Remember to include places you longed to see, careers you thought of having, lifestyles you wished for, things you wanted to try. If any of the following exercises remind you of more dreams, add them to this dream history, at the bottom of the page. And get some more paper ready. I want you to make your dream list as full as you can. A lot of dreams have fallen from your memory, of course, but when you move to the next steps, many of them will start coming back.

As soon as the list is as long as you can make it, take a look at the entries and ask yourself a question:

**What happened to those dreams?**

Maybe you got that puppy. Or maybe you had to wait until you grew up and could give it to yourself. Or maybe you never got it. *But something happened to every dream on that list.* Look at each dream, and right next to it write down what became of it.

There are two purposes for this step. One is that you may find out something about yourself and what happened to your dreams. Another is that this line of inquiry will remind you of more dreams. If it does, write them next to the age you remember dreaming them. If there's no particular age attached to the dream, add it to the bottom of the page.

Here are the kinds of things that may have happened to your dreams:

*1. You outgrew them.*

Maybe you got old enough to realize you probably weren't serious about being a movie star, for example. But was there anything in your childish dreams that is still attractive to you? If so, write it on the list, next to your present age.

*2. You didn't take yourself seriously.*

You loved something but the time came to grow up and forget about it. For example, say you realized that you loved to run as fast as you could.

"The thing I loved about running was that I was good at it. It was one of the few things I could do really well, easily. I knew I was special. It never occurred to me to stick with it."

Did you have something you loved like that? Can you re-

member what you loved most about it? Did you love being physical? Did you love being fabulous at something? Do you still feel
that way?

If you find something like that, write it on the list above,
beside your present age.

3. *Something happened to stop you, and you never got started
again.*

You moved to another place, or you made another choice, or
you got swept up with events and never got back to the same
place.

"I was offered an art scholarship when I was twelve, but my
dad got another job, and we had to move. I think it really bothered me that no one thought it was important, so I just gave up
on it."

"My older sister became very ill, and everything changed.
After that everything was focused on her, and I got forgotten. I
didn't think it was right to want anything, because I was already
the lucky one."

Do you have something like that in your background? Were
you so hurt or guilty that the spirit went out of you and you gave
up your dream? Do you think it had any effect on your willingness
to dream as you grew up? Can you think of what you might have
dreamed if the incident had never happened? If so, add it to the
list, next to the appropriate age.

4. *The pressure to conform was too great.*

Did you just assume you had to do what everyone else did
and never really think about what you wanted? Here's an excerpt
from a letter I received from a thirty-nine-year-old secretary:
"How narrow our choices have been. From my young adulthood
on, I have been consistently amazed at how my peers never see
that they have a choice in their life: that they don't have to
marry the first guy who proposes, that they don't have to have
children, that they don't have to get a corporate job and try to
get into 'management.' Sometimes it seems like our culture is a

big tribe, and when you reach adulthood there are three rites you have to go through to be considered part of the tribe; marriage, just to prove someone wanted you and that you are worthy; children, to prove you have a real stake in the tribe; and a good job, preferably 'in management,' to be impressive to the tribe. If you can't do these things, you will always be an outsider."

Were there any nonconformists in your earlier years? Did their paths look interesting to you, although you never felt you could also take them? If so, add them to the list.

*5. You chose one path and didn't get to take others.*

Even success can limit you. Perhaps you took one fork in the road but still thought longingly about some others. There may be an unmet dream still there, nagging at you.

"I loved astronomy when I was in school. I saved for a year to get my own telescope, and I'd have stayed up all night, every night, if my folks hadn't made me get some sleep. But after college I went to med school and didn't have time for it anymore."

Do you have something like that in your background? Do you still remember it with some feeling? Can you isolate the element you loved the most? Do you still love it? If you can, put it on the list.

*6. Your dreams have been tied to someone else's happiness.*

Are you living to accommodate someone else?

"My husband won't travel. He just refuses. He's happy at home, and that's that. And I don't think I'd like to travel alone."

"I wanted to be an artist, but my family wanted me to marry a businessman, so I went for an M.B.A in a top university. I didn't marry anybody because I didn't like businessmen very much. But school was expensive, so now I work in business myself."

What about you? Is the obstacle to one of your dreams another person? If that person changed, do you think you'd want to go back and get your dreams? If so, add it to the list above.

*7. You're still waiting.*

Many of us don't realize it but we've been waiting to be called on. We feel we were never asked to do what we were capable of. Perhaps you were taught not to be aggressive, and you played by the rules, sat politely, and waited for an invitation, and you're still waiting. What would you love to be called on to do?

Or maybe you're still waiting for your ship to come in, for your luck to change. Imagine you got lucky. What do you imagine happening? That's a dream and should be added to the list.

Sometimes you're trying to break into a field without success, sending résumés or screenplays or demo tapes of your music, and no one ever answers. You keep trying, but you assume you have no choice but to wait for a response, and you're beginning to think it's hopeless. It hasn't occurred to you that you can start without one and develop a reputation by following your dream on your own.

So the story isn't over. Put it on the list.

8. *You tried and failed.*

One time you gave it your best, but the gates were closed or the time wasn't right, and since then, you've assumed the dream is impossible. Search that dream and see if you'd still love to have it, if every obstacle were out of the way. If so, write it on the list.

Sometimes you were told by experts that you couldn't do what you wanted, and they seemed to be right, so you gave up your dream.

A young woman came to see me recently because she was never able to find anything she loved "except the one thing I'm no good at, music." She had gone to a music school but couldn't learn to read music no matter how hard she tried. After a while she came to hate her classes, and her advisers finally advised her to give up.

I couldn't help being curious because I've never met anyone who loved something without being talented at it. So I began to question her.

"What was your instrument?"

"Well, everyone has to learn piano, so I started there. But I tried clarinet, cello. I was terrible at everything. I could never hear intervals, could never read music. I guess I didn't have a natural feeling for it."

"But then why did you think you liked music?"

"You know, it was this TV commercial with horses running over these hills, and there was nice music, but what was really exciting was the sound of their hooves, I could hear all these different rhythms, all at the same time. It was just gorgeous." She looked a little sheepish. "That's a pretty stupid reason to think you're a musician, isn't it?"

"Not if you're a drummer it isn't. Could you possibly be a drummer?"

Then she remembered wanting drums as a kid, but since she wasn't in the school band, her parents begged off, and she forgot about it. In college you weren't allowed to specialize until you had mastered piano.

"Is there anyplace you could play drums without learning to read music?" I asked.

"In a band, in a rock band!" she said, getting excited.

The other day I got a flyer from her, an invitation to hear her play with a band in the East Village. There was a photo of the band, and she had a broad smile on her face as she posed behind the drum set.

What about you? Was there something you loved and might have abandoned by mistake?

9. *You never dared to try.*

Sometimes we shied away from our dreams for other reasons: We were afraid people would make fun of us because our dreams were unusual, or we were afraid we'd fail and that would destroy us. Or we knew our dreams were impractical because they didn't make money. Or we simply didn't know where to start because we didn't know anyone who could tell us how. If any of your dreams fell by the wayside for reasons like these, add them to your dream list.

*10. You had to give it up to support your family.*

Buddy, fifty-one, said, "I was an artist, but when I got married, I became an artistic director at a big ad agency, and then I just gave up on painting. I started my own ad agency, and the years went by as I tried to build it. I lost confidence in my ability to paint. Just couldn't get started again."

Sometimes, when we put our dreams away for a long time, we lose our nerve. We begin to tell ourselves we're not good at what we love, and if we're rusty or undeveloped, that seems to be confirmed. No matter how wrong we are about this—and believe me, we almost always are wrong (Johann Sebastian Bach had a twenty-year mid-career dry spell, and went on to write his greatest music)—our dreams fall by the wayside. If this could be you, add this dream to your list.

*11. You've never had enough money.*

"All I want is to travel and take photographs of people in small villages all over the world," a woman told me in one of my workshops. "But I'll never have enough money for that."

I got on the microphone and said, "Is there anyone in the audience who knows how to travel without money?" A dozen hands flew in the air. Here are some of the suggestions I remember.

"Pay for everything with a frequent flier credit card, and rack up the free miles."

"Stay at colleges all over the world. During the summer they've very cheap."

"I work free-lance for an international training company, and they send me all over the world."

"Be a courier and you can fly almost free."

"Join the Peace Corps."

"Come talk to our bank. We have to give money away, and we sometimes fund projects just like yours."

Before you assume that money is an insurmountable barrier, put your dream on the list.

*12. You're too old to do it anymore.*

"My first dream came true, and it was pretty damn good. I was a singer and songwriter and made two records. I loved to sing, loved the stages, studios, loved being applauded. But there's nothing grosser than an old pop singer. I can't compete with young people, and I don't want to."

"Comedy writing is a young person's business. It's all I know, and having to change my career at this late date is horrifying, but they won't hire me anymore."

Sometimes an industry, such as the world of TV comedy writers, really changes. This doesn't mean that there's no way to keep the heart of the dream, whatever that was, and transform into something you can do (doing stand-up comedy or writing a book or a screenplay, for example).

And sometimes you've got it all wrong, like the singer above who forgot to notice how many of the greats are older. Of course the songs she was used to singing were for young people. *But she's a songwriter. She could write for anyone, including herself and other women her age.*

What about you? Is there something you did, or always longed to do, but now it seems too late? If so, it goes on the dream list.

*Is your list getting nice and long?*

Take a casual look at it and see if you notice any patterns emerging. Do your dreams fall in the same general area? Or did you give them all up for the same reasons? Or are you having a very hard time thinking of any dreams at all?

**The dreams you didn't have.**

None of us dreams all the dreams we're capable of achieving.

For example, what would you have dreamed if you had been somebody else? What would you have dreamed if you'd been born into a different family? Or in a different country?

In another workshop I asked the men and women to pretend they were the opposite sex and see what kinds of dreams they would go for. I got some unexpected responses. Most of the women found themselves daring to be far more ambitious as men. And the men experienced a kind of freedom they weren't used to, as if they were allowed to go after what they actually wanted, not what they were supposed to want.

In so many ways we limit our dreams because of our limited experience. But to make your dream list complete, you need to know not only what you dreamed but what you *should have* dreamed. So, for the next step, try pretending you're someone else and see what you uncover. Ask yourself the following questions:

What if you were the opposite sex? Don't bother with what you imagine "any" man or woman would want. What would *you* want?

What if you had a magic wand and could pick a talent you don't have? Which talent would you pick? Why?

Pick someone famous, someone you admire. If you were that person, what would you do with your life that you never thought to do as yourself?

What if you were a character in a movie who came across the best "help wanted" ad imaginable. What would the ad say? For example: "Wanted, year-round caretaker for Italian villa," or "Wanted, kind, energetic person who likes to work outdoors," or "Wanted, someone who wants to make a difference," or "Wanted, someone who loves to hang around great art."

Those are dreams. Add them to your list.

I hope your list is getting very long. Let's scoop up just a few more for good measure.

**Try to remember some little dreams.**

Make a list of all the little things you want to do before you die.

"Before we die, my husband and I have to come up with an idea for lunch that involves a plane ride. And I have to see Bali. And I never had a horse. I'd want to go to Europe one more time. And I'd like to read all the books on my shelf."

**Now remember some bigger ones.**

"I'd really love to have a supernatural experience, a brush with the miraculous, something profound that makes me aware of a higher level. Like maybe to see a ghost, or have a dream and have it happen. I think there's something wonderful going on, and I'm afraid I'll miss it."

Okay, unless you can think of some more dreams, you can stop now. Now let's work that list down to a manageable size.

## EXERCISE 29

### *Shorten the list.*

Take a careful look at what you've got. Some dreams have passed their shelf life, but they stay in our minds out of habit. They have to be weeded out to make room for what you really want. Let's go through your list, and open some space for dreams that really matter to you.

*1. Cut anything you're certain you don't want anymore.*

"I wanted to be a stand-up comic because I liked making people laugh. I had to fight for it because everyone said it was so impractical. I was determined. But when I got up on the stage, I realized I wasn't that good, and I didn't really love performing. I'm almost embarrassed to admit it, but truth be known, if somebody gave me a job as a stand-up comic, I wouldn't take it."

"I wanted a hit record and a road tour. Nothing else mattered to me for years, but now I know a lot more about that life, and it's not for me."

Does that sound like you? Then cut that dream off the list.

*2. Toss dreams that you're certain no longer fit you.*

The writer K. C. Cole says that after thirty-five, "You can

stop worrying about the things you'll never do: win the Nobel Prize, star in the sitcom *Friends,* compete in the Olympics."*

I might quarrel with her about the Nobel Prize—as a matter of fact, I fully intend to do just that in the next chapter—but she's got the right idea. And there are other dreams you might give up on.

"I realized that those first romantic days of our marriage won't ever be back. That time is over. Even if something happened to Mel, I wouldn't want to start with someone else again. Relationships take so much work, you have to do so much caretaking. I'd probably want to be on my own, not worry about anybody else."

"I always thought I wanted my own children. Maybe if I'd had them, I'd have been very happy, but the time is past. I don't want children anymore. I'll borrow someone else's."

If you're not sure whether you still want an old dream, ask yourself this question: How much would I be willing to sacrifice for that dream? If the answer is "nothing," take it off.

*3. See if anything on the list is someone else's dream.*

"My mother always wanted me to be an insider in a group of rich people. I've always felt I'm not good enough because I didn't make it."

Off the list.

*4. Drop the dreams that consoled you but weren't real wishes.*

"I realized I wasn't doing a thing to become an actor. I just liked thinking about it because it made my life seem less drab. It wasn't a dream; it was an aspirin."

You can find out for sure what these "aspirin" dreams are by fantasizing yourself actually doing them. If the fantasy isn't fun, the dream isn't real. Take it off the list.

---

* "35 Things That Get Better After 35," by K. C. Cole, *Good Housekeeping,* November 1997.

*5. Make sure your dreams aren't a way of saying, "I'll show them."*

"I wish I were the handsomest guy in the world. I'd go out and break every beautiful woman's heart, because I was so badly treated by my first wife. So I work out all the time. I'm a fanatic, but I don't enjoy it like a lot of those guys do. If I woke up with a perfect body one day, I swear I'd never exercise again."

Take it off the list. Revenge is the same as dreaming someone else's dream. You need to let out some of the hurt so you can move on. To distinguish a real dream from a revenge dream, ask yourself a question: If no one had ever hurt you, would that dream still be on the list? If not, take it off. It will drag you down and never fix the wound anyway.

*6. Go looking for other dreams that you wanted for the wrong reason.*

"I think I went after the wrong goal. I got a lot of praise for being an actor in my small town, and I loved the praise, not the acting. In college I found out I wasn't nearly that special. But I stuck to it, wanting to feel that I was really fantastic at something."

"I dreamed of being a better writer than James Joyce. If I couldn't be that special, I would have felt worthless. I realized I didn't love writing itself."

You can't bother with anything you don't love. There's always another path to what you want, and you won't find it until you take these items off your list.

*7. Cut anything else that doesn't make your heart beat faster.*

I know you want to read all those self-help books on your shelf, and fix every broken appliance in the house, and get the garden looking great, but check it out with care: Those might not be real wishes, just some habitual "shoulds," and they don't belong on your list of dreams. They're about safety, not talent, and though there's definitely a place in your life for safety, this dream list isn't it.

An astrology buff friend sent me this clipping from a local newspaper:

> VIRGO: I implore you not to alphabetize the spices in the cupboard this week. I beg you not to wash and polish your bottlecap collection or read the VCR instruction book from cover-to-cover or count the cracks in the sidewalk as you take a perfectly-timed 22-minute walk. Your current surplus of good karma, rowdy chutzpah and incredibly precise luck is too valuable to channel into projects like that. On bended knee, I'm pleading with you to seek out instead adventures that make your knees wobbly, your heartbeat fluttery and your mouth absolutely speechless.*

If you feel that way about anything at all, that's a keeper.

**Dreams to keep.**

Remember, anything on that list, as long as it makes your heart beat faster, must not be taken off. You must keep the dreams you'd still go for if only it weren't too late, the ones that never had a fighting chance, the ones you got talked out of, and the ones you keep postponing because they scare you.

**All right, there's your list.**

You might end up with ten or even twenty dreams left on it. Or you might wind up with only one. But after a search like the one you've just made, I don't think your dream list will be empty.

*Now take a look at what has emerged.*

Look at the dreams that made the cut. What do they tell you about yourself and your life? What do you see that wasn't so obvious before? Has something emerged that wasn't visible before?

"I've changed, and I didn't know it. I always wanted to find

---

* Robert Breszny, *Real Horoscopes*, September 7, 1995, Boulder, Colorado, newspaper.

someone fabulous to love, someone with wit and glamour. I was willing to put up with a lot of unhappiness for that at one time. But now I know I'll never be happy unless I'm with loving people."

"I gave up my dreams because I didn't understand what was going on in this business. I could have hung on if only I'd known then what I know now."

"I gave up because I couldn't make my goal in one step. It never occurred to me that I could take lots of small steps."

"I always felt like I was showing off, trying to get attention, and so I gave up one thing after another. Now I know the message my family sent me was that I wasn't supposed to have *anything*. If I'd known then, I would have done whatever I wanted."

"I keep thinking I love running my import-export business, but the only things left on my dream list are about working with my hands, building things out of wood."

What does your dream list tell you? Write the answer on a sheet of paper, and tape it to your mirror. Read it whenever you pass by, and let the lesson sink in. Sooner or later you'll almost hear it speak. And here's what it will say:

**"Now you know better. Get moving."**

You see, working that list of dreams has done more than isolate what you love, important though that is. If you've done all the exercises on the previous pages, you've been handling and examining your dreams like never before, turning them over and over intently, as if they were pieces of ancient pottery that held the clues to the mystery of a little-known civilization.

All your dreams and the reasons you had them—or dropped them or even forgot to have them in the first place—show the existence of the long and complex path which your talent, like a seeker on a quest, has been taking throughout your life. And they also show very clearly the forces that pulled you off the path. I think you'll find that when they're reduced to their most common denominator, these forces are almost always characteristic of your first life, when other people's opinions and your own biology sent you after goals that turned out not to be really yours.

But now you've got to take those dreams very seriously. Some of them should be turned into goals, and there never was a better time to do it because that's what grown-ups are best at.

## DREAMS INTO GOALS

The difference between a dream and a goal is a plan, so let's take the first steps to create one. Anything left on your dream list qualifies as a message from your original self. But don't scare yourself by thinking you have to chuck your life out the window and start over. To turn a fantasy into a down-to-earth reality, you merely need to take some simple steps.

**Step one: Find the core of the dream.**

"My wife and I both work at large companies, but we dream all the time of owning our own deli. How we'd love it. But it's such a gamble we'd really be afraid to make that move."

Why do they want it? That "why" will show what's at the heart of the dream.

"We want people to be happy, not disappointed. Everything's a letdown. You can't fix people's whole lives, but you can give them a reliably fantastic moment, a big smile with eyes closed when they eat the cheesecake. I want them to know our place is special because we care."

Go looking for the core of love at the center of your dream. Don't trust reason right now, only feelings. We're talking about love, nothing else. As soon as you've found the most important part of your dream, call your friends and throw an idea party to get around any obstacles.

**Step two: Start small, start now.**

Don't wait, but don't do it all at once. Setting up strategies to turn a dream into a reality is like learning a language. You must always start on a small scale, and right away. Forget all-or-nothing high-risk thinking, one-step solutions, and splendid isolationism. Start small, start now, and get a lot of help.

That's what this couple did. They started coming up with small steps and alternative plans that would carefully conserve the heart of the dream. First, they brainstormed as many ideas as they could think of. Here's what they came up with: "Start a private dinner club in our home. Or cook desserts and deliver them to restaurants. Or get a weekend job in someone else's delicatessen, where we make the cheesecakes, and we work only on weekends and vacations."

Over the next two years they ended up doing all three, and kept their jobs too. Recently the deli owner asked them to become his partners because he wants to go into semi-retirement.

**Step three: Get support. Life is not a do-it-yourself project.**

Gathering friends together to help you with strategies is a wonderful technique for turning dreams into concrete goals. For one thing, the companionship will calm many of your unrealistic fears. Also, your friends can help you out in many ways. One of them might know an expert you can talk to. Another will have a skill to offer. And they'll always encourage you when you get stuck. Support might be the most important need you have at this time. Just knowing that people are on your side can be enough to get you rolling.

I often throw small "idea parties" for friends who are struggling with some part of a personal creative project. Just last week we found a way to finance a showcase of one woman's play, and we'll soon have a "mailing party" to send out the announcements. At another idea party we got pro bono help for a filmmaker friend to do the expensive processing of his completed feature film. Next Sunday I'm gathering together a few people who know something—or need to learn something—about foundation grants, and we're going to learn what opportunities exist for the artists in our midst.

I call these meetings "Support Your Local Genius Nights." Miracles come out of them on a regular basis, and they're fun too.

Sometimes the support that makes the biggest difference is very small and unstructured. Some years ago, when I was avoiding writing a book very near to my heart, my son became my support team. When I wasn't home, he took a small stuffed moose from his room, tacked it to the kitchen door, and made a sign with a Magic Marker in very large letters: WRITE OR WE KILL THE MOOSE.

When I saw it, I burst out laughing. But I was very touched that he cared because when you're lost in a problem that's the first thing you forget. For me it was a moment of truth. I wasn't alone and had to stop thinking that I was. Someone I loved wanted to help me. It was all I needed to start writing again.

**Step four: Jump-start your energy with a moment of truth.**

Go looking for the moment you woke up and realized you had to go for your dreams. Perhaps that happened while you were gathering and narrowing your dream list. Or maybe a lightbulb went on over your head when you were walking down the street. These moments vary in their details, but the one thing they have in common is that they make the fog drop away and bring back our clarity. The result is like having a jet engine attached to your shoulder blades.

Here are some examples of what I mean.

Rochelle is a gifted career counselor who has many clients. She always wanted to do something more glamorous, but she could never figure out what it was. And although she enjoyed every minute she spent with her clients, she resented how much time it took away from her search to find what she really wanted.

Then two thoughts hit her on the same day.

"I was wandering on the Internet, through the science fiction section, and saw a picture of a knight in armor on a white horse, and suddenly I realized I was waiting for someone to rescue me, some great maestro who would see my gifts and spirit me away to a finer world.

"And then I stumbled across a piece of writing by a science fiction writer named Spider Robinson. He said, 'It took me better than a quarter century to learn, the hard way, that hard work at something you want to be doing is the most fun that you can have out of bed . . . to learn that the smart man finds ways to make everything he does be work; to learn that "leisure" time is truly pleasurable (indeed tolerable) only to the extent that it is subconscious grazing for information with which to infuse newer, better work.'

"I was stunned. I realized I had to admit I love what I do, I love hard work, and I don't want to be rescued and carried away to a better world. I want to do what I'm doing."

*That's a moment of truth. It shoots you right into action.*

Marcelle, forty-six, a designer whose industry had closed down, was demoralized and without plans, until one evening when she was visiting a relative. "I took a friend to see my sixty-two-year-old aunt Dina, and my friend and I were going on and on about how awful our jobs were and how awful men were and out of nowhere, Dina stood up and said, 'Want to go to Turkey?' She left the room and came back carrying photos of this amazing village she had found, right in the middle of Turkey, where she would be fixing up a rented cave house the following spring. 'I've always wanted to start my own little school, and Turkey might be coming into the European Community, so I think I'll teach English. Just in the spring and fall. For free.' She gave us a big grin and said, 'Everybody thinks I'm crazy, but what can they do to me?'

"I was hit by a bolt of lightning," Marcelle said. "I just thought that's how I want to be feeling at sixty-two. And I started looking at all my insurmountable problems as if they were nothing but design problems that had to be solved."

"I was visiting a friend who had just recovered from a serious illness," said Bill, a thirty-nine-year-old football coach, "and I was complaining about my last relationship, and how I didn't know when to start looking for another one, and how I didn't know any new women, and she said, 'Bill, life is very tenuous. You should quit complaining and get into action.' What do you say to someone who almost died a few weeks ago? She was absolutely right. So I called a friend, and tonight we're going dancing at a disco!"

"I took early retirement with a pension," said Marta, an ex-government employee, "and wasn't sure what to do with myself. I didn't have extra money, but I could get along, and I didn't feel like getting another job. Then one day I was reading *National Geographic* and came on a story about an American woman who lived in a small village in northern Pakistan, and something clicked. It had never once occurred to me that such a thing was possible.

"I thought, 'I could do that!' I don't have a job or a family to leave behind, and I can easily sublet my apartment for a while. So I tried to tell my friends, but they thought it was crazy. For a while I was deflated and started to see it their way. After all, you can't just pick up and go live in a small village in a faraway country. *And then I realized I was asking for permission.* I saw it as clear as daylight. I was asking someone else to respect my dreams more than I did.

"So I saved some money, flew to Pakistan, and went to visit this lady. She was wonderful and directed me to a number of beautiful villages within a day's walk. I met so many kind people! I stayed for three weeks and came home, and all year I saved to go back again. Since then I've been home to earn extra money as a substitute teacher and gone back again three times."

How did she explain her decision to her friends?

"I didn't bother," she said. "For a long time they shook their heads as if I were crazy. Now they're asking to visit me."

"My old teacher was told in the hospital that she had only a few days to live," Beth, a massage therapist, told me. "She was brilliant, but such a terrible person. She scowled all the time and dressed in somber clothes. She was like a mean witch. But she was a genius, so she had a lot of students although she treated them all terribly. But when she found out she only had a couple of days left, she made this incredible change. She got stylish, had her hair done and put on makeup, got a beautiful robe, and then she called all of us and told us to bring champagne and crystal glasses. And we had a party in the hospital. I was toasting her and thinking, 'Was that inside her all those years? How sad that she only got this one party.' And then I thought, '*What makes me think I'll be any different?* I'm not changing anything either!' That's when I woke up."

Your moment of truth, like your list of dreams, will reveal what's been standing in your way and reduce it to a simple obstacle, one you can create a strategy for.

Now, where's that box of obstacles?

## EXERCISE 30

### *Troubleshooting obstacles.*

Remember the box you kept beside your chair? It should have pieces of paper in it, each one describing what stands between you and your dream. Some of these obstacles don't matter anymore because you've already cut those dreams from the list. Find the remaining obstacles, and lay them out on the table.

Obstacles are problems to be solved, so pull out some paper and pencils, roll up your sleeves, and get ready to solve them. Now look at your list of dreams and all your obstacles, and frame them into this very special sentence. I call it an "Idea Generator": "I want to do _____ [fill in the blank with your dream], but I can't because of _____ [fill in the blank with your obstacle].

What's so special about this sentence? It creates an irresistible urge to solve the problem in anyone who hears it. What you shouldn't do is say the first part of the sentence without the second. If you say, "I want to do x," others will supply obstacles, most of which have nothing to do with you.

Okay, get ready. *You're going to run your obstacle past as many people as you can.* So have your personal phone book nearby, and keep a piece of paper and a pencil ready so you can write down every suggestion, good or bad. Now pick up the phone and start calling your friends and present them with the Idea Generator: "I want to do x, but I can't because of y." And then say, "Have you got any ideas?"

That's all.

Say it to anyone, and you'll find, nine times out of ten, they'll start coming up with solutions. Watch the ideas rain down. And your phone won't stop ringing for days, as your friends come up with more and more solutions.

The following ideas came in from phone calls I made as an experiment, using my clients' problems as the obstacles to be solved.

**Moonlighting.**

*Dream Obstacle:* "I want to be a singer, but it doesn't pay enough."

*Suggestion:* Do it after work. You won't mind even an uninspiring job if it pays for your dream.

That's a first-rate solution, more useful than you might think. Take for example, a patent clerk who loves to dream about physics. We have a nicely documented case, Albert Einstein. By his own account, he was often entertained in his day job looking at people's applications to patent their inventions. When his mind would wander, he'd be thinking about problems of physics, searching out mysteries that thrilled and gripped his imagination. You could hardly call him a clerk. He was a physicist.

But he could equally have been a playwright. Or an architect. Or someone who was building his own sailboat. Or developing a new breed of wheat. Or deciphering ancient Aztec writing.

You don't have to be Einstein to understand you're more than your job when a passion colors everything you do.

**Wing walking.**

*Dream Obstacle:* "I want to start my own business, but I can't get along without a paycheck."

*Suggestion:* A friend faxed me an article from his copy of *National Business Employment Weekly:* "Professional temping lets you snoop. . . ."

"Wing walking" refers to people who launch their own businesses on company time. This can be a necessary first step if you need a steady paycheck and health insurance until you're solid, but the writer advises you not to take advantage. Your boss owns your time and his materials and phone and has the right to sue if you use them for your own business.*

**Piggybacking.**

*Dream Obstacle:* "I was a speech teacher who wanted to write, act, and produce plays. But I needed time to write, a theater, actors, and I had no way of getting them."

*Suggestion:* Parlay your present situation into a better one.

Elliot, the speech teacher, searched for almost a year until he found a job in a theater school that would allow him to write and produce and act in his own plays, using the students and the facilities of the school.

**Climb down the ladder to the right job.**

*Dream Obstacle:* "I want a job I love, but I'm a top executive, and there's nowhere to go but down."

*Suggestion:* A man from western Montana told me that he left his high-powered job in Chicago when a merger threatened to close down his department and went looking for "someplace that felt good." Montana was the place. Instead of finding the

---

* "Employment Briefs," *National Business Employment Weekly,* Maura Rurak May 18–24, 1997.

same kind of work, which he'd never liked, he found a job with the highway department (to the horror of his friends and his successful ex-wife, a reaction that secretly pleased him). "I realized that I wanted to work outdoors, and I wanted physical work. I feel better than I have in ten years."

**Take a sabbatical.**

*Dream Obstacle:* "I wanted to be a singer, but I had a business to run."

*Suggestion:* A woman closed down the office-cleaning business she'd started and run for ten years. "I was making money, but the headaches weren't worth it, and the kids were out of college. At forty-five I decided it was my turn, so I sold the business, socked away half the money, and I'm giving myself two years to go after an old dream. I've started a jazz band where I'm the lead singer, and we travel to small clubs and colleges all over the country. In two years I might try being a free-lance business consultant."

**Get a job with normal hours and build a dream after work.**

*Dream Obstacle:* "I want to do what I love, but my present job eats up all my time and energy."

*Suggestion:* Get a job that allows you the time to make changes.

If you're working more than forty hours a week, your chances of making any changes are severely hampered. Olivia loved geology, although she didn't think she wanted to do it for a living. Occasionally she'd catch a documentary on television, but for the most part her life was spent working long hours at a small newspaper.

"I love geology more than I can say, but I guess it's just a hobby, and I don't have any time for hobbies. If I had any time at all, I'd be out socializing, trying to go on dates," she said. "Two years ago, on my fortieth birthday, something snapped. I spent almost a year running around in a panic, dyed my hair, went to singles clubs, the works. All in addition to this time-consuming job. And then one day I came home exhausted, sat down, and said, 'No more.' It felt like the end of the road.

"I opened my bag and took out a travel magazine I'd bought during the day, with a picture on the cover of a desert with beautiful rock outcroppings, and I almost started to cry. I didn't have the time or money to go back to college, and anyway, what would I do that for? I've seen what geologists do, and it doesn't appeal to me.

"But something happened. I could feel it. I decided I was going to give myself what I loved, one way or another."

She quit her job and went to work for the post office so she'd have normal hours. After work she went to bookstores and libraries, and read books about mountains and deserts. One of them interested her so much she called the author, found he taught nearby, and began to take his class. Now she goes on outings with the school's Geology Society and has produced a geology lecture series at the local library.

"I'm already designing my own expedition for next summer, following in the footsteps of an early explorer in the Rockies. I'm going to try to put together a lecture series with slides when I get back," she writes. "I've met the greatest people too, and they love to talk about geology."

**Fit your dream into your present life.**

*Dream Obstacle:* "I have a great job and would never want to lose it. But it doesn't leave me any time to do anything else."

*Suggestion:* Find a dream, and strategize ways to fit it into your life.

"I wanted a year off, my wife quit her job, and we were ready to go. But my boss gave me two months as a present, and that was it. We went on vacation to Italy and had the best time of our lives. But I didn't have the nerve to quit my job. It's a great job, and I'm good at it. But I want something more, something for me. I had this totally impractical dream about having my own vineyard in Italy or in northern California. But I don't want to own a business and move overseas, and I don't know enough to make it work. Still, it was such a strong dream."

He got together with friends, and together they came up with a plan where he'd be able to ask for time off every few months if he first became so good at his job that he was indispensable. During that time he and his wife searched wine magazines and networked until they found a small family vineyard that needed financial help. He became a silent partner. "I'm getting faxes every day on how the new equipment is working, how good this year's grapes will be. I'm flying over next month for a week. Sometimes I think I died and went to heaven."

**Find a job that lets you leave and come back again.**

*Dream Obstacle:* "I'm not rich enough to travel, but if I work full time, I'll be tied down."

*Suggestion:* Find the job that supports your dream.

I know a taxi driver who works six months and travels the world for six months on his earnings. I know a chef who takes cooking jobs on yachts heading for someplace she'd like to see and stays in the new location when the trip ends. I know a lawyer who partnered up with another lawyer so she could leave her firm for six months of every year to live at the seashore and write.

Or you can become a professional temp or try professional contract work, like Masami Shigematsu. She worked in fashion, but the hours were too long, the pay was too low, and something wasn't right. For one thing, there wasn't enough overseas travel. One day she asked herself: "Is this what I really want to do with my life?" The answer was no.

So she started doing contract work, taking jobs on a project basis and being free when each project was complete. It allowed her to take vacations on short notice and earn enough for a nice apartment. Over the course of a few years she took time off to study horticulture in Pennsylvania, practice organic farming in southern Oregon, and be a volunteer at Guadalupe Mountain National Park.*

**Develop chutzpah.**

*Dream Obstacle:* "I know what I love, but the bridges got burned. I can't get back."

*Suggestion:* Be shameless.

Margo lost the job she loved and didn't think she could find anything like it again. "I was a senior producer in a small German film production company. The job ended badly; my boss closed down the business without paying me, after I'd worked my heart out for him. I ran everything, traveled everywhere, had meetings with the biggest people, and did great work. Nothing's ever been as right as that job."

Why didn't she try to find another one like it?

"That was such an unusual situation I don't think I could find it again."

"Have you looked?"

"Well, no. You see, the only way to look is to go to film festivals in Germany and Poland. I avoid them because I know he'll be there. I wouldn't want to run into him again. I couldn't stand that."

"How old are you?" I asked.

"I'm turning forty next week," she said, looking unhappy.

"Would you like to be in the same place when you're fifty?"

"Oh, God," she cried, horrified.

"Go looking for him," I said. "You can't let someone like that keep you away from a dream. Find him when he's surrounded by people he wants to impress, slap him on the shoulder with a big smile, and say, 'Hey, get me a pass to the good parties, and we'll call it even.' Turn to the others, and say, 'I was Dietmar's

---

* Michael De Senne, "How to Have It All," *National Business Employment Weekly,* July 27–August 2, 1997.

top hand years ago; forgive me for intruding, but it's great to see him again.' That way you'll impress them too."

She took a deep breath, looking scared, and then she said, "I guess it's now or never."

Last time I spoke to her she was on her way to Frankfurt, to her second film festival. She hasn't encountered her ex-boss yet, but she's already gotten job offers from other production companies.

**Make a long-term plan.**

*Dream Obstacle:* "I'm stuck in a corner of my company, but I can't just walk out and do what I want."

*Suggestion:* Start slowly working your way out of your present situation, step by step, until you've changed everything that's not right.

That's what a banker decided to do. He is the son of a farmer and still loves working in agriculture. He's developing relationships with farmers and the manufacturers who buy from them, helping them in any way he can as an informal adviser. "That's the world I really love, not the area I have to handle for the bank. I'm learning as much as I can and helping as much as I can. One day there will be an opportunity to buy into a manufacturing plant, and I'll take it."

A saleswoman took a similar path. "I've been selling advertising space to tourist hotels for my magazine for years, but my job was getting worse and worse. I knew I had about a year left before the hatchet fell. But I realized I knew so many people in the field that I had ten directions I could take. So I kept the job as long as I could and simply met with everyone I knew. Before the year was up, I quit to take a new job with a hotel chain in Tanzania!"

**Liftoffs and springboards.**

*Dream Obstacle:* "I love quilting, but there's no money in that."

*Suggestion:* Do it part-time, and it might grow into something bigger. If it doesn't, keep doing it anyway. After all, you love it.

I recently read a story about a woman who did exactly that and who now has a business of her own, selling quilts.

**Get a job.**

*Dream obstacle:* "I just want a good job, but they're not hiring people over forty."

*Suggestions:* Look again.

The people I called for ideas sent me some interesting items from newspapers and magazines. If you think you're too old to compete with the new crop of lower paid college graduates, look at what Janet Tweed, CEO of Gilbert Tweed Associates, a recruitment firm in New York, has to say: "Younger workers may be cheaper, but older workers give you better value." Many companies have gotten a bit too mean and lean, and they're looking for people with experience.

There are hundreds of ways to get around any obstacle and move straight toward your dream. Anytime you feel stuck and want your mind to fire up again, try this exercise.

## EXERCISE 31

### *Idea Wizard to the rescue.*

This is a role-playing exercise using two chairs. One chair is for you whenever you're out of ideas for how to overcome an obstacle to getting your dream. The other chair is for the imaginary Idea Wizard. The Idea Wizard is a special kind of consultant. His firm pays him a thousand dollars for each idea he can persuade you to consider seriously.

Here's how to play:

1. First, sit in your chair, and explain what you want and why you can't get it.
2. Then, change chairs, and become the Idea Wizard. Answer the first chair as if you were still in it, and come up

with as many ideas as you can for overcoming the stated obstacle. Remember, you're being paid a thousand dollars for each idea that genuinely interests the other party.

3. Change chairs again, and evaluate, as fairly as you can, all the ideas given you by the Idea Wizard. This is not a contest to you, and you're not trying to shoot his ideas down. Consider each one, and explain what looks interesting to you and what you object to in each suggestion.

4. Change chairs again, become the Idea Wizard, and use your best ideas to solve the objections or enlarge on the interesting ideas.

Change roles at least three or four times.

Write down every interesting strategy you come up with. Remember, even if you don't find anything you can use right now, your thinking will be stimulated and will soon get you unstuck on its own.

Incidentally, if you've got a video camera, it can be fascinating to record this exchange. For fun, make a wizard's hat and wear it when you play that role. Then turn the chairs so they half face each other and half face the camera. When you watch the conversation later, you're almost certain to get some startling insights into yourself, so keep a pen and paper available for notes.

I think you're going to discover that it's possible to get any dream you want, without wrecking your life.

*All your excuses are gone.*

Chat time is over. You must change your life.

You see, the terror and the blessing of arriving at the middle years are that you must answer the biggest question of your life:

**How do you live now that you know you will not live forever?**

"Do you think it a small thing, to know how to live?" asked St. Bernard of Clairvaux.

A challenge like that rings in our ears through the centuries. This is a tough question, but there's no ignoring it. Whatever you answer, even if it looks deceptively commonplace at first, will be far more significant than it appears.

## EXERCISE 32

*How do you live now that you know you will not live forever?*

Sit down with pencil and paper and quickly write down as many answers as you can without thinking. Then take a look at the answers I got in a small survey I took.

Franklin, forty-two, a successful stockbroker: "When I graduated from college, the only thing I wanted to do was study political science. It was my passion. But I went after a bigger success I cared less about because in my family you're nothing if you don't make a lot of money. Now I have a family of my own, and I don't think I can give up this career. But when I look at that question, the only thing that comes to mind is one sentence: *I have to have my passion in my life.*"

After that insight Franklin realized something that hadn't occurred to him before: "I saw it wasn't an either/or situation. I could do both!" He kept his lucrative job, and with his wife's encouragement, he returned to graduate school to study political science. His goal is to write a book before he's fifty.

Janice, forty-six, a downsized banking executive: "I fell into banking, and I never liked the environment although I was good at the work. Once I quit for three years and went into the world of nonprofit to pursue my love of art, but that wasn't the kind of full-time work I really wanted either, and for a long time I was in bad financial straits. So I went back and stayed for a long time. But now I'm looking for a new job, because my answer to the big question is this: I know three things about how to live, and I swear never to forget them. One, I will never work in a corporation again. Two, I don't ever want to be broke again. Three, and this is the most important, *I have to have fun in my daily work.*"

Janice is getting her dream. For the last two years she's been enthusiastically consulting for small businesses, helping them grow up to the next level.

"These are the people I wanted to help when I worked for the bank, but I wasn't really allowed to do it," she said enthusiastically. "Now I charge a small consulting fee, and I take a percentage of my clients' profit increases. If they don't make a profit, neither do I. And that's the way I like it." Janice continues to take business courses to sharpen her skills, but her real gift comes from her love of what she does; she wants her clients to succeed with all her heart, and two of them have already had impressive successes.

Gary, forty-one, a physical therapist: "I was torn between what looked like a great opportunity and staying on track toward the work I really love. Here I was finally beginning to get some free time from my job to pursue my dream of writing again, and I got discovered! I'm being offered an office in a major hospital; they want me to train their physical therapists and see all their patients who have a particularly tough problem that I've been successful with. It's a great jump in my career. But there goes my time. It was very confusing until I asked myself the question: How do I live now that I know I will not live forever? And the wheels started turning.

"I knew that working night and day, no matter how much money I made, was making me miserable, so I asked myself what I thought people would say about me at my funeral if I took the offer. What came up in my mind immediately were the words *responsible, concerned, hardworking, professional*. But that's not what I'd want them to say.

"I'd want them to describe me as a creative, ingenious man who developed a lot of new ideas and wrote some great novels," he smiled. "And that was that. I immediately put a sign up on my wall that said I'M FORTY YEARS OLD, AND MY HAPPINESS MATTERS."

Gary didn't have to throw away his opportunity, however. He realized he simply had to hire some assistants, and he could continue to work his usual hours while still developing a reputation in the field and taking care of his future security.

And Alix Kates Shulman answers the big question beautifully in her book *Drinking the Rain*: "Finally, invoking my fifty years, a number shockingly old to most of them, I announce that henceforth I intend to do only what I love regardless of what anyone thinks."

What did *you* answer? How will *you* live now that you know you will not live forever?

**There you are. No more excuses.**

*You can't ask that question and stay the same.* Even if you don't have a clear answer, you can see very clearly that the time has come to set a target date and make a plan. And a target date with a plan transforms a dream into a plan of action.

But are you ready?

Oh, yes. And you're getting more and more ready with every day that passes. Every day there's less to stand in your way, because once you spot the wonderful possibilities in your future, your fear of leaving your youth rapidly diminishes.

**And now you have time on your side.**

"I do? We're talking about not living forever, and I have time on my side?" you might say. Yes, exactly. Time is on your side precisely *because* you will not live forever. Now you won't waste any more of it. But time has become your ally for more reasons than that. We've talked about time in many places through these chapters. Let's do a brief review, and I think you'll agree that time is definitely in your corner.

As you read in Chapter 3, "Time Limits," time has given you rich experiences and increased not only your knowledge of the world but your own depth of character. Time limits, your midlife awareness of mortality, have brought you to your "now or never" moment, where standing still becomes more dangerous than daring to move ahead. And in Chapter 9, "Power," you realized that letting go of your power fantasies has allowed you to be in each moment instead of always rushing past with your eye on the next crisis. Chapter 10, "The Courage to Live Your Life," reminded you that you need courage to live your life and be all you can, and the courage to say no has given you some open time in which to grow your dreams.

If you look closely in these pages, you'll see even more ways time has become your best ally when it comes to going after your dreams.

So turn your back on the dreams of youth, and turn your face into a future of finding what you really love. If you dare to follow your dream, and if you're willing to take the time to develop the genius that lies under every dream, you're looking at some very happy years ahead.

And the first moment you begin, you'll notice something astonishing. Your midlife crisis has disappeared like the twenty-four-hour flu.

# 12
# Going for Greatness

"Everything we do is music. Everywhere is the best seat."
John Cage

"In adolescence, when our public and private
selves divide, these studies see authority rather than
self regulating our behavior and life is lived out
automatically and compulsively rather than freely and
consciously. . . . Studies have shown that midlife
rather than childhood or adolescence represents
the pivotal time of individuations, autonomous
self-definition and conscious choice. . . ."
Betty Friedan, *The Fountain of Age*

*N*ow *you're headed in the right direction. You've opened your eyes
and can see through the illusions that kept you locked in your
first life. Now you're ready to go after the dreams no one but you
could ever dream, and they'll lead you into your future and away from
your past.*

*Of course, a big part of you still looks over your shoulder with
youthful yearnings from time to time. Inside, you can't help occasionally wishing you were eternally young, the most beautiful and popular
and successful, to say nothing of being all-powerful and immortal. I
know you now see things very differently from the way you did at the
beginning of this book, but you're still pulled by impulses you don't
even believe in anymore, and that's a humbling experience.*

*Have you entered a permanent battleground between what the
grown-up in you knows and what the adolescent wants? Are you*

doomed to be a sadder but wiser adult who forever aches at the loss of youth? Or will your heart soon follow what your wisdom already knows and let you comfortably grow into your full stature?

Will you ever change?

Happily the answer is yes, you're changing every day. You see, transformation is the miracle of midlife. The discomfort you're feeling is nothing more or less than growing pains. What's ahead is your coming of age, as you change from someone propelled by predictable drives into a very unpredictable, authentic, and unique individual. And this won't be another of those "sane intermissions" we discussed earlier. This time you can stay this way for good; clear, untormented, and honest forever. Even though your physical side is still subject to biology's whim in many ways, nature isn't nearly as interested in making you crazy anymore. And so with every passing year you'll become more and more free to go your own way.

But what will drive you if not ambition, competition, or the passions of youth?

**The answer to that question is the best part of everything you've read from the first page of this book until now. And I love being able to tell it to you.**

The force that will drive you in your second life is the love of what is new, the magnetic pull you feel when every project feels like a treasure hunt you can hardly bear to interrupt, the energy generated by your fascination with new enterprises, the robust exhilaration of exercising your underused talents and watching your skills improve every day, the delight of being a genius and doing the things you were born for.

You have reached the age of great undertakings. You're on the path to greatness.

Greatness? I just wanted to get past my midlife crisis!

Sorry. There isn't any other way to get past it. There isn't even any other reason to get past it. Not because you need fame and glory; actually, because you don't. As a matter of fact, the only time you can possibly attain true greatness is when you've given up your dreams

*of glory. Your midlife crisis has happened precisely because your narcis-*
*sism is crumbling like an unsafe old structure, and what that structure*
*was hiding is a self so original you can no longer ignore it.*

*Originality is genius. If you respect and care for it, it will take you*
*on the ride of your life. And whenever work you love is undertaken*
*with the simplicity and directness of a genius or a child, you're going*
*for greatness. There's nothing to be done about it.*

*But don't let it worry you. You don't have to gear up for some*
*marathon-size effort. There's nothing special to do that you won't*
*already be doing the moment you follow your heart. Because greatness*
*isn't an attainable goal; it's simply a by-product of real happiness.*

*So why am I bothering you with all this? Because you should*
*know you've got something of enormous value on your hands, so you'll*
*take proper care of it.*

––––––––

What is greatness? Well, contrary to what we've all been taught,
greatness has nothing to do with your profession or with fame.
You don't need to be a world-famous singer or the president of a
country or a prizewinning scientist; you can be a carpenter and be
a great man. If you're a teacher who knows how to make children
feel proud of themselves or if you're a person with the gift of true
compassion you've also been touched by greatness. You can be on
the road to greatness if you're simply someone who stands outside
one snowy morning and finds the day so beautiful that you cancel
all your plans and go walking outdoors for hours.

Because greatness is all about trusting what feels important
to you.

"What is the real reason why we want to be big, to be creating geniuses? For posterity? No. To be pointed out when we stroll
in crowded places? No. *To carry on with our daily toil under the*
*conviction that whatever we do is worth the trouble, is something*
*unique . . . for the day, not for eternity,*" says Cesare Pavese,
MacArthur "Genius" award recipient.

There are many definitions of greatness, but for our purposes, greatness describes both a person and the first-rate kind of work he or she produces. Because great work is invariably the result of an original mind pursuing an intense interest with great patience.

An original mind. An intense interest. Great patience. *That's the prescription that will turn the years ahead into the sweetest time of your life.* And you've already got, or will soon have, every one of those three qualities. They come with the territory—if you learn to know and respect what you're looking at.

I think we've established that you have a highly original mind. There will never be another one like it. But where does a "great interest" come from, and why is it significant? Interest appears when your inborn gifts are stimulated by something they have a special sensitivity for. When something holds strong interest for you, you obviously have a unique way of perceiving it. *It means you can see things in it that other people don't see.* That's why you love things that other people have no feeling for. Your fascination is a clear sign of unique perceptions, and those unique perceptions obviously give you unique abilities; if you choose to develop them, you can become a master.

As Nobel Prize–winning physician Albert von Szent-Gyorgyi says, "Discovery consists of looking at the same thing as everyone else and thinking something different."

And that's what happens every time an original mind focuses on something that interests it.

*And patience? Well, patience simply comes from being in love with what you're doing.* When you're in love, you're willing to give each detail all the attention it needs. Does that mean that creating great work requires unending amounts of tedious labor? No, it means exactly the opposite.

**Let's blow the whole "self-discipline" and "hard work" philosophy out of the water right now.**

When Thomas Edison said, "Genius is one percent inspiration and ninety-nine percent perspiration," he wasn't telling the whole truth. Before you start arguing with me, think about this for a moment: *You could say exactly the same thing about sex with just as much accuracy, but no one ever does.* Why not? Because, just like inspired sex, when you're using your gifts, the work you do is enormously pleasurable. The perspiration *is* the inspiration.

"The first time I encountered the act of writing poetry, which means the first time I managed to make contact with something that I didn't know before and could only discover by the act of writing the poem—that experience was so intoxicating that I was willing to give up everything in life to have it again," says the acclaimed contemporary poet Jorie Graham.

Can you imagine anyone who feels this way complaining about hard work? Of course not. In fact, anyone with experience will tell you that when you're doing what you love, it's much easier to keep working than to stop! That's why every time I hear warnings and admonishments that talent doesn't go anywhere without lots of hard work, I'm bewildered. Why the sour note? Why the grumpy, preachy tone? It's as if they were saying, "Remember, this is serious stuff. Nothing important is easy, nothing important is fun."

*But the only point in being a genius is that it's fun.*

And you can't honestly say hard work isn't easy because when you love doing something, hard work is the only thing you *want* to do!

Of course you can't just fantasize your dream and have it materialize. You actually have to get started, and that can be a bit scary. Stepping from easy familiarity of normal life into the intense novelty of something that fully engages your gifts is nothing less than a change of thought universes, and the first moment is like a leap into an ice-cold lake: You remember the jolt of contact from the last time, and you hesitate.

"It's the oddest thing. My canvas is waiting in the next room, and all I want in the world is to go in there and start painting. But I know once I get absorbed, I won't want to come out. So every morning I circle around, avoiding and avoiding, until I finally just go in and paint. And then I'm so happy I don't know why I waited!" a friend told me.

Structure and support are essential to help us pass through this electric field that separates the two universes. We need to know someone's there and something is expected of us at a certain time, to make us feel a bit safer. Structure and support will lower the animal apprehension that rises in us whenever we embark on unknown journeys, no matter how delightful they may be. You might need to work with a partner and a deadline or to sign up for a class with an instructor you respect. You'll need the company at the beginning, just as an athlete needs a coach with a stopwatch. *But once you're involved in an activity that wakes up your talent, they may have to get out of your way because you'll be unstoppable.*

So don't be put off by grim reminders of how hard it is to write or paint, or take photos or start a home business, or climb Mount Everest, for that matter. If you love what you're doing, you'll love every part of it, even the hardest. And if you find yourself perspiring at something that's just not fun, you probably haven't found your gift yet.

**So how do you find your gifts?**

What makes one person feel drawn to poetry and another to music or weather or machinery? It's a kind of giftedness that is almost certainly genetic. When people say they were "born" to do something, they're probably right.

But what if you don't know what your gifts are? How do you find them?

Well, if you know what your dreams are and you follow them, you're already tracking your gifts. Remember, *dreams are messages sent by talent.*

But sometimes you can't see your dream in advance, and you don't know what will strike the kind of chord that will set your genius on fire.

That just means it's time to go exploring.

You've got to start visiting many worlds and trying out many activities. You're shopping for something you don't know exists yet, but you'll know what it is when you see it. This time you're scouting for something that fits your genius like a glove. How will you know when you've found it? *Pay attention to your reactions.* Your responses always provide solid evidence of gifts, but it's evidence we typically ignore.

"I unexpectedly spent the weekend helping an old friend repair an antique motorcycle, and I was amazed at how I loved it. But I'm no specialist," you might say.

*But you would be if you stayed with it.* There's no other possibility. You see, if you weren't gifted, you wouldn't love it at all. You'd find it tiresome. And your feeling of enjoyment is not only a dead giveaway, it's the *only* way to discover what you're gifted at. Never forget that what you love is what you are gifted at. There is no exception.

Any experience can be a very efficient research tool and has the potential for changing your life.

"My uncle was over fifty, playing on the floor with his two-year-old grandson, making a little figure for him out of children's plastic clay," an editor told me. "He said that once he picked up the clay, he simply couldn't put it down. Something in him that had never before been touched came to life. Within weeks he was in an art class, and after a few years he'd had his first show. He ultimately was able to buy himself a studio in Paris, which he has to this day."

So ignore the conventional wisdom that advises you to focus on what you already know. You should focus only on what you already *love.* And if you haven't found what that is, start opening up your life to new experiences. Talk and, more important, *listen* to people you don't ordinarily meet. Visit conventions and conferences, audit courses in subjects you never considered before, hang out with people whose interests are different from yours.

*And never let your feelings of inadequacy in the presence of experts keep you away.* Perhaps they will welcome an outsider, and perhaps not. Just keep in mind, they were once beginners too. Anyway, your expertise isn't the issue here. Remember, when it comes to genius, there is no competition. You're one of a kind. That's that.

So try new experiences as a matter of course. When someone invites you to pitch in on a project or do some kind of volunteer work, or to attend a performance or an exhibit, or go on a hike or to a quilting bee—anything you're unfamiliar with—start saying yes instead of no. You might walk right into the work you love.

You'll know the moment you do because it will feel like play.

**When work is play: The return of the child you once were.**

Different people see genius in different ways, but everyone agrees on one thing: When you're engaged in the work your genius loves, it feels like you're playing. Because originality and creativity come from the child inside each of us.

Look who has play as their primary driving force: scientists, writers, filmmakers, oceanographers, and choreographers, and anyone else who's having a good time when they work. Most of them will admit without any hesitation that they're playing, and you can see it in their eyes and their attitudes because they're just like kids. Child's play included curiosity, building, creating, learning in an unstructured way, being alive with feeling as we hugged our dogs or walked through a park, being completely absorbed as we fixed a bike or took apart an alarm clock, or bounced our personalities off those of our friends as we ran through the schoolyard or pitched pennies or told jokes. We didn't play simply because we hadn't learned self-discipline yet. We did it because we instinctively understood the importance of fun.

*Fun indicates the presence of a gift. It's the first beacon of talent.*

When you begin doing work that feels like play, you'll wonder where the time went. Without knowing it, you'll be creating a never-before-seen body of work that shows who you really are.

You'll be making an important and original contribution to this world because you're incapable of doing anything else. When you let yourself focus on what you love, you'll be brilliant at it. And because you love it, you won't stop until you're completely satisfied that you've taken your project as far as it can go. Inspiration and persistence, that's the path to greatness. That's how genius works.

**Genius, master. Those are pretty big words, aren't they?**

No, they're just big enough to take seriously. But don't be intimidated by them. The people we call great rarely call themselves geniuses. And they don't expect to be perfect either.

Listen to the painter, Robert Henri: "It's a wrong idea that a master is a finished person. Masters are very faulty; they haven't learned everything and they know it. Finished persons are very common—people who are closed up, quite satisfied that there is nothing more to learn. A small boy can be a master. I have met masters now and again, some in studios, others anywhere, working on a railroad, running a boat, playing a game, selling things. Masters of such as they had. Have you never felt yourself 'in the presence' when with a carpenter or a gardener? When they are the right kind, they do not say, 'I am only a carpenter or a gardener and therefore not much can be expected from me.' They say or they seem to say, 'I am a Carpenter!' 'I am a Gardener!' These are masters. What more could anyone be?"

*The essential element, the ingredient that must not be missing, is that you have the deepest faith, just as a child does, that your happiness signifies something important.* Not just so you can walk around smiling all the time but so you can tap into your genius.

You'll be helped by another miracle of midlife.

**Trusting happiness becomes easier at midlife than at any time since childhood.**

"If time is short, happiness is important," said a forty-year-old woman. Well, time probably isn't as short as she assumes, but at midlife this can be an enormously productive thought all the

same. The fact that your awareness of mortality shows up at midlife is wonderful, because it pushes you as nothing else will into
respecting your own happiness, and your happiness will unerr-
ingly draw you to your genius like metal is drawn to a magnet.

The moment you decide that it's important to enjoy what
you do, you're hot on the trail of your gifts. Before you were forty
you wanted to be happy, of course, but you didn't fully understand that this was of primary importance.

*Will you look at this timing!* Everything comes together as if
we were programmed to seek our genius actively at the very moment our reproductive usefulness begins to dwindle. Here is the
fork in the road that we come to at midlife. To the left is a sign
that says STAY AS YOUNG AS YOU CAN AS LONG AS YOU CAN. The
"selfish gene" that wants us to help our species reproduce pulls us
back to the cosmetic surgeon and the exercise machine and tells
us to hang on to the illusions of our youth. But to the right is a
sign that says IF TIME IS SHORT YOU MUST MAKE YOURSELF HAPPY, and
each day that direction becomes more compelling.

It feels like that unselfish gene swinging into action again,
doesn't it?

Perhaps you always wanted to sing or take photographs or
make movies or raise grasshoppers or crack language codes, but
until now, you had to worry about how you'd look to others, how
well you'd do, or how much money you'd make, so these wishes
had to be put away like children's toys. But now that you have no
time to waste, you care less each day what the world says. And
now these desires are reappearing and revealing their true nature:
not trivial little impulses but the earmarks of a talent that will
make you very happy indeed.

**What a pity someone didn't help us find our gifts long ago.**

Don't waste your time fretting. It probably wasn't possible.
For one thing, the job of any family and society is to make you
useful to them. They have to train you into the values and skills
of the tribe. *But more important, nobody ever knew who you were.*

For the most part your brain, unlike your body, is unexplored territory. And there's not a skills test or an exam that can help. Because no one knows what world you really live in.

Not even you.

You're so completely accustomed to the unique way you sense time, height, or distance, and the colors you see and the sounds you hear, that to you they're perfectly normal. And no one but you knows what emotions are stirred when you hear trumpets or violins or bassoons. You could have a special sense of shiny things or silences, or understand with unexplainable intimacy the heft and balance of heavy things. You could have an unusual awareness of what's really going on in social situations, or you might feel some unusual connection between song and shape, between rhythm and number, between math and music. No one senses these things about you. And you're not aware of them either because you have nothing to compare them with.

But if you begin to respect your style of thinking instead of criticizing it, you'll allow it to grow. You'll give your thinking apparatus whatever it needs.

**Your potential for greatness requires you to create the environment you need to do your best work.**

You've already learned that you need uninterrupted time for yourself, but we haven't yet spoken of something you need just as much, and that's the right environment for you. Like any rare bird, you need suitable surroundings.

You might need a special place or change of location, for example. To help you remember to take free time in the beginning, you might want to make appointments with yourself to go to the library, the back porch, the woods, or on a long drive. When you do, remember, you're in a place of reverence and thought and work, like a chapel or a studio.

Some people need absolute silence to think, but a film editor I know says silence makes him nervous. When he edits, he has to have music playing; it gives him a feeling of galloping, of moving forward. Some of us can't think if we're not talking and even imagine conversations when we're in public. (Of course, if we get a few strange looks, that means we were moving our lips.) Others can think only when they're walking. Some people need to organize their surroundings and have a plan before they can begin to work, but the filmmaker Federico Fellini detested plans and couldn't think if he wasn't surrounded by chaos.

"Myself, I should find it false and dangerous to start from some clear, well-defined, complete idea and then put it into practice. I must be ignorant of what I shall be doing and I can find the resources I need only when I am plunged into obscurity and ignorance."

You'll find yourself fascinated at the way your own mind sees your surroundings.

"If the average person goes to Yosemite and sees a rock wall, there's nothing inherently exciting about it," says Mihaly Csikszentmihalyi, author of *Flow*, "but if the visitor is a climber, the rock means a certain action potential. To him, it's the most important part of the environment—perhaps of his life."

Interviews with dancers tell us that they think with their bodies, that they are highly sensitive to gravity, and that instead of seeing objects in a room as we do, they're keenly aware of the space between them. When you or I hear music, we want to move our bodies too, but a dancer's awareness is different.

"When I hear a strong rhythm, I start pushing empty space around the room with my hands, my shoulders, my hips. I can almost feel the weight of the air I'm pushing."

**You must honor the unique way your particular mind works.**

No one understands very clearly how we think, but at least people are beginning to understand that variety, far from being a problem, often signals a special brilliance. Take learning "disabilities," for example.

If you think you don't have any, all you need to do is take a look at the classes in school that you had the most distaste for—

there must have been something from geometry to gym that you didn't like—and you're probably looking at the same thing. Not a disability at all, just the evidence of a brain designed for something else.

The best educators are trying to get the word out, but there's a lot of resistance. And I can think of nothing that proves their point better than looking at some of the people who were afflicted with these "disabilities."

Albert Einstein is said to have started speaking very late, but some educators think this allowed him to view and conceptualize the world in a less conventional way. Turner, the painter, might have been color-blind and had other vision problems as well. Leonardo da Vinci had mirror vision, maybe dyslexia. Others who had some kind of learning "disability" connected to attention deficit disorder (ADD) or dyslexia include Thomas Edison, Alexander Graham Bell, Walt Disney, General George Patton, Winston Churchill, Whoopi Goldberg, Danny Glover, and Greg Louganis.

Not a bad lineup for people with thinking "disabilities."

Some experts say this evidence should make us wonder if disabilities aren't always indications of style or even survival traits.

Thom Hartmann, author of *Attention Deficit Disorder: A Different Perception*, maintains that the condition, with its constant scanning for stimulation, its impulsiveness and willingness to risk, is a kind of thinking that was perfectly suited to hunters in the million years of human existence before agriculture came on the scene.

"Because of picture thinking, intuitive thought, multidimensional thought, and curiosity, the dyslexic's creativity is greatly enhanced," says Ronald D. Davis, author of *The Gift of Dyslexia*.

Neurologist Oliver Sacks suggests that unusual brain chemistry might even be a *requirement* for creativity.

*What a difference it would make if any variations from the aver-*

*age were seen as nothing but the pointer to a different kind of thinker.* We might pay more attention to assisting the development of talent than rehabilitating it. Imagine if, instead of treating these differences as problems, we drafted these unique geniuses into doing work they're better at than the rest of us!

Someday maybe.

Until then we're going to rescue just one genius. You.

**How to go for greatness.**

The rules are simple.

1. Find what you love.
2. Do it only because you love it.
3. Stick with it.
4. Start now.

Let's look at each of these more carefully.

1. Find what you love because greatness is based on great gifts. If you love something, you can count on the fact that you are genetically gifted at it.

2. Do it only because you love it, not for any other reward, because only then will you go to the limits of your gifts. There will be nothing to hold you back. If someone wants to pay you, that's fine. If they want to change you, it's not.

3. Stick with it, because that's the only way to learn your craft. Don't be overwhelmed, be steady. Remember the instructions for how to eat an elephant: one bite at a time.

4. Start now. You thought it was too late? I think you now understand that was an illusion. Entering your middle years means only one thing: You can't stall anymore.

*It's only too late if you don't start now.*

**Now let's talk about that Nobel Prize for a minute.**

You could get one. Especially if you're so in love with what you're doing, you realize you already have the biggest prize: happiness. But you're definitely poised to do something outstanding.

You'll be able to give everything your best effort precisely because you don't care what people think. Critics won't distract you, and competition won't interest you because you don't have to try to be the favorite anymore.

*Do you understand the freedom that gives you?*

You now have the freedom to grow to your full height. The freedom to fall in love with your life. The freedom to do something extraordinary.

You have reached the age of great undertakings, and greatness will simply come along for the ride. You don't have to buy a microscope and come up with a cure for cancer either. And you might make headlines, but you might not. I promise you'll be so satisfied you won't care one way or the other.

"It is really not important whether [one artist's] vision is as great as that of another. It is a personal question as to whether one shall live in and deal with his greatest moments of happiness," the painter Robert Henri tells us.

Does that mean your vision might not be as great as someone else's?

Nope. Not possible. If you don't love to paint and you try to be a painter, like Henri says, you might not have great vision. You might still have a very good time, of course. But to go for greatness, you must follow your own path.

**And how will it feel to be one of the greats?**

Ask anyone who's done it. It doesn't feel like you're on a stage getting an award. It's better than that.

"It's a feeling of being who you were meant to be, of being fully human and alive and unselfconscious while you do your work," a photographer told me.

"You're in love with the tools you use, the pins and scissors. It feels fantastic to handle the fabric, to see how it falls and drapes, to learn what it can do," said a costume designer.

"I love to type," a writer told me once. "I'd type a laundry list and enjoy it. The keyboard is my piano."

Peter Meinke, the poet, would find that a good sign: "If you're hooked on the physical act of writing, there's a good chance of your hanging in there long enough to say what you were born to say. . . ."*

**Ready to begin?**

Anytime you wonder, "What do I want to be when I grow up?" change the question. Because you already are someone. It will take longer than one lifetime to use everything that's in you, *which is why it's so exceptionally wonderful that you've been given a second life to play with.*

So the question should be: What do you want to *do* when you grow up? What do you want to *know?* To *see?* To *build?* To *discover?* What do you want to *change?* What do you want to *create?* Those questions will give you the right answers. Go looking for what makes you happy, and that will be your guide.

And greatness?

It will come like the warmth on your bare arms when you're at work in your garden. You won't notice it because you'll be so busy having a good time.

Your first life may have belonged to nature, but now you have reached the age of great undertakings. Your warehouses are bursting with talent and experience. This is your second life and it belongs to you.

Go out and claim it.

---

* "On Judging Poetry," Sept. 1997 *The Writer.*

# EPILOGUE

How about a travel poster for your second life?

"Look around you at this splendid place! See the stunning beauty of a world you don't need to exploit. Fall in love with your life! Be who you were born to be! Forget that you ever despaired at turning forty!" (Or fifty or sixty or any age!)

Far from what you were programmed to believe, this is the launch into the most exciting time of your life.

I hope I've successfully trashed the old ideas of the stages of life—you know, the ones that say you start out as a baby, you become an adult, and then you go into your decline. If that was ever true, and I seriously doubt it, it isn't true anymore.

Here's how it looks to me: You start out as a lovable but narcissistic baby fighting to maintain your original position as fate's favorite creature who will never have the misfortunes that befall ordinary humans. You stay that way throughout adolescence and young adulthood, heroically ignoring the battering your narcissism keeps taking from real life. By your forties it's becoming apparent the battle is lost.

*At some point you glimpse your own mortality and grow up real fast. And then the fun begins.*

Because then you get young again.

"The day I buried my youth, I grew twenty years younger," said George Sand.

**How to begin the journey into your second life.**

None of us knows everything we need to know at the begin-

321

ning of a journey. But you must make some crucial promises to yourself.

*Promise yourself that you'll always fight the lockstep of mindless conformity and never let someone else tell you who you are or who you're supposed to be. Promise you'll never let yourself down by ignoring your dreams.*

And while you're at it, here are some more. You might want to say them out loud each morning:

*I promise to try to be open to my new life by being in touch with my feelings.*

*I promise to find time, come hell or high water, in which to wake up my creativity.*

*I promise to seek out the company of generous, interesting people.*

*I promise to keep my life fresh and new and interesting.*

*I promise never again to believe that it's over before it's over.*

Never forget them. Because you have promises to keep and miles to go before you sleep.

**Okay, are you ready for your final exam?**

Would you say the following sentences are true or false?

1. Time is a thief, and it has stolen the best years from you.
2. Death is the enemy of life.
3. You know exactly what "old" means, and you never want to be it.
4. Beauty will get you love and happiness.
5. Romantic passion equals love.
6. Success in the eyes of the world is important for happiness.
7. You can escape the dullness of middle age by running away to sea.
8. You have unlimited personal power and can do anything if you only try hard enough.

*I hope you put a "false" after every one.*

But you knew that.

\* \* \*

322

**Now here are the exam answers to the cosmic questions in Chapter 1.**

Finally, let's ask those terrible questions again, the ones I posed in the very beginning—you know, Why am I here? Where am I going? I told you your answers would be very different by the end of this book. See if I'm right by comparing your answers to these.

Q: *Where am I going?*

A: Wherever your energy, originality, and love of life want to take you.

Q: *Did I do the right thing with my time so far?*

A: Of course. That's how you got so smart.

Q: *What's ahead?*

A: A fresh adventure, a new life built on who you really are.

Q: *What are my greatest fears?*

A: That you won't have enough frequent flier miles to see every place on earth.

Q: *What do I really want in my future?*

A: Work you love, people you love, creativity, and laughter.

Q: *What do I definitely not want any more of?*

A: A meaningless grind, a lack of courage, a new diet.

Q: *Why am I on this planet?*

A: To live a rich and exciting life by using your loving heart and your big brain and your amazing gifts to the fullest extent possible.

Do you agree? Then there you have it. I told you this would all look different by now.

**Congratulations. You've graduated.**

Now where's that terrible bogeyman in the closet that scared you to death on your fortieth birthday: the vision of the bored and depressed fifty-year-old, the arthritic, useless sixty-year-old, the forgotten, eccentric seventy-year-old, and the pathetic, burdensome eighty- or ninety-year-old you thought you must inevitably become?

Nowhere to be found.

By the time you hit those ages you'll be writing best-sellers on economics, or rebuilding wells to bring water to small villages in Central Asia, or working on your fifth film, or chiseling marble in your studio in Sedona or heading up a music festival in Italy. Or you'll be selling your business and looking around for another one, or running for state senator, or discovering a new virus, or teaching adults to write their autobiographies, or filming a documentary, or building a new house.

*Oh, and quit assuming your personal life is going to dry up.* Read some books about the artists and explorers and adventurers and scholars and filmmakers and philosophers and senators and businessowners who sailed through their sixties, seventies, eighties and nineties as though they didn't exist. They never lacked for companionship. They were magnetic people, and everyone—lovers, friends, and family—wanted to be around them. As you shrug off nature and society's definitions of who you should be and turn into your highly original self, you will become equally magnetic.

*There you are: passion and adventure, gifts and greatness, brains and body. Now where did that midlife crisis go?*

From now on, whenever you hear someone say, as you so recently did, "Is that all there is? Is the party over? Is it too late?" I hope you'll smile and wonder why you ever felt that kind of dread. And I hope you'll answer them, "Too late? Not by a long shot.

"The party's just beginning."

Would you like to write me? I'd love to hear from you with any comments, reactions, personal stories, or good advice for others. Send all mail to me in care of:


Barbara Sher
Box 20052
Park West Station
New York, NY 10025


I may not be able to answer each letter, but I promise to personally read every one. I learn something new from every person I meet, so I eagerly look forward to hearing from you and promise to pass on any new insights to future readers.

I thank you in advance.